SEMANTIC FACTORS
IN COGNITION

SEMANTIC FACTORS IN COGNITION

Edited by

JOHN W. COTTON
ROBERTA L. KLATZKY
UNIVERSITY OF CALIFORNIA, SANTA BARBARA

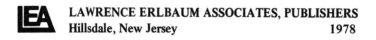
LAWRENCE ERLBAUM ASSOCIATES, PUBLISHERS
Hillsdale, New Jersey   1978

DISTRIBUTED BY THE HALSTED PRESS DIVISION OF

JOHN WILEY & SONS

New York   Toronto   London   Sydney

Lawrence Erlbaum Associates, Inc., Publishers
62 Maria Drive
Hillsdale, New Jersey 07642

Distributed solely by Halsted Press Division
John Wiley & Sons, Inc., New York

Library of Congress Cataloging in Publication Data

Main entry under title:

Semantic factors in cognition.

Papers presented at a conference held on May 26 and 27, 1976 at the University of California, Santa Barbara.
Includes bibliographical references.
1. Cognition—Congresses.   2. Semantics—Congresses.
I. Klatzky, Roberta L.   II. Cotton, John W.
BF311.S44   153.4   77-21022
ISBN 0-470-99340-5

11-30-78

Printed in the United States of America

Contents

Preface

This book is the edited collection of speeches presented at the conference on Semantic Factors in Cognition held on May 26 and 27, 1976, at the University of California, Santa Barbara. This conference grew out of our conviction that the psychological study of cognition owes much of its recent progress to developments in linguistics and to psycholinguistic theorizing and experimentation. It was our intention that a conference presenting theoretical and experimental work relating semantic memory to cognitive processes should be informative both to scholars who could be present at the original presentations and to others who would depend upon a subsequent record of conference proceedings. This book is the vehicle by which the second group is to be served.

The organization of the book corresponds to the structure of the conference, which was held in three half-day sessions. Each session is represented by four chapters of the book, presenting two major speeches followed by two sets of discussants' remarks. Each discussant commented on both featured presentations of the session, permitting comparison by the reader of two analyses of each paper being discussed.

The first two chapters of this book, Hunt's "Imageful Thought" and Rumelhart and Norman's "Learning, Memory, and the Acquisition of Knowledge," are highly theoretical contributions. Hunt presents a comprehensive theory of cognition in which computer science concepts describe sensory, memory, and thought processes. Sequences of sensory images of external and internal phenomena are the pre-eminent concepts in Hunt's theory. Then Rumelhart and Norman expand their own computer-oriented general model (Norman, Rumelhart, & the LNR Research Group, 1975) to include preliminary hypotheses about the way learning occurs, providing mechanisms for the development of memory networks for storing information and for the modification of such networks as learning proceeds. Their central concept is of schemata within which memories may be organized. If these schemata are adequate, learning proceeds by accretion to them. Otherwise, minor (tuning) or major (restructuring) modifications of the schemata must take place. Despite differences in the process assumptions of the two chapters, Rumelhart and Norman's chapter can serve as an amplification of Hunt's section on long-term memory and pattern recognition.

Hintzman evaluates the Hunt chapter and the Rumelhart and Norman chapter with psychological criteria, for the most part; a hint of controversy is discernible in his remarks. In contrast, Kendler primarily judges these two models on the basis of their adequacy in the light of a contrasting pair of philosophies of science.

The next two conference papers and discussions thereof are presented in Chapters 5–8. The papers are "Visual Information and Semantic Information Processing," by Klatzky and Stoy, and "Some Factors Involved in the Recognition of Words," by Conrad. These papers were discussed by Keenan and Revlin. The final conference session is contained in Chapters 9–12. During that session, Fillenbaum's and Smith, Balzano, and Walker's papers were presented. Discussants for these papers were Wexler and Munro.

In contrast to the metatheories presented in the first session of the conference, the four papers by Smith et al., Fillenbaum, Conrad, and Klatzky and Stoy report empirical studies. In these papers can be found a common task – to compare semantic processing and processing with other informational systems. This theme is well set by Conrad, who postulates the existence of isolable visual–orthographic, nominal–phonemic, and semantic subsystems. Each of these systems is assumed to play a role in word recognition, with the importance of the role varying according to the recognition task. Smith et al. also investigate the roles of visual, nominal, and semantic information; their investigation occurs in the context of a picture-categorization task. Again, they conclude that the relevance of each type of information to the categorization task depends in part on the nature of the task itself. Klatzky and Stoy contrast the visual and semantic systems in picture comparisons. They conclude that semantic information plays an important role, even when there is much overlap in the visual properties of the pictures. Fillenbaum departs somewhat from the information-processing framework of the other authors. Yet, he too compares semantic processing to an alternative – in this case, a logical, truth-table analysis of the connective *If*. Fillenbaum concludes that such an analysis cannot account for performance; he argues that the meaning of the connective depends instead on the semantic context in which it occurs.

Thus, each paper in this group focuses on the relevance of semantic information in cognition and compares its role to that of information in other systems. The papers differ in the empirical context in which they discuss this question and in the relative importance they ascribe to semantic data.

The discussants of these four papers share a somewhat different theme: Whereas the authors of the papers examine semantic processing in specific contexts, the discussants call for a metatheory to combine those contexts. Were they to call for a common theory, the problem might be solved, but each discussant suggests a distinct theoretical approach. Munro, who discusses the work of Smith et al. and Fillenbaum, proposes that procedural semantics might provide the theoretical framework to integrate the two papers. One psychological model that incorporates this approach is that of Rumelhart and Norman. Wexler, reading the same two papers, suggests that the conversational rules of Grice may provide at least a solution for the seeming polysemy of *If* in Fillenbaum's research. In discussing the papers by Conrad and by Klatzky and Stoy, Revlin introduces the Distributed Memory Model of Hunt as an integrative theory. Thus, different discussants of the later papers recommend one or the other of the unifying theoretical approaches presented in the earlier part of the conference. Keenan's suggestion is that encoding processes form the basis of a theory of memory; the task for a conference like the present one then becomes the analysis of semantic encoding operations.

A conference like the present one is intended to provide a forum for the dissemination of information. It can also produce some integration of that information; it can point to emerging trends or reconcile discrepant areas of endeavor. In the case of the present conference, participants repeatedly returned to the need for an integrative cognitive–semantic theory and to the requirement that such a theory address itself to a broad range of empirical studies. We feel that if this conference provides an emergent theme, it can be found in its articulation of this desire for a symbiotic relationship between research and theory in the area of semantics and cognition.

We are appreciative of the support of Professor David Brokensha, Director of the UCSB Social Process Research Institute, which sponsored the conference on which this book is based. We also thank Dean Henry W. Offen of the UCSB Office of Research Development, which funded that conference. Mrs. Patricia Griffith, Administrative Assistant of the Social Process Research Institute, was very helpful in conference planning and in the preparation of the final book manuscript, and Kim Guenther prepared physical facilities and assisted participants at the time of the conference. Dr. Robert Bortnick, formerly Assistant Professor of Education at UCSB, participated in early formulation of the conference plan but was unable to continue work on the conference after accepting a new position in the Midwest.

We thank the following authors and publishers for permission to reproduce copyrighted materials from earlier books and articles: P. F. Strawson and John Wiley & Sons for material from Strawson, P. F. *Introduction to logical theory.* New York: Wiley, 1952, pp. 231–232; R. Gerritsen, L. W. Gregg, and H. A. Simon for material from Gerritsen, R., Gregg, L. W., & Simon, H. A. Task structure and subject latencies as determiners of latencies. Carnegie Mellon University, CIP Working Paper *292,* 1975; D. Wilson and Academic Press for material from Wilson, D. *Presuppositions and non-truth-conditional semantics.* London: Academic Press, 1975.

Finally, we thank all conference participants for excellent presentations and for timely preparation of manuscripts in original and later in partially revised form.

JOHN W. COTTON
ROBERTA L. KLATZKY

SEMANTIC FACTORS
IN COGNITION

Section I

1
Imageful Thought

Earl Hunt

University of Washington

Students in human information processing classes learn about detailed models of letter recognition, pitch identification, memory scanning, signal detection, and depth of processing. Can there be anything else? There is. One of them asked me "Does cognitive psychology have anything to do with thinking?" I had two choices. I could say "No, it probably doesn't." Or I could write a paper. I have chosen the cowardly alternative. This paper outlines a general theory of the thought process. Such efforts were more popular in the 1930s and 1940s than they are today. Those who wish to develop historical trends will find the ideas expressed here somewhat akin to Bolles' (1975) modern version of Tolman's stimulus–stimulus connectionism, but any philosophical communality is well buried under an avalanche of concepts borrowed from computer science.

The theory needs a name. I will call it *semantic-image theory*. It rests on a single basic assertion:

Cognition proceeds by an orderly sequence of sensory images.

A "thought" is a coherent sequence of internal events that we could perceive if the appropriate external events occurred. Whether the events themselves are physically possible is quite beside the point. There is no claim that we see full-blown sensory recreations in the mind's eye. The key concepts are *sequence* and *image*. At any instant, our attention will be focused on an internal representation of an amalgamation of inputs from external perception and aroused memories. This abstraction of present and past experiences constitutes the *image,* in the sense in which I use the term. An image will, in turn, serve as an input to a pattern-recognizing system that somehow provokes the arousal of new memories, to be merged with new sensory input, creating a successor image.

Figure 1.1 illustrates the basic cycle of thought. The image is seen as the product of the output of sensory feature generators and thus is an abstraction of the environment rather than a direct record of it. The feature generators, and

3

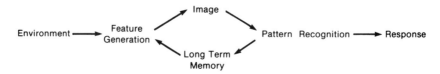

FIGURE 1.1   The cycle of thought.

hence the image, can also be activated from memory. Once the image is formed, the pattern-recognition system maps it into memory, simultaneously changing the state of memory and determining the next input from memory to the feature-generating system. The feature generators merge memory input with new environmental input and re-form the image, and the cycle continues.

This is not a theory; it is a theme underlying a theory. Is it adequate for thought? The argument that it *is* adequate draws upon concepts in computer science and in particular upon the logical relationship between abstract automata, formal languages, and programs.

A *Turing machine* is an abstract computer that, being in some internal state, reads a symbol from an input tape and, depending upon the combination of state and symbol, writes a symbol on the tape and moves to a new state. The steps of reading, writing, and moving constitute the Turing machine's basic cycle and correspond to the cycle illustrated for the mind in Figure 1.1. If a real computer is loaded with a program, then it can be looked upon as a specific example of a Turing machine. It is for this reason that Turing machines are interesting; the set of Turing machines is equivalent to the set of all programs that can ever be written. Therefore, if a function is defined that a Turing machine cannot compute (which is possible), then no program for that function can ever be written. Our argument about mind and image has been carried forward thus far at that level. It is asserted that man can only have those thoughts that can be translated into abstractions of our sensory experience.

The next level of specificity in the theory of computation is the programming language. A programming language also defines a set of specific machines, the set of all programs that can be written in the language. This is a subset of the set of all Turing machines. For instance, the FORTRAN language provides a way of describing machines that have certain elementary capacities, such as the ability to do arithmetic and to manipulate vectors, but do not have the capacity to perform other elementary functions, such as using a "push down stack" for the storage of symbols during intermediate calculations.[1] At a still greater level of specificity, individual programs define particular computing machines, each of which use some of the language capacities in a certain order.

Semantic-image theory is a construct at the same level of specificity as a computing language. It defines the operations that are available to "program" a

[1] For amplification, see Hunt (1975), chapter 2.

specific action, whereas a model of an experimental task is the program itself. The theory exists within the world view that man is a device for computing stimulus–response mappings. As seen later, this paper falls short of the goal of defining a complete language for cognitive models. Hopefully it provides a start toward such a language by describing the operations and data types that seem to be sufficient to describe many of our experimental paradigms and our subjects' reactions to them.

STRUCTURAL ASSUMPTIONS

What sort of machine structure is envisaged by semantic-image theory? Figure 1.2 illustrates the major components of the device. The figure displays three boxes, which appear in virtually all modern theories of cognition: an *active memory*, a *long-term memory* (LTM), and a *buffer system*. The two memories provide a stage for the representation currently in attention and a repository for the background information required to construct it. The buffer system is needed to decouple cognition from the real-time demands of the environment. These ideas are common enough. What is uncommon, although probably not unique, is the method of communication between the boxes. The state of active memory, the *image,* is maintained by input from a sensory feature-generation system, which is in turn driven by the sensorium and memory. This provides our technical definition of "image"; an image is simply that subset of feature generators whose activity exceeds a threshold value at a given time. This definition (which is to be further restricted) should be kept in mind as our argument develops.

Active Memory

Because active memory is the stage for the center of our actions, it is appropriate that the description begin there. Active memory is *not* to be thought of as "memory elements above some level of activity"; it should be thought of as a physically distinct location that receives selected input from the feature-generation system. Furthermore, active memory representations are thought of as

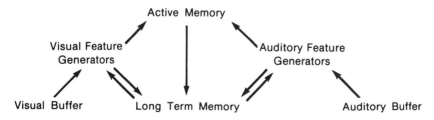

FIGURE 1.2 The structures of memory.

having isomorphic relations to some dimensions of conceivable physical stimuli, although, *in toto,* the representations need not provide sufficient information to define a complete external stimulus.

It is a fact that images have sensory modalities and that the modalities have dimensions of their own. Visual and auditory images are separate. Visual images are ordered by the normal three spatial dimensions, plus color, whereas auditory images vary in time and sound quality. To formalize this, the concept of *memory fields* will be used. This is the first of a series of "semi-rigorous" mathematical definitions that are to be offered in an attempt to be precise about the relationships between elements of the theory.

Let $S = [s_j]$, where $j = 1, \ldots, s$, be the set of feature generators, and let F^* be a partition of S into mutually exhaustive subsets, $F_{a1} \ldots, F_{aa^*}; F_{v1}, \ldots, F_{vv^*}$. Each cell of this partition (i.e., the F_{ai}, F_{vj}) is called a *field*. As the notation indicates, the fields themselves are partitioned into two sets, the set of visual fields $[F_{vj}]$ and the set of auditory fields $[F_{ai}]$. (Presumably there are other fields corresponding to the other senses, but we do not deal with them here.) Within a field, one feature generator at most is permitted access to active memory. The percept consists of all those feature generators that are active at any one point in time. The problem is to explain how a feature generator is selected for activation within its field. A number of models of the selection process might be considered. It would not be appropriate to comment on any of them in detail at this point. It is worth considering what properties seem desirable in any selection process.

Let us divide time into discrete instants, $t = 1,2, \ldots$, even though feature generators are assumed to vary continuously in their level of activation. Define $q_j(t)$ to be the activity level of feature generator s_j at time t. A minimal assumption is that the probability that s_j will be the active generator in the field F_{ai} which contains it $(s_j \in F_{ai})$ is a nondecreasing function of $q_j(t)$. All this says is that, "other things being equal," the probability of selecting a feature as part of the percept will increase or remain constant as the strength of activity in the associated generator increases. "Other things" in this context refers to the activity levels in the other feature generators which compete for access to the same field.

The fiction of discrete time intervals is not just a convenient mathematical device; it can be given a psychological interpretation. At any given moment, t, the set of feature generators will have the collective strengths $[q_j(t)]$. After some period of real time, the feature-selection process will choose a new feature for some field, thus reforming the percept. (This should include the case in which a feature is chosen to replace itself; the important point is that the image is re-formed.) Each new image in active memory serves as an effective stimulus for LTM, i.e., it has the potential of changing the feature-generator strengths, $[q_j(t)]$. A similar change could be caused by changes in the environmental input to the feature-generator system. Changes in the image thus provide a natural unit for psychological time. A new time interval is initiated at each change of the image with the associated changes of feature-generator activity levels.

"What has not been said" is an important part of the definition of an image. There is no requirement that there be active feature generators in every field. In fact, this is unlikely if an image is generated largely from memory. Thus we permit the imaging of faces detached from bodies and the many other phenomena of mental imagery that have no exact correspondent in the physical world. It is in this sense that we speak of an image as being an *abstraction* of present or past stimuli.

Changes in the image are not restricted to changes associated with the provision of new information from either the environment or long-term memory. Sparked largely by the work of Shepard and his associates (cf. Cooper & Shepard, 1973, for a review), numerous experiments have shown that the image may be transformed, within limits, to highlight information that was present in the original image but muted in its original form. The best example of such a transformation is our ability to perform a mental process analogous to rigid rotation of the image. Such phenomena are not easily associated with memory, because they may be used to produce images of scenes never experienced, e.g., the rotation of a nonsense figure that has been seen in only one orientation. There are a number of less dramatic transformations that have the same property; they are best interpreted as transformations of the image rather than augmentations of it. Perhaps the simplest of these transformations is the ability to detect that corresponding parts of two imaged objects are, or are not, identical.

To account for such findings, it is necessary to assume the existence of a set of primitive operations associated with the visual and auditory fields. Conceptually, these constitute the machine instructions of the human computer. They also provide a conceptual Pandora's box, because all we have to do to explain any phenomenon is to postulate another primitive operation. Fortunately, it appears that a wide variety of cognitive phenomena can be handled using only three primitive operations: *rehearse, move,* and *test for identity.*

The *rehearse* process is used within an active memory field to maintain the activity of those feature generators currently having access to memory. Note that this is only one possible meaning of "rehearse," the meaning "maintain the image." A sequence of items, such as a poem, could be rehearsed by sequential activation of the associated concepts in LTM. This would involve changing the image in a repetitive manner, which is not the same as image maintenance.

The *move* operation permits the movement of feature-generator output from one field to another within a set of sensory fields. The operation makes little sense across sensory-field sets. This operation permits transformations of images within a sensory-field set as, for instance, in the image rotations studied by Shepard's group.

Finally, the *identity* operation permits a test for identity of two composite images within the same sensory-field set.

Obviously a great deal needs to be done before making the claim that a complete theory of the active memory process has been offered. Indeed, this could easily require a book relating perception to memory and problem solving. The outline just given is sufficient to continue the discussion here.

Feature Generation

In semantic-image theory, an image is a sort of jigsaw puzzle. It is formed by specifying which piece goes into each of several regions. The active memory fields represent the regions, and the feature generators associated with each field represent the range of choices of pieces for that region.

What are the inputs that dictate the choice of a feature generator? As we have seen, there are basically two sources. The feature-generation system is assumed to be able to "view" the sensory buffers, which are more directly driven by the sensory transducers. The feature-generation system thus functions as an abstractor, which reports the approximate presence of prototypes in a messy input. In addition, LTM may issue commands for the activation of certain sensory features. The functional relations between feature generation and LTM are expanded upon considerably in the next section; here we simply note that they exist.

The result of activation of feature generators will be an analogical representation of some portion of the external world in active memory. This does *not* imply a commitment to a similar analogical representation for records in LTM. Indeed, the opposite is the case. LTM is assumed to contain propositional information associating sets of sensory features with certain engrams. This assumption does not deny the fact of imagery, which is an active memory process, but it does avoid postulating the existence of two separate, context-dependent memory coding systems in the brain.[2]

Long-Term Memory and Pattern Recognition

The long-term memory and pattern-recognition systems are dealt with here as one, because they are thought to involve the same physical structures. Collectively "long-term memory" consists of a set of *engrams,* i.e., records of past experiences. The logical relationship of the engrams to each other is discussed in some detail in the next section. Here we are concerned only with the structural role. Engrams are viewed as devices that can execute a pattern-recognition

---

[2] See Pylyshyn (1973) for an expansion of this point.

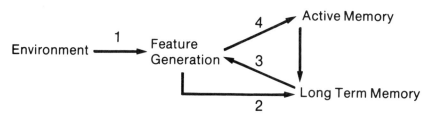

FIGURE 1.3 Stages of memory arousal. Environmental signals (1) arouse feature generators that (2) send signals arousing engrams in long-term memory. The aroused engrams activate (3) feature generators, until the combined inputs (1 and 3) to the feature-generating system are strong enough to force input (4) into active memory.

process upon their input. Thus, if a signal is broadcast blindly into LTM, it will be recognized by only some of the engrams and thus may produce a highly specific response.

But what is the input to long-term memory? A strong assumption of the theory is that there are two sources of input signals, with quite distinct properties. The signal sources are the feature generators and active memory. Signals from the feature generators serve as arousal signals, which can bring engrams to an increased level of activity. The engrams of memory can, in their turn, arouse the feature generators, the two systems form a positive feedback loop, as depicted in Figure 1.3. The necessary damping signals are discussed subsequently. Because the feature generators can be aroused by either a long-term memory or an environmental signal, the image formed in active memory will be an amalgam of the two.

Whereas the role of the input from the feature-generation system is to arouse LTM, the role of input from the active memory system is to change it. The topic of learning could justify volumes, as it has. The general principle of learning in this theory of thought is that learning consists of the creation of stimulus–stimulus bonds (expectations), where the stimulus is defined as the ensemble of features currently in active memory. Thus the theory at once contains the strong assumptions that learning is of the S–S variety and that it is limited to associations that are, in some sense, noticed consciously. Although the term "S–S" is used because it is conventional, the bonding between stimulus representations is not necessarily pairwise. It would be better conceived of as the formation of a chunk cementing together several components of the image. The situation in which one of these components is the label for an abstract relation is particularly interesting. For example, suppose that active memory contained features corresponding to the labels *dog, cat,* and *opposite.* This could lead to the storage of an engram that was equivalent to the proposition "The opposite of *dog* is *cat*" even though it is not at all clear in what sense *cat* is the antithesis of *dog.*

FUNCTIONAL RELATIONS

Our attention now shifts from a concern with the structural relations between temporally defined traces to a concern for the logical relations between hypothetical engrams. As in the last section, but with increasing frequency, mathematical formalisms are introduced. Again, the level of discussion is best described as "semi-rigorous;" hopefully this does not become psuedo-rigorous. There are two reasons for using formalisms here: to make verbal statements more precise and to illustrate the contention that the theory is potentially expressable as a computer program. No attempt is made here to develop theorems, although in principle it should be possible to do so.

Semantic Organization in LTM

Functionally LTM consists of the engrams and the relations between them. We consider, in turn, what it means to say that there are "relations" between engrams, a formalism for stating those relations, and some distinctions between engrams that are related only to other engrams and engrams that are connected to feature generators.

Obviously humans link their memories to each other. The simplest experiment in controlled association can show that these linkages are varied. "Red" has one set of associates in the context of colors, another in the context of politics. How does the memory *implanting* mechanism know which link to establish? In the theory being presented, this problem is "solved" by asserting that bonds are established on a "vertical" basis. Two or more engrams are linked together when they are associated with a common, labeled chunk. The chunk label establishes the context. Furthermore, for this to occur, the chunk label must itself have been temporally contiguous with the engrams in active memory. The result is a set of undifferentiated bonds, as shown in Figure 1.4(a). What the theory does is use the concept of a chunk label plus undifferentiated bonds to produce the functional equivalent of a labeled arc between engrams, as is shown in Figure

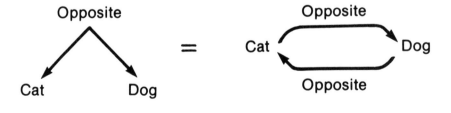

(a) Explicit chunk   (b) Labeled association

FIGURE 1.4   An illustration of bonds between engrams in LTM.

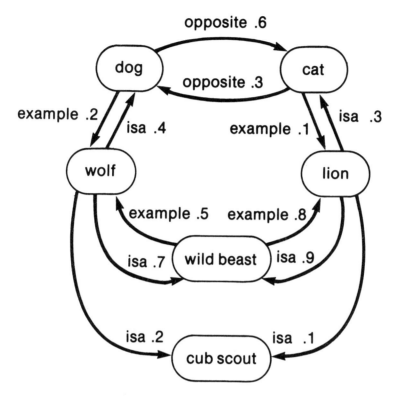

FIGURE 1.5   A frament of a semantic network.

1.4(b). In general, the labeled arc notation is easier to use in describing LTM organization, and it is used here.[3] This part of the theory expands upon some of the ideas about semantic memory organization expressed by Collins and Loftus (1975) and thus could be considered one of several possible formalizations of their model. It is perhaps worth noting that even the minimal attempts at formalization here highlight some specific questions that are not easily distinguished in a completely informal presentation.

LTM can be visualized as a network of nodes, representing the engrams, and arcs, representing the relations between them. Each arc is labeled and directed and has a strength index associated with it. The strength index is a measure of the closeness of the relationship. A fragment of such a memory structure is shown in Figure 1.5. To formalize these concepts, LTM is specified by a set $M =$

---

[3]Note that the labeled chunk ties engrams together much in the same way that the verb ties concepts together in a case–grammar-oriented memory system, such as the ELINOR model of Norman and Rumelhart (1975).

$[m_i]$, where $i = 1, \ldots, m$ of engrams, and a set $A = [a_j]$ where $j = 1, \ldots, a$ of arcs between engrams. Each arc is a quadruple,

$$a_j = < h_j, t_j, l_j, v_j > \qquad (1.1)$$

where h_j, t_j, and l_j are members of M, called the *head, tail,* and *label,* respectively of arc a_j, and v_j is a positive real number representing the *strength* of arc a_j. There is no limit to the number of arcs having the same head and tail, but no two arcs may have the same head, tail, and label.

We distinguish between two types of engrams: *symbols* and *concepts.* It is important to realize that these engrams are distinguished strictly by the definitions that follow. No meaning should be attached to the names used to refer to engram types.

Let $D = [d_i]$, where $i = 1, \ldots, d$, be the set of symbols, and let $C = [c_j]$, where $j = 1, \ldots, c$, be the set of concepts. Taken together, C and D partition M. The functional distinction between symbols and concepts is that symbols have connections to feature generators and concepts do not. These linkages are illustrated in Figure 1.6. Note that in the figure, some symbols, such as "brown,"

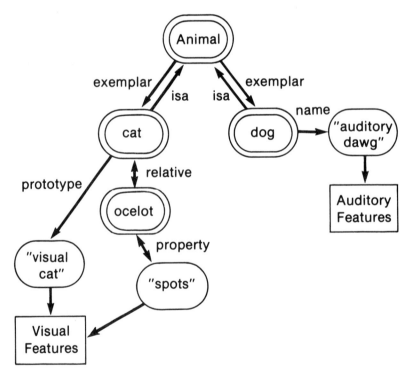

FIGURE 1.6 Relationship between concepts and symbols in long-term memory. (◯ = symbol; ⬭ = concept).

are linked to a very small set of uniform feature generators, whereas other symbols, such as "dog," may be linked to a varied, comprehensive set of generators, which, when activated together, form a coherent image.

Turning again to formalisms, for every $d_j \in D$, there is an associated set, $F(d_j) \subset F$, of feature generators. The associations between d_j and the members of $F(d_j)$ are bidirectional but not necessarily equal valued in each direction. Therefore it is easier to represent the connections by pairs of arcs in a graphic display. Algebraically it is more convenient to consider the set $P = [p_a]$, where $a = 1, \ldots, p$, of *prototype arcs*, where

$$p_a = <f_a, d_a, x_a, y_a>, \tag{1.2}$$

with $f_a \in F$, $d_a \in D$, and with x_a, y_a as positive real numbers. The strength of association from symbol to feature is indicated by x_a and from feature to symbol by y_a.

Activation

We have assumed that at any instant each engram has some potential for arousal. This potential is usually referred to as the *activation level*, although the term carries some unfortunate neurophysiological connotations. In the formal theory, it is simply a positive, real valued variable $w_i(t)$, defined at any time t and for each engram $m_i \in M$, which appears in certain equations.

The major point in having a network theory of memory is to account for the fact that arousal of one memory will lead to the arousal of another related memory in some orderly fashion. To this we must add another more puzzling fact: The orderly fashion of memory arousal will vary at different times. It is always orderly but not always the same order! The only way a network theory can handle both phenomena is for the network to be permanent in structure but somehow capable of rapid temporary reorganization. These antithetical ideas are combined by presenting a network in which the labeled arcs are relatively permanent, but the effectiveness of labels may change over time.

Figure 1.7(a) shows a simplified fragment of a "permanent" semantic network that ties two engrams, A and B, to each other by two arcs, with labels C and D respectively. As dictated by our previous discussion, a value is associated with each arc and an activation index with each engram, including the label engrams C and D. What is the effective connection from A to B at this time? The answer depends upon the rule used for combining labeled arcs into a single association. One possible rule, which is offered for illustration only, would make each labeled arc's effectiveness the product of (a) the value of the arc, and (b) the relative level of activation of the label engram. To determine the total bond from A to B, the effective level of each of the labeled arcs would be summed. It we let $e_{AB}(t)$ be the effective association from A to B at time t, and let v_{ABC}, v_{ABD} be the values of the labeled arcs, then

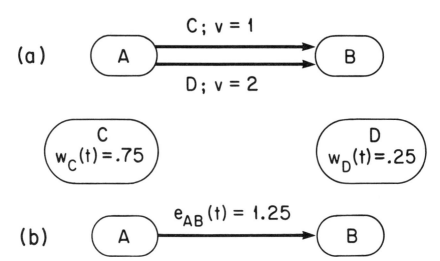

FIGURE 1.7 Derivation of effective connections at time t. (a) shows state of network; (b) shows effective connection.

$$e_{AB}(t) = \frac{w_C(t) \cdot v_{ABC}}{w_C(t) + w_D(t)} + \frac{w_D(t) \cdot v_{ABD}}{w_C(t) + w_D(t)} . \qquad (1.3)$$

The resulting unlabeled effective association from A to B is shown in Figure 1.7(b).

Equation (1.3) is one of several possible combinatory rules that might be considered. They all lead to the following "hydraulic analogy" for a semantic network. Imagine that each engram is a reservoir, with its activation level corresponding to pressure in the reservoir. The arcs represent pipes between reservoirs, and the values are the diameters of the pipes. Each pipe, however, is fitted with a valve named by its label. The pressure in the reservoir representing the label engram is used to open the valves with that label.

Let us reword this more formally and more generally. Consider a matrix, $E = [e_{ij}(t)]$, where $i, j = 1, \ldots, m$, representing the momentary effective association from engram m_i to m_j. To determine the value of $e_{ij}(t)$, let f and g be nondecreasing, positive-valued functions of their arguments, and let l_s be the label of arc a_s with activation level $w_s(t)$. Define

$$A(i, j) = \text{"set of arcs such that } m_i \text{ is the head and}$$
$$m_j \text{ the tail of each arc in the set."} \qquad (1.4)$$

Then

$$e_{ij}(t) = g\left(\sum_{a_s \in A(i, j)} f[l_s, w_s(t)] \right) . \qquad (1.5)$$

The value of $e_{ij}(t)$ determines the momentary strength of association between m_i and m_j.

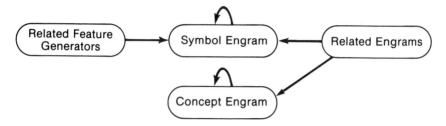

FIGURE 1.8   Sources of activation level.

Engram activation stems from three sources: (a) a residual level due to the engram's own previous activation level, (b) activation that has spread from related nodes, according to the rule expressed by Equation (1.5), and (c) in the case of symbol engrams only, input from the feature-generating system. The situation is demonstrated in Figure 1.8, which shows the potential routes for spread of activation in the memory network.

The information in Figure 1.8 can also be expressed in a mathematical summary. For a concept engram, $c_i \in C$, the activation level at time t is

$$w_i(t) = \alpha w_i(t-1) + \sum_{j=1}^{m} e_{ji}(t)w_j(t-1), \quad \text{where } 0 \leq \alpha < 1. \quad (1.6)$$

For a symbol, $d_j \in D$, an additional input is provided from the feature generating system. Let $q(t) = [q_1(t), \ldots, q_s(t)]$ be a vector defining the activation levels of the s feature generators at time t, and let $B = [b_{ij}]$, where $i = 1, \ldots, s, j = 1, \ldots, m$, be a matrix whose elements are the (semipermanent) values of the directed arcs from feature generator i to symbol engram j. By convention b_{ij} is 0 for all i if engram j is not a symbol engram. The activation index of a symbol engram is given by

$$w_j(t) = \alpha w_j(t-1) + \sum_{r=1}^{m} e_{rj}(t)w_r(t-1) + \sum_{k=1}^{d} b_{kj}q_k(t-1). \quad (1.7)$$

Feature Generation

In this section we discuss the functional role of the feature-generation system in engram activation rather than its structural role in the creation of active memory.

Figure 1.9 presents a simplified illustration of the three roles played by the feature-generation system. Most obviously, the feature-generation system blends input from the environment, via the sensory buffers, with input from long-term memory. The result of the blending process is a particular state of activity within the feature generators as a group. This is what provides input to the LTM system and therefore guides arousal of particular engrams. Finally, but no less importantly, the feature-generator state is subject to a selection process, which determines the features that will capture each field of active memory. The

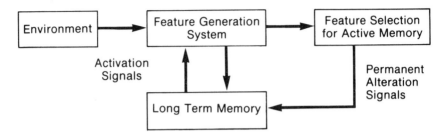

FIGURE 1.9   The role of feature generation.

selected features define the image and provide the input to a contiguity-based learning system, which is capable of adding new links to the LTM network.

Because environmental input is independent of the theory, we simply assume that at any point in time there will be some input, $i_j(t)$, to feature generator s_j. The input from memory will be determined by the state of the symbol engrams, as interpreted by the association matrix $C = [c_{ij}]$, where $i = 1, \ldots, m$, $j = 1, \ldots, s$, which specifies connections from the engrams to the feature generators. As before $c_{ij} = 0$ if engram i is not a symbol engram. Let $q'_j(t)$ be the input to feature generator s_j exclusive of any input from the feature-generation system itself. Because environmental input and memory input are additive,

$$q'_j(t) = i_j(t) + \sum_{i=1} c_{ij} w_i(t). \tag{1.8}$$

Before considering the input to a generator from other feature generators, we must consider the more complex question of how a feature generator is selected to be the active generator within its field. (To avoid circumlocution, a feature generator is said to *capture* its field when this occurs.) We have already made the minimal assumption that the probability that a generator will capture its field is a nondecreasing function of the generator's activation level. Within this general restriction, there are obviously many selection and comparison models. Although it is unnecessary, and perhaps unwise, to commit to any one of them, we outline one model, based on some earlier speculations about network activity (Hunt, 1966), which has some attractive characteristics.

The example is one of the class of "mutual inhibition" models, in which feature generators within a field provide positive feedback for themselves and negative feedback (i.e., inhibitory signals) to all other feature generators in the same field. The situation is outlined in Figure 1.10. Given a constant input, one feature generator will stabilize at a relatively high level of activity, whereas the other generators will be driven to low activity levels and eventually to quiescence.

At least, it can be proven that this is true (Hunt, 1966) for the following formal system.

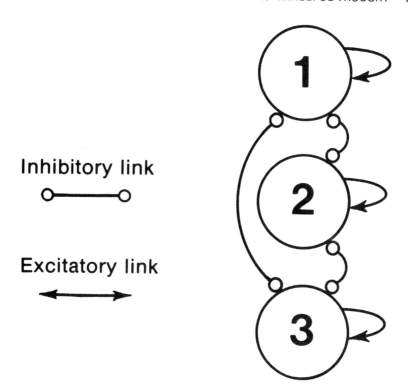

Inhibitory link

o———o

Excitatory link

←———→

FIGURE 1.10   Spread of activation within a three-unit feature-generation system, showing positive feedback and inhibition of competitors.

Let $U = [u_{ij}]$, where $i, j = 1, \ldots, s$, be a matrix of connections from feature generator to feature generator. We require that $0 \leqslant u_{ii} < 1$ for all i and that $u_{ij} \leqslant 0$ for $i \neq j$. Furthermore, $u_{ij} = 0$ if s_i and s_j are not in the same field, and $u_{ij} \neq 0$ otherwise. Denote the input from the feature-generating system to the j th feature by $q_j''(t)$. We have

$$q_j''(t) = \sum_{i=1}^{s} u_{ij} q_i(t - 1), \tag{1.9}$$

and the current state of activation of a feature generator is found by combining Equations (1.8) and (1.9),

$$q_j(t) = q_j'(t) + q_j''(t). \tag{1.10}$$

Finally, we assume that the selection process permits feature s_j to capture its field if and only if $q_j(t)$ exceeds some field threshold, θ and if no other $q_{j'}(t), j \neq j'$, within the field also exceeds θ.

We have effectively moved from a theory of memory to one of perception, which is as it should be, because cognition requires both. Two aspects of the perceptual theory are worth comment. One is that it assumes a form of lateral inhibition as a property of the perceptual system's response to states both of the external world and of the memory system. The other is that semantic-image theory uses memory to account for coherent perception of scenes. This requires amplification.

If feature generation took place in a completely independent fashion, we should perceive mosaics, unless we were fortunate enough to live in an amazingly regular world. The alternative of permitting positive correlations between the arousals of feature generators in different fields (formally, permitting u_{ij} to be nonzero for s_i, s_j in different fields) is not attractive, because it places within the feature-generating system macrofeatures for such concepts as "my grandmother" or "the yellow Volkswagon." We do not want to deny the existence of percepts for grandmothers or VWs, but we do want to derive them from memory.

Consider how the present theory handles the problem of coherent perception of familiar objects.

1. Some feature generator can be assumed to have its activation level raised. This causes a lowering of the activation level of other features within the same field and the raising of the activation level of all symbol engrams associated with the generator.

2. Arousal of the symbol engram(s) causes activity in both the original feature generator, through positive feedback, and in those feature generators in *other* fields that are associated with the symbol engram.

3. Repetition of the cycle will increase the activation level of all feature generators, in all fields, which are associated with the symbol engram. This, in turn, lowers the activity of those feature generators that are in a field associated with the engram but are not themselves tied to the engram. The lowering, in turn, lowers the activity of those symbol engrams that are associated with the "depressed" feature generators, relative to the activity level of the original engram.

4. As the cycle continues, those feature generators associated with the engram capture their fields, leading to a coherent percept associated with the engram. Because environmental input is a separate factor, however, the percept is modified. In particular, modification by the environment is easy in those fields in which the symbol engram does not have a strongly associated feature generator.

At least at the verbal level, this manner of linking perception to memory provides a basis for explaining several perceptual phenomena. One is the Gestalt concept of "goodness"; an ambiguous or sloppy figure is pushed toward the percept associated with the symbol engram. If there are two possible symbol engrams, the formation of a coherent percept is slow at first, and then proceeds rapidly as one engram and its associated features gain dominance over the other. Finally, perception is obviously very much influenced by the current state of memory, providing a link to the "set" phenomenon, where current perception is linked to memorial events.

EVALUATION AND EXTENSION

Semantic-image theory permits derivation of multiple models for specific experimental situations, so it is unlikely that the theory can be brought into direct confrontation with data. How, then, are we to evaluate it? This question can be answered when we consider the purpose of the theory. It provides a way to organize our thoughts about cognition without direct recall of all the experiments that have ever been done and without a compulsion to do all the experiments that might be proposed. There are three questions we can ask in evaluating such a device. Is the theory adequate to describe the phenomena of interest at an appropriate level of specificity? In doing so, does it lead to the development of general principles that can be applied to the analysis of related phenomena? To illustrate, a general theory of cognition ought to have something to say about cognitive development and mental retardation. Finally, and paramount in the eyes of many scientists, within the framework of the theory is it possible to develop specific models that can be used to generate the data from specific experimental situations?

Can the Theory Encompass Thinking?

Earlier it was maintained that thinking is equivalent to computability. Reviewing briefly, a computer program defines a Turing machine. A programming language, then, defines a class of Turing machines equivalent to the class of programs that can be written in the language. Every computer language has an execution sequence, which specifies how the elementary instructions in the language are to be realized. This is our point of contact. We ask if there is a programming language whose execution sequence can be given a psychological interpretation. Assume that such a language exists. If the Turing machines it defines compute the same set of functions as "human thought," then the language and the psychological theory used to interpret it constitute a model of human reasoning.

The next step in the argument is that Newell and Simon's (1972) *production system* notation provides such a language. The basic unit of this language is the *production,* an operation defined on strings of symbols. Let A, B be strings of symbols. We call A the *active string.* A production is written

$$A \rightarrow B;C \qquad (1.11)$$

where C is some action that can affect the environment. A production is interpreted "If A is the active string, then replace it with string B, and make external response C." A and B may be general statements that have to be instantiated in any one situation, in the sense that "2 + 3" is a special case of "X + Y." C may involve a recording action, such as taking notes, which can later provide cues for other productions.

A *production system* is an ordered set of productions. System action is initiated when one of the productions in the set can match its left-hand part (A) to the current active string. The active string is then replaced by the B part of the production, and any necessary action is taken. The cycle continues until the action "Stop" is taken.

Without introducing any further restrictions, the production system notation is equivalent to the class of Turing machines and is clearly too general to be a psychological theory. Newell and Simon and their associates have shown that one can establish limits on the permissible productions and still develop interesting simulations of human behavior. The limits they impose are essentially on the lengths of the strings A and B and correspond to limits to the contents of active memory. This still permits the writing of simulation programs for a wide variety of complex cognitive tasks, including chess, the solution of difficult mathematical problems, the solution of Piagetian conservation tasks in the manner in which they are solved by children at different ages, and the solution of mathematical puzzles.

Evaluating the accuracy of any given simulation often becomes quite difficult. Because of the precision of the predictions, conventional statistical tests may be beside the point. In principle it is possible to produce accurate descriptions of human thought processes using the production system notation.

Two conjectures are needed to tie production systems to psychological theory. Can the rewriting of one string into another be interpreted as a notation for the replacement of one set of active feature generators with another? Is there a correspondence between subgraphs of an LTM network and the finite set of productions in a production system? The formal proof or disproof of these conjectures would be an exercise in the theory of computation, which would have substantial implications for theoretical psychology.

Concrete and Abstract Thought

One of the common objections to the use of a programming notation to state psychological theories is that cognition is then restricted to abstract symbolic reasoning. This is a misconception. Abstract and concrete reasoning must proceed by the same mechanisms, so any notation that can describe the mechanism must be able to describe either process. It is at this point that the concept of imagery is helpful. A symbol is itself a physical stimulus.[4] The imagery

---

[4] Hayes (1973) has shown that mental arithmetic is sensitive to the physical variables that affect imagery.

involved in visualizing "7 + 2 = 9" is not different in its method of production from the imagery involved in visualizing a dog chasing a cat and a cat up a tree. In both cases, the associations stored in long-term memory force the replacement of one active memory image by another. The only difference is in our own arbitrary distinction between "semantic" associations, which have been established by learning about events in "the real world," and "syntactic" associations, which have been established by learning about formal languages. It is unlikely that the brain makes this distinction.

Even though the same mechanisms are involved, the choice between the imaging of symbols and the imaging of situations has many implications for the content of thought. Thinking, using images that stand in reasonable perceptual correspondence to the objects that they represent, permits the observation of a variety of scenarios from which the thinker can choose when the probable consequences have been observed. Such a method of planning would not be advised for mathematics, but it might be excellent for choosing a restaurant or a dinner companion in the restaurant. Whether this is idle daydreaming or social perceptiveness depends on your point of view. By analogy to a sort of playwriting by Walter Mitty, let us call this *scenario thinking.*

The other side of the coin is *abstract thinking,* in which the sequence of images is a sequence of symbols that follow the association rule of a formal system and not the associations of their real-world referents. The imagery involved in mental arithmetic is a simple example. If you are asked "What is 3 X 4 X 8?," the answer is computed in your head by visualizing a sequence of numbers (or names of numbers) that is controlled by the rules of arithmetic. You arrive at the image for "ninety six," and the question "Ninety six whats?" is obviously nonsensical.

The imagery of language forms an interesting intermediate case. Here we have a system of symbols and formal rules, but many of the symbols are closely tied to real-world referents, so that it is impossible to suppress semantic associations. Verbal reasoning, then, involves a play back and forth between the rules of syntax and semantic associations.[5]

Abstract reasoning is much loved by academics, who tend to consider it a higher form of thought. Indeed, abstract reasoning has become the definition of intelligence. Although there are excellent reasons for retaining this definition within some cultural settings, there are many situations in which either abstract or scenario thinking can be used. Consider the following problem:

"A boy went into an ice-cream store and ordered a cone. He asked for a vanilla scoop, then he decided he wanted a big cone, so he asked the clerk to add a strawberry scoop. As the boy went out of the store the vanilla fell off. The clerk

---

[5] For illustrations of how syntactical and semantic reasoning might unite, see Schank's (1975) collection of papers on the topic.

felt sorry for the boy, so he put a free chocolate scoop on. How many scoops were there on the cone?"

If you are an abstractionist, it is obvious that $1 + 1 - 1 + 1 = 2$. If you are a scenarist you may have noticed that the bottom scoop fell off of the cone, and very likely took the top scoop with it.

The point is not that abstract thinking is better or worse than scenario thinking. They both have their place. The power and precision of abstract thinking makes it preferable when it can be used properly. When abstractions fail to capture some important part of the real situation, or when abstraction leads to such a plethora of symbols that image transformation is unmanageable, then scenario thinking is preferable. The decision rules that lead a person to choose one or the other form of thought in a given situation will depend both on situational variables and the person's ability to manage each type of image.

Verification in Specific Situations

The argument for the theory thus far has been what Newell and Simon refer to as a "sufficiency analysis"; we have stressed what the theory can handle. An alternative way to approach the verification question is to conduct "Gedanken experiments" on the theory itself to show that it will display the gross phenomena of human behavior over a wide variety of experimental situations. Such studies differ from the Gedanken experiments of the last century in that the Gedanken itself may be a burdensome task that is feasible only with the aid of computer simulation. Where might we meet with success if such simulations were constructed? Let us consider a few situations.

Stages of Processing Models

Many experiments require the manipulation of highly overlearned material in some way designed to reveal (a) the presence of stages in information processing, and (b) the extent to which different processes can proceed independently. Let us consider briefly the way in which a simulation might be constructed to handle the basic findings.

Identification of Various Levels of Abstraction

In these experiments, subjects are required to compare highly overlearned arbitrary associations to different physical stimuli. The simplest case is a situation in which the subject must identify "A" and "a" as naming the same letter. It has been found that the time required to identify an association is a function of its abstractness. For instance, it takes longer to identify "A" and "a" as naming the same letter than it does to realize that "A" and "A" are two different examples of the same physical pattern (Posner, Boies, Eichelman, &

Taylor, 1969). It takes longer still to identify "A" and "E" as both naming vowels. Interpreting this theoretically, the identification of two stimuli as "same" requires that identical representations be fetched into corresponding fields of active memory. The further the search of the semantic network must be from the original stimuli before the identical symbols are produced, the longer the reaction time should be.

Scanning Studies

We next consider two paradigms that, though only slightly different, give quite different results. In a *visual scanning* task, subjects are given a target set of from two to six letters and are then asked to scan an array of printed symbols for examples of the target set (Neisser, 1967). Providing that the subjects are highly practiced, the time to scan the array is independent of the size of the target set. The correct items appear to spring out at the observer, whereas distractor items are hardly noticed. The situation is markedly different when we use the *memory-scanning* paradigm first developed by Sternberg (1966). In the *constant memory set* procedure, the subject first memorizes a small number of target items, as before. A single *probe item* is then presented, and the subject is asked if it is or is not in the memory set. In the *variable set* procedure, a new memory set is presented on each trial, followed by a probe item. In both cases, the time required to make the identification is a linearly increasing function of the number of items in the memory set. When we contrast this to visual scanning, we see that a minor change in procedure can lead to markedly different results.

What is the theoretical explanation for these paradoxical results? In both cases, assume that the memory set will have aroused its associated verbal and visual symbol engrams. The treatment of probe items in the two experiments will be quite different. In visual scanning, the eye is swept rapidly over the array of probe items. This has two important results. The first is that the name codes for letters in the arrays being scanned will compete with each other for the auditory fields of active memory, thus keeping any one of them from capturing the percept easily. The second effect is that rapid scanning will restrict environmental stimulation so that this, unaided, will not force a clear visual percept into active memory. In the case of target stimuli, however, only a small visual input is needed to assist the already partially activated feature generators. Thus the target letters "leap out" against a blur of distractors.

In memory scanning, a single probe item is presented for a sufficiently long time so that its closely associated name code will be aroused. Indeed, in some studies auditory presentations are used. If this happens, the comparison in active memory will be based on the auditory rather than the visual fields. The natural auditory dimension is time, because response competition from symbol engrams forces the subject to activate the items on the memory list one at a time in order to compare them to the *auditory* code of the probe item.

Studies of Semantic Organization

The next illustration deals with experiments that attempt to unravel the semantic organization of long-term memory. Three classes of experiments are discussed.

Clustering

In free recall, subjects often impose their own organization upon initially randomly ordered lists. To take an oversimplified example, if a person is asked to recall the list,

>"Apple, diamond, snake, fish, coal, peach, cherry, bird,"

recall may be in the order,

>"Apple, peach, cherry, snake, fish, bird, diamond, coal."

Recall is said to be clustered into semantic categories. To relate this to the theory, assume that somehow the first item is recalled. This will activate related items, including the items on the list that share a semantic category with the first item. The association will be particularly strong if the subject has activated the category names at the time the list is presented, thus permitting learning in context. In any case, as the associated words are recalled, the task shifts from recalling words presented to the easier task of recognizing which semantically associated words were presented.

The time between successive recalls (inter-response time) in this task is of some interest. Typically inter-response time is short between recall of two items of the same category and is long when a category boundary is crossed (e.g. between "cherry" and "snake" in the above example). In theory this effect should occur, because the first word in the new category could not be recalled until activation spread from the "list to be recalled" concept node, whereas successive recalls within a category could benefit from activation of previous examples of the category.

Category Activation

Collins and Loftus (1975) described studies from the category-activation paradigm (e.g., Loftus & Cole, 1974) as one of the pieces of evidence for a somewhat simpler spreading-activation model. In a category-activation study, two terms are presented in sequence. Each term names a set of items in long-term memory. The task is to produce the name of an item in the intersection of the sets. Reaction time (RT) is measured from presentation of the second set name to the initiation of the response. In the simplest variant of the paradigm, one set name restricts the semantic category of the response, and the other restricts its spelling. An example is "Name a *fruit* beginning with *A.*" Call these terms the *semantic restrictor* and the *name restrictor,* respectively. Responses may be as much as 500 msec. faster if the semantic restrictor precedes the name restrictor by one or two seconds, compared to the reverse ordering.

Collins and Loftus argued that the semantic restrictor raises the activation level of close associates of the category name, i.e., of good examples of the category. The name restrictor is not assumed to do this because, with a few exceptions such as "A is for apple," names are not associated with letters. The names that are associated with letters may often not be members of the required semantic class. Thus partial activation of the ultimate response is possible only when the semantic restrictor is first.[6]

A similar but more detailed explanation is offered here. As do Collins and Loftus, we assume the existence of associations from the semantic restrictor's engram to those of its examples but not between a letter engram and most of the words that begin with the letter. (The reverse arcs, from the word to the letter, must exist, or the word could not be spelled.) This simply rewords the Collins and Loftus assumption; the real question is why the assumption itself is justified. The answer forces us to consider the effects of stimulus–stimulus learning. It also highlights some of the distinctions between symbol engrams and concept engrams.

Recall that, theoretically, learning occurs when there is a simultaneous presence, in active memory, of the referents for two or more engrams and the referent for the conceptual relation between them. There are two ways in which the name of a category and its exemplars should, by this process, be more closely linked than the name of a letter and the words with which that letter begins. One of these two associations might simply be more frequent, or there could be some source of bonding between a category name and its exemplars that is not available to the letter name and its associated words. Although we cannot reject the frequency argument, it also seems a hard one to prove. We argue that the additional bonding source does exist.

By definition, the symbol node of a category will share feature generators with the symbol nodes of good examples of the category. A "dog in general" looks like a German Shepherd (Smith, Shoben, & Rips, 1974). Presentation of a category name, then, will have the effect of priming symbols for good examples. Now consider the case in which the name restrictor, a *visually* presented letter, is

---

[6] This model is an example of Kantowitz's (1974) simple serial model for double stimulation. Let A be the time required to activate a category name given the semantic restrictor, and let B be the time required to select a response from a set of activated item names. Finally, let t be the interstimulus interval. If the name restrictor is first, then $t < 0$. Applying the simple serial model, we have

$$RT = A + B; \qquad t \leqslant 0$$
$$= A - t + B; \qquad 0 < t < A$$
$$= B; \qquad A \leqslant t$$

shown first. This will arouse two types of feature generators, those associated with the visual pattern and those associated with its pronunciation. These may not be the same feature generators associated with the symbols for names in the language. The sound "El" does not have a close phonetic representation to the first syllable in "lemon." In addition, the perceptual features of letters in isolation are not identical to the perceptual units used in recognition of written words (Spoehr & Smith, 1974). Therefore advance warning of the name restrictor should not provide a focal point for the arousal of feature generators associated with the eventual response.

Of course, this does not mean that people cannot list words within a category that begin with a given letter, because they obviously can. We argue that the initial word produced in such a list must be located by a directed search through the conceptual network, possibly first locating a syllable beginning with the required letter, and then words beginning with that syllable. This should be a slower, more diffuse process than the process of finding good examples, given a category name.

The analysis suggests an interesting restriction on the "category first" effect. Rosch et al. (1976) have shown that only certain "basic" categories have clearly defined prototypes. "Animal" is an example of a basic category; "furniture" is a counter-example. The category activation paradigm should work only when dealing with basic categories. Similarly, it should be possible to identify some letter-response pairs in which the features of the letter are, indeed, suggestive of the response, as in "D, academic officer = Dean." If the letter-response similarity was strong and the category involved not basic, it might be possible to reverse the usual finding.

Classes and Prototypes

The hallmark of human reasoning is the ability to reason about abstract classes. Obviously such reasoning depends on the ability to recognize specific objects as class exemplars. Sometimes this distinction can be made with legal precision. In other situations, class membership may be a "fuzzy" concept, in which membership is a matter of degree rather than a logical proposition that is true or false. Many classes can be thought of as regions of a hypothetical Euclidean semantic space, in which a class prototype is located somewhere in the center of the region. For example, the set of animals appears to be representable by a three-dimensional space defined by size, domesticity, and ferocity (Rips et al., 1973). Within that space, classes of animals correspond to regions.

Smith et al. (1974) maintain that decisions about class membership are made in two stages. If the item to be classified is located in the semantic space at a point very close to, or very far from, the class prototype, an immediate decision is made. In intermediate cases, the decision is made logically, by comparing the characteristics of the example to the defining characteristics of the class. This accounts for the fact that class-membership decisions involving good examples

("Is a robin a bird?") are made more rapidly than decisions involving bad examples ("Is a penguin a bird;"). Collins and Loftus point out that such findings are compatible with a network model, because good examples should be linked more tightly to the class name. To continue the illustration, the concepts *robin* and *bird* are linked through *fly,* whereas *bird* and *penguin* are not. We shall expand on this notion, again considering the effects of feature generation.

An object can be identified as a class member if that specific fact is incorporated in the LTM network because of some past contiguity of class name, example name, and membership relation. In other situations, one can deduce class membership by retrieving the definition of a class and then by searching memory to find whether or not the required relationships exist with respect to the test item. These situations appear to be extremes of the Collins and Loftus argument. The intermediate case is of somewhat more interest.

If two items are identical, then each is equivalently an example of the other. "Identical," in the context of this theory, can only mean "If the active memory representations of two items correspond to each other by some criterion of identicality, then the concepts being represented are identical." Now consider the situation in which a class concept has a prototype whose symbol node generates a coherent set of features in active memory. If this representation is close enough to the representation associated with the symbol of a particular example, then that example will be judged as identical to the prototype, and class membership will be assigned quickly. This accounts for the *robin–bird* example. The argument also implies that the rapid classifications discussed by Smith et al. must be based on dimensions that have perceptual interpretations. All the dimensions uncovered in studies of this type (of which we are aware) do, indeed, lend themselves to imaging, either of the animal itself (size), its actions (ferocity), or its context (domesticity).

Rosch et al. point out that only some classes, i.e. their *basic* classes, have prototypes. Rosch et al. offer several highly correlated ways of defining a basic class, the most effective of which is to define a class as having a prototype if there are a large number of perceptual features shared by most members of a class and *not* shared by members of related classes. In semantic-image theory, "perceptual feature" would be reinterpreted as "feature generator." The definition makes possession of a prototype a matter of degree, for two pairs of symbol nodes could vary in the extent to which members of each pair had the same generators associated with them. It also makes definition of a prototype a matter of experience; class prototypes can exist only when there has been enough experience to establish a symbol node. Furthermore, prototypes can only exist for classes that refer to concrete, perceivable objects.

Classes and Collections

Rosch and Mervis (1975) and Vygotsky (1962) have distinguished between two collectives of our thought: *classes* and *collections.* An object is in a class if it possesses the defining features of that class. An object is in a collection if it bears some relation to another object previously defined as in the collection. To illustrate, we can divide humanity into the sexes, obviously two classes. Alternatively, we can partition humanity into the collections that we call *legal families*, because a given individual is a member of a family if she/he stands in one of a small number of relations to some known member(s) of the family. The class-collection distinction is apart from the abstract—concrete dimension. As our examples show, classes and collections may both refer to concrete objects. Mathematics contains examples of abstract classes (the prime numbers) and abstract collections (the Fibonacci numbers). In some situations, however, it seems to be easier to reason about collections than about classes (Markman & Seibert, 1976). How would a network *cum* feature generator model deal with collections?

Within semantic-image theory, the mechanism for establishing links between engrams is the same for engrams representing class names or exemplars. In each case, we simply have a labeled arc between nodes. Whether a particular set of concrete objects is to be treated as a class or a collection, then, depends largely upon the individual's experience. Prototypes, and from them classes, form to the extent that the objects in a set have common features. Collection linkages form if the objects do not have common features, as a group, but within the set any object is close to at least one other object in some definable perceptual space.

The situation is somewhat more complex with regard to abstract classes and collections. All members of an abstract class will have a common linkage path to the engram representing the class, whereas members of an abstract collection may be tied each to only one other member. This suggests that the relative difficulty of dealing with classes and concepts may depend upon whether the subject matter is abstract or concrete. At present there is no data against which this conjecture may be tested.

PRINCIPLES AND CONCEPTS

Theories are of general interest if they permit abstraction of a few principles that can be applied to many phenomena. Semantic-image theory has been developed by considering laboratory studies of cognition. What are the principles that apply to everyday life?

Encoding and Pattern Recognition

The succession of images in thought must be both appropriate and timely. Consider the time dimension first. When a representation is constructed in active memory, its associates must be called up before another representation replaces it. We typically think under time pressure. In the simplest conversations, the listener must keep up with the speaker. In several experiments in our own laboratory, we found that those persons who are rapid at recognizing the meaning of arbitrary physical patterns are likely to have high scores on the verbal comprehension factor of a conventional intelligence test. This factor is perhaps the most pervasive psychometric measure of general intellectual performance (Hunt, Frost, & Lunneborg, 1973; Hunt, Lunneborg, & Lewis, 1975; Hunt, 1977). Looking at the other end of the spectrum, mildly retarded children are very much slower than normal children in associating a highly overlearned name with a pattern (Warren & Hunt, 1976).

Being fast is not enough; the succession of images must be correct. This is apparent when one thinks of thinking as a production notation program. The first step in the production cycle is recognition of the active string as an example of the left-hand side of a production. If this fails, thinking cannot proceed.

The relevance of this to human thought can be illustrated by considering two extreme cases. G. Polya, one of the great mathematicians of this century, wrote eloquently on how to solve mathematical problems (Polya, 1954). Although his examples show clearly that a fine mathematician can recognize appropriate analogies, they provide no information at all about how he does so. Polya's wide-ranging generalizations of previously learned principles are in striking contrast to reports of problem solving in the mentally retarded. Even after very detailed training on strategies for solving simple problems, retardates often fail to show transfer of training to only slightly modified situations (Robinson & Robinson, 1976).

Image Manipulation

Some problems we encounter can only be solved by manipulating an active memory representation without reference to LTM engrams. In the laboratory, the rotation problems studied by Shepard and his colleagues are good examples. Many real-world problems can be solved either by direct reference to stored information or by image examination. To illustrate, does the state of Florida have a substantial coastline facing south? Introspect on how you answer the question. Different people will choose different ways to solve such problems.

The importance of active memory manipulation, however, is not limited to processes that proceed independent of long-term memory. The "Florida" example just given required recall of an engram and, if you visualized the problem, an examination of its representation. We might have to manipulate a representation as well. To show this, let us conduct another *Gedanken* experiment. Figure 1.11 is an upside-down outline of the state of Texas. What is the state that borders on Texas at the point marked by the arrow? A possible way to solve the problem is:

1. Rotate the active memory representation of Figure 1.11 180°, placing the map in its proper orientation.

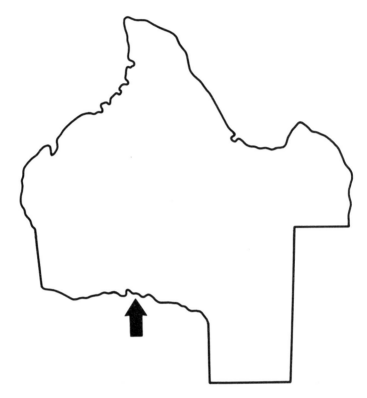

FIGURE 1.11   Outline of one of the United States, 180° out of usual orientation. What state touches on the point marked by the arrow?

2. The rotated map can now be recognized as an example of a prototype "Texas" map, because the engram for maps of U.S. states are equivalent to their visual outlines in normal orientation (Shepard & Chipman, 1970).

3. Examine the active memory representation of the engram for "Texas and the surrounding area," and identify Oklahoma as the state sought.

The point of the illustration is that it is unlikely that the sensory image of a physically present object will be an exact match to the image associated with the LTM engram. The two must be matched by manipulating the images into a congruent representation. In many cases, the manipulation must be done in an internal representation of an object, apart from the representation of other objects physically present at the same time. The many studies of "field independent thinking" can be interpreted as an indication of wide individual differences in the performance of this sort of mental task.

There is a tendency to equate *image* with *visual imagery*. The theory does not require any such restriction. In fact, manipulation of auditory images may be even more important, because they may be a key step in language comprehension. Clark and Chase (1972) have pointed out that language comprehension requires that statements with varying surface structure be placed in correspondence with each other so that they can be compared. This is a step logically analogous to the manipulations of visual images discussed previously, even though it is probably carried out by different physical structures in the brain.

Information

Experimental psychologists are understandably biased toward the study of reactions to information presented under controlled conditions. We tend to forget that most thinking is guided by the thinker's idiosyncratic past experience. This seems a serious mistake, because the possession of knowledge cannot be separated from the act of thought. The role of knowledge is to organize the semantic network, both by establishing the identity of the engrams and by determining the connections between them.

Very little can be said beyond pointing out these obvious facts. Traditionally the study of how knowledge affects cognition has been the province of education rather than psychology. We can point out two avenues for future research. One is the study of individual differences in cognitive style as a function of age. Problem solving is an amalgamation of information handling and knowledge utilization; in most situations there is an opportunity to stress one or the other. Combining this with the equally trite observation that as people grow older, they learn more, we conclude that information-processing capacities should be relatively more important in the problem-solving performance of children than of adults. Making the point more concretely, the studies cited from our own laboratory, and those of others, have shown that various measures of encoding and active memory capacity have a correlation of from .2 to .5 with the performance of young adults on a global intelligence test. We should find an increase in these correlations if we repeat the studies on children and a decrease if we repeat them on older adults. (In the latter case, it would be necessary to allow for the major changes in information-processing capability due to physical injury to the brain.) There is a hint of such a phenomenon in the reported shift in problem solving from "fluid" to "crystal" intelligence with increasing age (Horn, 1968), but considerably more work needs to be done to establish the point.

It should be possible to use this phenomenon to construct tests of the effect of different intellectual experiences. A test of "education" is typically a test of the engrams a person has acquired. "Do you know who commanded the Confederate army at the battle of Atlanta?" Why not try to find out more about how these facts are organized inside the person's head? The idea is not a farfetched one. Loftus and Loftus (1974) found indications that graduate training in psychology had some effect on a person's semantic organization of information about scientific psychologists. Mapping a student's semantic network is certainly not considered as a replacement for conventional fact testing. It may be a more appropriate way of assessing the psychological implications of an educational or social experience than is the conventional test of knowledge possession.

The Representation Issue

To think about Canadian geese, one can image a flight of them or image words about migratory birds. To think about the nonreal numbers, one may image $(-1)^{1/2}$, a Cartesian coordinate system, or words about the properties of numbers. In each case, thought depends upon the manipulation of an internal representation of an external reality. The choice of an appropriate representation, i.e., one that is easy to manipulate but captures the essential points of the problem, is probably the most important single decision a problem solver makes.

The representation decision takes place in two stages. In the first, a choice is made of sensory modes of presentation. Within modes, a particular analogy must be chosen. We then must decide whether to react to the imaged representation of the problem in a piecemeal, analytic fashion or to react to a wholistic impression. Each of these decisions has implications for the engrams that will be activated and the active memory mechanisms that will be called into play.

Human problem solving is clearly influenced by such decisions. Environmental cues can force people toward one form of representation or another. Experience modifies the way two individuals handle the same problem, even to the extent of determining whether some recognitions of auditory pattern are handled as right- or left-hemisphere tasks (Bever & Chiarello, 1974). There are apparently stable individual differences in whether wholistic or analytical approaches are applied to fixed problems in visual stimulus identification (Hock, Gordon, & Gold, 1975). At present, we know that representation choices are important and that people make them in different ways. Semantic-image theory may be of help in stating why representation choices are important, although practically any other reasonable theory of thought would come to the same conclusion. If the theory can be developed to indicate *how* the choices are made, this will be a major contribution indeed.

CONCLUDING REMARKS

Experimental psychologists have developed powerful models of isolated aspects of cognition. This is necessary, for many grand theories in psychology have failed because they could not be applied to any specific situation. Psychoanalysis is perhaps the best example of a far-reaching idea unable to come to grip with facts. Scientific psychology has been appropriately cautious about such grandiose notions.

It is possible to overreact. Human cognition is a unified phenomenon. We see as we hear, and we talk to ourselves as we visualize. All these things are done inside one's head and depend on the physical structures the skull contains. Furthermore, there are great individual differences in the way we go about thinking. These differences are both qualitative and quantitative. We must deal with the fact that some people are bright and some are not and that some people are bright in one way and others are bright in another. We also have to explain why minor changes in a stimulus make a problem easy or hard. Why, for instance, can humans deal so easily with complex linguistic structures in natural language and yet have so much difficulty with the much simpler syntactical structure of formal mathematics? Why is it that 10 to 15% of the citizens of our most advanced industrial societies are functionally illiterate, although every human being learns to speak without any formal instruction? These are the real issues of cognition. We cannot even talk about them coherently in the absence of a unified theory of thought.

This paper is an outline of such a theory. It is based on two assumptions: that active thought is physically a succession of sensory images and that long-term memory is functionally a network of semantic associations. The theory is not complete. At best, a sketch has been offered of its applications. The next step in theoretical development should probably be construction of a computer simulation to demonstrate that the theory is internally consistent and that it actually does lead to the derivations that have been conjectured. In parallel, the general theory should be used to develop specialized models for specific paradigms in cognitive psychology. The models should encompass problem solving, decision making, and individual differences; they should not be microspecialized models of very limited situations. Studies of the specifics of memory and attention are vital and must give results consistent with any broad theory. They are not sufficient. There must be more study of the broad questions if we are ever to have a significant theory of thought.

ACKNOWLEDGMENTS

This research was sponsored by the National Institute of Mental Health, grant MH21795, to the University of Washington. I would like to express my thanks to Dr. Colin MacLeod for his painstaking comments. I am also indebted to Professor Douglas Hintzman for pointing out the importance of distinguishing between the meaning of "image" as used in this paper and the popular connotation of the word as "visual image."

REFERENCES

Bever, T. G., & Chiarello, R. J. Cerebral dominance in musicians and nonmusicians. *Science*, 1974, *185*, 537–539.

Bolles, R. C. Learning, motivation, and cognition. In W. Estes (Ed.), *Handbook of learning and cognitive processes, Vol. 1.* Hillsdale, N.J.: Lawrence Erlbaum Associates, 1975.

Clark, H., & Chase, W. On the process of comparing sentences against pictures. *Cognitive Psychology*, 1972, *3*, 472–517.

Collins, A. M., & Loftus, E. F. A spreading activation theory of semantic processing. *Psychological Review*, 1975, *82*, 407–428.

Cooper, L., & Shepard, R. Chronometric studies of the rotation of mental images. In W. Chase (Ed.), *Visual information processing.* New York: Academic Press, 1973.

Hayes, J. R. On the function of visual imagery in elementary mathematics. In W. Chase (Ed.), *Visual information processing.* New York: Academic Press, 1973.

Hock, H. S., Gordon, G. P., & Gold, L. Individual differences in the verbal coding of familiar visual stimuli. *Memory and Cognition,* 1975, *3*, 257–262.

Horn, J. Organization of abilities and the development of intelligence. *Psychological Review,* 1968, *75*, 242–259.

Hunt, E. B. *Artificial intelligence.* New York: Academic Press, 1975.

Hunt, E. B. We know who knows, but why? In R. C. Anderson, R. J. Spiro, & W. E. Montague (Eds.), *Schooling and the acquisition of knowledge.* Hillsdale, N.J.: Lawrence Erlbaum Associates, 1977.

Hunt, E. B. *A model of information acquisition and organization.* Proceedings of symposium on human information processing. XVIII International Congress of Psychology, Moscow: 1966.

Hunt, E. B., Frost, N., & Lunneborg, C. Individual differences in cognition: A new approach to intelligence. In G. Bower (Ed.), *Advances in learning and motivation, 7.* New York: Academic Press, 1973.

Hunt, E., Lunneborg, C., & Lewis, J. What does it mean to be high verbal? *Cognitive Psychology,* 1975, *7*, 194–227.

Kantowitz, B. H. Double stimulation. In B. Kantowitz (Ed.), *Human information processing.* Hillsdale, N. J.: Lawrence Erlbaum Associates, 1974.

Loftus, E. F., & Cole, W. Retrieving attribute and name information from semantic memory. *Journal of Experimental Psychology,* 1974, *102*, 1116–1122.

Loftus, E. F., & Loftus, G. Changes in memory structure and retrieval over the course of instruction. *Journal of Educational Psychology,* 1974, *66*, 315–318.

Markman, E. M., & Seibert, J. Classes and collections: Internal organization and resulting holistic properties. *Cognitive Psychology,* 1976, *8*, 561–577.

Neisser, U. *Cognitive psychology.* New York: Appleton, 1967.

Newell, A., & Simon, H. *Human problem solving.* Englewood Cliffs, N. J.: Prentice-Hall, 1972.

Norman, D., & Rumelhart, D. *Explorations in cognition.* San Francisco: Freeman, 1975.

Polya, G. *Mathematics and plausible reasoning.* Princeton: Princeton Univ. Press, 1954.

Posner, M. I., Boies, S. J., Eichelman, W. H., & Taylor, R. L. Retention of visual and name codes of single letters. *Journal of Experimental Psychology,* 1969, *79*, #1, part 2, 1–16.

Pylyshyn, Z. W. What the mind's eye tells the mind's brain: A critique of mental imagery. *Psychological Bulletin,* 1973, *80*, 1–24.

Rips, L., Shoben, E., & Smith, E. Semantic distance and the verification of semantic relations. *Journal of Verbal Learning and Verbal Behavior,* 1973, *12*, 1–20.

Robinson, N., & Robinson, H. *The mentally retarded child* (2nd ed.). New York: McGraw-Hill, 1976.

Rosch, E., & Mervis, C. Family resemblances: Studies in the natural structures of categories. *Cognitive Psychology,* 1975, *7*, 573–605.

Rosch, E., Mervis, C. B., Gray, W., Johnson, D., & Boyes–Braem, P. Basic objects in natural categories. *Cognitive Psychology,* 1976, *8*, 382–439.

Schank, R. *Conceptual information processing.* New York: American Elsevier, 1975.

Shepard, R., & Chipman, S. Second order isomorphisms of internal representations: Shapes of states. *Cognitive Psychology,* 1970, *1*, 1–17.

Smith, E., Shoben, E., & Rips, L. Structure and process in semantic memory: A featural model for semantic decisions. *Psychological Review,* 1974, *81*, 214–241.

Spoehr, K., & Smith, E. The perception of printed English: A theoretical perspective. In B. Kantowitz (Ed.), *Human information processing.* Hillsdale, N. J.: Lawrence Erlbaum Associates, 1974.

Sternberg, S. High speed scanning in human memory. *Science,* 1966, *153,* 652–654.

Vygotsky, L. *Thought and language.* New York: Wiley, 1962.

Warren, J., & Hunt, E. *Information processing in medically defined groups of retarded children.* Paper presented at 9th annual Gatlinburg Conference on Mental Retardation, Gatlinburg, Tenn., April 1976.

2
Accretion, Tuning, and Restructuring: Three Modes of Learning

David E. Rumelhart
Donald A. Norman

University of California, San Diego

It is somehow strange that throughout the recent work on semantic memory, the study of learning has been slighted. The term *learning* has fallen into disuse, replaced by vague references to "acquisition of information in memory." It is easy to fall into the trap of believing that the learning of some topic is no more than the acquisition of the appropriate set of statements about the topic by the memory system. According to this simple view of things, to have learned something well is to be able to retrieve it from memory at an appropriate time. We believe this view is much too simple. Learning can be more than the simple acquisition of statements. We believe it is time to examine learning again, to evaluate just what does happen when people acquire information about a topic and use it appropriately.

The study of learning differs from the study of memory in its emphasis, not necessarily in content. Learning and memory are intimately intertwined, and it is not possible to understand one without understanding the other. But the difference in emphasis is critical. There are many different kinds of learning, and the characterization of the learning process most likely varies according to the type of learning that is taking place. Some forms of learning—especially the learning of relatively simple information—can probably be characterized correctly as a simple accumulation of new information into memory. However, especially when we deal with the learning of complex topics where the learning experience takes periods of time measured in months or even years, learning is much more than the successful storage of increasing amounts of information.

Complex learning appears to have an emergent quality. This learning seems to involve a modification of the organizational structures of memory as well as the accumulation of facts about the topic under study. At times this modification of the organizational structure seems to be accompanied by a "click of comprehension," a reasonably strong feeling of insight or understanding of a topic that makes a large body of previously acquired (but ill-structured) information fit into place. Thus the study of the learning of complex topics is related to the study of the understanding of complex topics.

This paper does not satisfy our desire for increased knowledge about the process of learning. Instead we simply hope to whet the appetite of our audience (and of ourselves). We present an analysis of learning and memory, attempting to examine some possible conceptualizations of the learning process, hoping thereby to guide the research of future years. We ourselves are just beginning the study of learning, and the start has proven frustratingly elusive. Indeed, it is the very elusiveness that has given rise to this paper. We now realize that simple characterizations of the learning process will not do. In this paper, we attempt a coherent account of the process of learning within our conceptualizations of a theory of long-term memory—the theory we have called *active structural networks* (cf. Norman, Rumelhart, & LNR, 1975). Our goal is to indicate how different forms of learning might be integrated into one conceptualization of the systems that acquire, interpret, and use information. This paper only sets the stage for development of theories and observations about learning. Hopefully, the stage is new, with useful characterizations that can be used to guide future developments, both of ourselves and of others.

LEARNING AND THE ACQUISITION OF KNOWLEDGE

Accretion, Restructuring, and Tuning

It is possible to learn through the gradual accretion of information, through the fine tuning of conceptualizations we already possess, or through the restructuring of existing knowledge. We find it useful to distinguish between these three qualitatively different modes of learning. Although we are not ready to propose a formal, rigid classification of learning, let us informally talk as if we could indeed classify learning into these three categories: *accretion, tuning, and restructuring.*

Learning through accretion is the normal kind of fact learning, daily accumulation of information in which most of us engage. The acquisition of memories of the day's events normally involves merely the accumulation of information in memory. A person's knowledge base is merely incremented by a new set of facts. Accretion is the normal learning that has been most studied by the psychologist. The learning of lists, dates, names of presidents, telephone numbers, and related things are examples of learning through accretion. Such learning presumably occurs through appropriate exposure to the concepts to be acquired, with the normal stages of information processing transforming the information being acquired into some appropriate memory representation, which then is added to the person's data base of knowledge. In this case there are no structural changes in the information-processing system itself.

Learning through tuning is a substantially more significant kind of learning. This involves actual changes in the very categories we use for interpreting new information. Thus tuning involves more than merely an addition to our data base. Upon having developed a set of categories of interpretation (as seen in the following, we call these *schemata*), these categories presumably undergo continual tuning or minor modification to bring them more in congruence with the functional demands placed on these categories. Thus, for example, when we first learn to type, we develop a set of response routines to carry out the task. As we become increasingly better typists, these response routines become tuned to the task and we come to be able to perform the task more easily and effectively. For another example, presumably an analogous phenomenon is going on as a young child learns that not all animals are "doggies." Slowly his "doggie" schema becomes modified into congruence with the actual demands on his interpretation system.

Learning through restructuring is a yet more significant (and difficult) process. Restructuring occurs when new structures are devised for interpreting new information and imposing a new organization on that already stored. These new structures then allow for new interpretations of the knowledge, for different accessibility to that knowledge (usually improved accessibility), and for changes in the interpretation and therefore the acquisition of new knowledge.

Restructuring often takes place only after considerable time and effort. It probably requires some critical mass of information to have been accumulated first: In part, it is the unwieldiness and ill-formedness of this accumulated knowledge that gives rise to the need for restructuring.

We are impressed with the fact that real learning takes place over periods of years, not hours. A good deal of this time can be accounted for by the slow accretion of knowledge. There is an extensive amount of information that must be acquired and elaborate interconnections that must be established among all the information, fitting it into the general web of knowledge being developed within the memory system of the learner (see Norman, in press). But a good deal of time must also be spent in the development of the appropriate memory organizations for the evolution of existing memory structures (tuning) and the creation of new ones (restructuring). This learning requires new structures. Indeed, often the point of the learning is the formation of the new structures, not the accumulation of knowledge. Once the appropriate structures exist, the learner can be said to "understand" the material, and that is often a satisfactory end point of the learning process. The accretion of information would appear to be a necessary prerequisite for restructuring; there must be a backlog of experiences and memories on which to base the new structures.

Note the long hours of study that seem to accompany the learning of many tasks. In intellectual domains, we expect students of scholastic topics to spend years of study, from undergraduate instruction, through graduate school, and then afterward, either through postdoctoral studies or as "budding young scholars," acquiring the knowledge and understanding of the field. The acquisition of intellectual knowledge probably continues throughout the lifetime of a scholar.

In skill learning, similar time periods are found. To our mind, the classic result in the literature is Crossman's (1959) study of cigar makers, whose performance continues to improve for at least ten years, with each cigar maker producing some 20 million cigars in that duration. Reaction time tasks in the laboratory have been carried out to at least 75,000 trials, again with continual improvement (Seibel, 1963). Similar figures can be produced for the learning of skills such as language, psychology, chess, and sports. People who are engaged in the serious task of learning a topic, whether it be an intellectual one or a motor skill (the difference is less than one might suspect), appear to show continual improvement even after years of study. As Fitts (1964) put it, "The fact that performance ever levels off at all appears to be due as much to the effects of physiological aging and/or loss of motivation as to the reaching of a true asymptote or limit in capacity for further improvement [p. 268]."

Learning, then, has several different components. In this paper, we concentrate primarily upon the qualitative differences among accretion of knowledge, restructuring of memory, and tuning of existing knowledge structures. Moreover, our discussion is primarily concerned with the latter two modes of learning. Restructuring involves the creation of entirely new memory structures, whereas tuning involves the evolution of old memory structures into new ones. Each of these processes—evolution and creation—can itself be performed in a number of different ways, each way being relevant to a different aspect of the learning process. But, before we can discuss the details of the learning process, we need to discuss our views of the structure of memory and, in particular, the organized memory units: *memory schemata.*

MEMORY SCHEMATA

General Schemata and Particular Instances

Memory contains a record of our experiences. Some of the information is *particular* to the situation that it represents. Other information is more *general*, representing abstraction of the knowledge of particular situations to a class of situations. The memory of eating dinner yesterday represents particular information. Knowledge that people eat meals from plates (using knives, forks, and spoons) represents general information that applies to a large class of situations.

A psychological theory of memory must be capable of representing both general and particular information. We believe that general information is best represented through organized information units that we call *schemata*. To us, a schema is the primary meaning and processing unit of the human information-processing system. We view schemata as active, interrelated knowledge structures, actively engaged in the comprehension of arriving information, guiding the execution of processing operations. In general, a schema consists of a network of interrelations among its constituent parts, which themselves are other schemata.

Generic concepts are represented by schemata. These schemata contain *variables:* references to general classes of concepts that can actually be substituted for the variables in determining the implications of the schema for any particular situation. Particular information is encoded within the memory system when constants—specific values or specific concepts—are substituted for the variables of a general schema. Our representations for specific events are thus instantiations of the general schema for that event[1] type. In some sense, one could consider schemata to represent prototypes of concepts.

A General Schema

A schema can represent an entire situation, showing the interrelationships among component events or situations (or subschemata). Thus we might have a schema for a concept such as *farming* that would contain the following information:

A partial schema for farming. [2]
A plot of land is used for the raising of agricultural crops or animals.
Some person cultivates the soil, produces the crops, and raises animals.
Typically farms raise some crops and have a few animals, including cows, horses, chickens, and pigs.

---

[1] This formulation leaves open the question of whether particular representations result from general schemata or general schemata from particular ones. It is possible that our early experiences with some class of events give rise to a set of particular representations of those events. Then we generalize from these experiences by substituting variables for the aspects of the events that seem to vary with situations, leaving constants (particular concepts) in those parts of the representation that are constant across the different events in the class. The result is a general schema for a class of events. Alternatively, we can take a general schema and apply it to a new, particular situation by replacing the variable with constants. We presume that both of these directions continually take place: General schemata are formed through the process of generalization of particular instances; particular knowledge is derived from the principles incorporated within the general schemata.

[2] Note that this is a personal schema, one relevant to the conceptualizations of one of the authors (D.A.N.), who is horribly ignorant of real farms. This is proper: Schemata within the memory system of a given person reflect (constitute) his beliefs and knowledge. A schema may be wholly inaccurate as a description of the world, but it corresponds to the inaccuracies and misconceptions of the possessor of that schema. Assume that the author of this schema learned about farms through nursery rhymes.

Usually tractors and automated machinery are used to work the fields, and specialized buildings are used to house the products and animals.

... (etc.)

Once we have some general schema for farming, we can use it in a variety of ways. The general schema for farming can be viewed from several different perspectives. In so doing, we learn that:

The land is called a farm.
A farmer is the person who cultives the land or raises the animals.
Livestock are animals kept on a farm for use or profit.
Farming is the act of cultivating the soil, producing crops, and raising animals.
Agriculture is the science and art of farming.
The barn is the building for housing farm animals.

Variables

The general schema for farming contains variable terms that can be further specified whenever the schema is used. Thus the general schema has the following variable terms:

land
crops or animals
some person
machinery
products
specialized buildings.

The particular values that get substituted for these terms depend upon the purpose for which the schema is being used. On different occasions, different substitutions will be made. If we learned that the Stewards have a carrot farm, then we substitute our concept for the Stewards as the group that plays the role of farmers in the schema, and we substitute carrots for the crops and products. We have substituted constants for these variables; however, some variables, such as *land, machinery,* and *buildings,* are still unspecified. Our general knowledge of carrots tells us something of the size of the farm and the kinds of machinery likely to be involved. Our schema for the growing of plants tells us that water and fertilizer are required. Our general schema for farming still has some free variables, but these are not without some constraints: We expect that there will be some animals, probably cows, chickens, horses, and pigs.

Constraints and Defaults

The different variables in a schema are often constrained: We do not expect to find all possible plants or animals on a farm. Tigers, eels, and poison ivy are animals and plants but not within the normal range of possible crops or livestock. Many of the variables in schemata have *default* values associated with them. These are particular values for the variables that we can expect to apply unless we are told otherwise. Thus we might expect cows, pigs, horses, and chickens to be on a farm, and if nothing is said, we assume their presence. Similarly, we use the schema for *commercial transaction* for interpreting an occasion in which some person *A* has purchased item *O* from some other person *B;* we assume that money was transferred from *A* to *B*. We could be wrong. Money may not have been involved. Or, in the previous example, any particular farm may not have those animals. Nevertheless, these are the default values for our general understanding of the situations in question.

Variables (and their constraints) serve two important functions:

1. They specify what the range of objects is that can fill the positions of the various variables.

2. When specific information about the variables is not available, it is possible to make good guesses about the possible values.

The values for the variables for a schema are interrelated with one another. If a farm raises cattle, we expect a different size for the farm and different machinery and products than if the farm raises wheat, peanuts, or carrots. We would expect the buildings to look different. Similarly, if someone purchases an automobile, we expect a different amount of money to be involved than in the purchase of a pencil.

Schemata and Comprehension

We view a schema as a general model of a situation. A schema specifies the inter-relationships that are believed to exist among the concepts and events that comprise a situation. The act of comprehension can be understood as the selection of appropriate configuration of schemata to account for the situation. This means that there will be some initial selection of schemata and verification or rejection of the choices. A major portion of the processing effort involved in comprehension is directed toward determining the appropriate schemata for representing the situation. Once an appropriate configuration of schemata has been found, the constants of the situation have to be associated with (bound to) the variables of the schema. The schema that is selected will determine the interpretation of the situation. Different schemata will thereby yield different interpretations of the same situation, and different features of a situation will take on more or less importance as a function of that interpretation.

Like a theory, schemata vary in the adequacy with which they account for any given situation. Schemata both account for existing inputs and predict the values of others. If the account for the early observations is sufficiently good (and no other candidates emerge in subsequent processing), the schema will be accepted, even though there might be no evidence for some of its predictions. These predictions, then, constitute inferences about the situation that are made in the process of comprehension.

When a schema is sufficiently poor at describing the situation, a new schema must be sought. If no single adequate schema can be found, the situation can be understood only in terms of a set of disconnected subsituations—each interpreted in terms of a separate schema.

Schemata Are Active Data Structures

Although this is not the place to go into the details, we believe that the selection and use of schemata is controlled by the schemata themselves. We think of schemata as active processing units, each schema having the processing capability to examine whatever new data are being processed by the perceptual systems and to recognize data that might be relevant to themselves. Schemata activate themselves whenever they are appropriate to an ongoing analysis, and they are capable of guiding the organization of the data according to their structures. Schemata then can control and direct the comprehension process itself. We further suppose that the output of a schema (evidence that the concept represented by the schema is in the input) can then be introduced into the data pile for use by other schemata.

Perhaps the best way to view this is to think of all the data being written on a blackboard, with the schemata examining the blackboard for data relevant to themselves. When a schema sees something, it attempts to integrate the data into its organizational structure and then puts new information onto the blackboard. Other schemata may react to these new data. Thus schemata are *data driven* in the sense that they respond to the existence of relevant data. Schemata perform *conceptually driven* guidance to the processing by using their internal conceptualizations to add new data to the blackboard, thereby guiding the processing of other schemata. Thus each schema is data-driven and provides conceptually guided guidance to others. Further details of this system can be found in a number of sources: The blackboard analogy comes from the work of Reddy (see Reddy & Newell, 1974); active demons are familiar concepts in modern computing systems, from the demons of Selfridge and Neisser (1960), to the actors of Hewitt, Bishop, and Steiger (1973), to the production systems of Newell (1973); descriptions of those concepts relevant to this discussion are to be found in some of our works, in particular Norman and Bobrow (1976), Rumelhart (1977) and Rumelhart and Ortony (1977).

LEARNING

The Accretion of Knowledge

One basic mode of learning is simply the accumulation of new information. We analyze the sensory events of our current experience, match them with some appropriate set of schemata, form a representation for the experience, and tuck the newly created memory structures away in long-term memory. The newly created data structures are *instantiations* of the previously existing ones, changed only in that the representations for particular aspects of the current situation have been substituted for the variables of the general schema.

This is learning by accretion: learning by adding new data structures to the existing data base of memory, following the organization already present. Learning by accretion is the natural side effect of the comprehension process. In it, we store some interpretation of the actual experience. If later we retrieve the stored information, we use the instantiated schemata to reconstruct the original experience, thereby "remembering" that experience. The schemata guide reconstruction in much the same way that they guide original comprehension.

Accretion, and later retrieval through reconstruction, is the normal process of learning. It is the sort of learning that has traditionally been studied by psychologists, and it is most appropriate to the current developments in the study of memory. Learning through the accumulation of new memories allows the data base of information to be built up. It allows for the acquisition of the large amount of specific knowledge that humans acquire about topics in which they are specialists and about the operation of the world in general. Learning by accretion assumes that the schemata required in the interpretation of new input already exist. Whenever this is not the case, the sheer accretion of knowledge is not effective; there must be a modification of the set of available schemata. This can be brought about either by the evolution of existing schemata (tuning) or the creation of new ones (restructuring). Learning by tuning and by restructuring probably occurs much less frequently than does learning by accretion. But without these other learning processes, new concepts cannot be formed.

Learning by Restructuring

When existing memory structures are not adequate to account for new knowledge, then new structures are required, either by erecting new schemata specifically designed for the troublesome information or by modifying (tuning) old ones.

Both the creation and tuning of schemata go hand-in-hand in the learning process. Thus in learning a skill such as typing, new schemata for the appropriate actions must be developed. But once the basic motor schemata have been developed, then further increases in proficiency will come about through the tuning of the existing schemata. Similarly, in the learning of some complex topic matter, probably the first step is the accretion of a reasonable body of knowledge about the topic, followed by the creation of new schemata to organize that knowledge appropriately. Then, continued learning consists of further tuning of those schemata (as well as continued accretion of knowledge and possibly creation of other new schemata, which in turn then have to be tuned).

If the only learning processes were memory accretion and tuning, one could never increase the number of conceptual categories over those initially given. Thus it is essential that new schemata be created. Logically, there are two ways in which new schemata can be formed. First, a new schema can be patterned on an old one, consisting of a copy with modifications. We call this process *patterned generation* of schemata. Second, new schemata can be induced from regularities in the temporal and/or spatial configurations of old schemata. We call this process *schema induction.* It is a kind of contiguity learning.

Patterned generation of schemata is doubtless the source of a good deal of ordinary concept formation.[3] Perhaps the simplest form of patterned generation occurs through the use of analogies. Thus, even if we never had direct experience with a *rhombus,* we could develop a schema for one by being instructed that a rhombus has the same relationship to a square that a parallelogram has to a rectangle. The rhombus schema can be created by patterning it on the square schema, modifying it in just the way the parallelogram schema differs from the rectangle schema.

Note that this is creation of a new schema by generalizing an old one. The modification involves replacing a constant term of the square schema (the right angles at the corner) with variables to produce a new, more general schema. Patterned schema generation can also occur through modifying old schemata, replacing some of the variable components of a schema with constants. Thus, for example, we might very well form the concept of a "cocker spaniel" by modifying the schema for "dog." In this case, we would pattern the cocker spaniel schema on the dog schema but with certain variables much more tightly specified.

Schema induction is a form of learning by contiguity. If certain configurations of schemata tend to co-occur either spatially or temporally, a new schema can be created, formed from the co-occurring configuration. Learning of this kind is probably the least frequent mode of learning (or equivalently the most difficult). Yet it is an important procedure for learning. The difficulty with induction is in the discovery of the regularities. We suspect that most schema creation occurs through patterned generation. Experienced teachers find that analogies, metaphors, and models are effective teaching devices. We do not often (ever) see temporal contiguity as an effective teaching tool in the classroom or in the acquisition of most complex topics. Temporal contiguity is the fundamental principle of most theories of learning, but it seems to have amazingly little direct application in the learning of complex material. As far as we can determine,

---

[3] Note that we are *not* referring to the concept identification tasks that have been studied within the laboratory. The normal experiments on concept formation probably involve very little learning. Probably these tasks have been more concerned with problem solving, where the subjects are asked to discover the rules that will properly classify the particular stimulus set under study.

most complex concepts are learned because the instructor either explicitly introduces an appropriate analogy, metaphor, or model, or because the learner happens across one. We believe that most learning through the creation of new schemata takes place through patterned generation, not through schema induction.

Schema Tuning

Existing schemata can often serve as the base for the development of new ones by minor changes: by "fine tuning" of their structure. We call this process *tuning*. We restrict the use of the term *tuning* to those cases where the basic relational structure of the schema remains unchanged, and only the constant and variable terms referred to by the schema are modified. These terms can be changed in four ways:

1. *Improving the accuracy.* The constraints of the variable terms of the schema can be improved to specify the concepts that fit the variables with more accuracy.

2. *Generalizing the applicability.* The range of a given variable can be generalized to extend its range of applicability. Either the constraints on a variable can be relaxed, or a constant term can be replaced with an appropriately constrained variable term.

3. *Specializing the applicability.* The range of a given variable can be constrained by adding to the constraints of the variable, in the extreme, by effectively replacing the variable with a constant term.

4. *Determining the default values.* The values of the variable that normally apply can be discovered and added to the specification of the schema. Whenever a particular variable is not specified, the default values provide intelligent guesses that can be used in making inferences and guiding further processing.

The adjustment of variable constraints must be an important mechanism of learning.[4] We must learn over what ranges variables vary; we must learn how the various variables co-vary. Our processing increases in efficiency if a schema specification is accurate and if we are not wasting time attempting to fit it to improper situations. Moreover, our understanding of a situation is more com-

---

[4]Note that there is really very little difference between constrained variables and constants. Schemata refer to terms with differing amounts of constraints upon the concepts that can be used in those terms. When the constraints are minimal, we have a free variable: Any concept can be substituted. Usually, the constraints specify some reasonable range of alternative concepts that can be used, excluding certain classes and allowing others. When the constraints are so restrictive that only a single unique concept can be used, then this is the equivalent of having a constant rather than a variable. In the normal case, schemata take variables that are partially constrained and thus provide some structure while at the same time represent a reasonable degree of generality.

plete if we account for it by a more, rather than less, specific schema. With more experience we can determine the typical values for the terms, providing information about default values to be used in the absence of further specification. The literature of language acquisition provides good illustrations of the role of variable adjustment. Let us look briefly at them.

Tuning to improve accuracy. The child must learn the range of conditions over which particular syntactic rules are applicable. Consider the child who can count and who realizes that the adjective meaning of the i-th element of a sequence can be formed by adding the suffix *th* to a number i. The child will correctly generate such words as *fourth, sixth, seventh,* etc. The child will, however, also generate words like *oneth, twoth, threeth, fiveth,* etc. The child has too broad a rule: the rule is over regularized. The child must tune the general rule so that it has the correct constraints on its applicability. The process whereby the restrictions are learned involves adjusting the variables of the schema to permit its invocation only for the appropriate conditions. The schema must be tuned to improve its accuracy of application.

Tuning to generalize the applicability. Bowerman (in press) reports that young children use action words first only about themselves, then later generalize them to other people and animals, and finally use them for inanimate objects as well. This would appear to be a case where the schema must be tuned by loosening the variable constraints to make it more generally applicable.

Generalization of schemata occurs when an existing schema is modified so as to apply to a wider range. One example is when the meaning of a term is *extended* to cover other cases. This process, called *metaphorical extension* by Gentner (1975), was illustrated by her use of the word "have" in the following examples:

1. Sam *has* a large kettle.
2. Sam *has* a nice apartment.
3. The kettle *has* an enamel coating.
4. Sam *has* good times.

Presumably the verb "have" gets a primary meaning of something like "own." By extension, aspects of the owning relationship become inessential to the application of the concept of "having." Originally "have" would seem to require the owner to be one with complete control over the object in question. As the usage gets extended, the requirement of having complete control is loosened until finally, by sentence (4), it appears to require only that the object in question be strongly associated, in some way, with the subject.

Although it is much more common in language acquisition to find cases of children overgeneralizing a concept, which then must be restricted in its range of application, there are cases reported in which children first over-restrict the application of a term and then must *generalize* its use to the entire conceptual category. Thus, Dale (1976) reports a case in which a child first applied the word "muffin" to only blueberries and blueberry muffins but not to other muffins. The process whereby the word comes to be extended to other muffins involves generalization of schemata.

In general, reasoning by analogy would seem to involve the generalization of a schema. In this case, a schema that is applicable in one domain is extended to a new domain by modifying one or more of its elements but maintaining the bulk of its internal structure. Thus, for example, when we consider fog "creeping on little cat's paws," the "creep" schema must somehow be extended to fog. Although this extension probably doesn't involve much learning, it follows the same principles that we have in mind.

Tuning to specialize applicability. A common occurrence in the child's acquisition of language is to overgeneralize the words, to use one word for a much larger set of circumstances than is appropriate. Thus a child may call all small animals "doggie" or all humans "mamma." Clark (1973) summarizes much of the literature on this phenomenon. Overgeneralization probably occurs because the child has selected too few features to identify the concept, when so many things will satisfy the definition. The child must specialize its understanding of the schema by either restricting the range of the variable terms or by adding more terms that must be followed before the schema is acceptable. Specialization by the first method fits our notion of tuning. Specialization by the second actually would be a form of patterned generation of schemata: forming a new schema based upon the old but modified by adding a few more terms.

Children may learn to use the term "ball" to apply to all small objects. They must learn to restrict the class of objects to which the term applies. Similar examples have been reported with the use of relational terms like "more–less," "long–short," "big–wee," etc. (cf. Donaldson & Wales, 1970). Children first learn to apply either term when the appropriate dimension is in question and then learn to restrict the application of the concepts to the appropriate direction on the dimension. Again, additional structure is inserted into the relevant schemata.

A similar process may very well be involved in becoming skillful at a motor task. At first when we learn to carry out a complex motor task, there is broad variation in the movements used to accomplish the task, but with experience in the situation, the variability of the movements is reduced. Consider, as an example, learning to juggle. At first we have great difficulty. We often toss the ball too high or too low. Our catching hand has to reach for the balls as they fall. With practice, our throws become increasingly precise. We come to be able to anticipate where the ball will fall with increasing accuracy. It would thus seem that at the early stages of learning to juggle, the appropriate schemata are only loosely interrelated—any of a variety of components may be configured together. With practice new constraints are added to our juggle schema, and it becomes an increasingly precise, well-tuned schema (see Norman, 1976).

LEARNING IS NOT A UNITARY PROCESS

One major point of this paper is that learning is not a unitary process: No single mental activity corresponding to learning exists. Learning takes place whenever people modify their knowledge base, and no single theoretical description will account for the multitude of ways by which learning might occur. Indeed, we do not believe that we have necessarily described all the varieties of learning in this short classification. But we have attempted to demonstrate a reasonable variety of the classes of learning that might occur, with a description of the mechanisms that might be responsible for them. The classification is summarized in Figure 2.1.

It is interesting to note that the different kinds of learning occur in complementary circumstances. Memory accretion is most efficiently done when the incoming information is consistent with the schemata currently available. In this case, the information is easily assimilated. The more discrepant the arriving information from that described by the available schemata, the greater the necessity for change. If the information is only mildly discrepant, tuning of the schemata may be sufficient. If the material is more discrepant, schema creation is probably required. Of course, in order for restructuring to occur, there must be recognition of the discrepancy. But when mismatched by the available schemata, the learner may so misinterpret (misunderstand) the material that the discrepancies might not even be noted. The need for restructuring might only be noted with mild discrepancies when the misfit is glaring.

This discussion has concentrated on descriptions of the changes that take place in the memory schemata during learning. We have not discussed the mechanisms that might operate to cause these changes. The mechanisms for accretion are reasonably well developed: This is the process most frequently studied, most capable of being described by most theories of memory. We suspect that schema tuning is also a relatively straightforward operation, one that might not require much different mechanisms than already exist in theories of memory. But the restructuring of memory through the creation of new schemata is quite a different story. Here we know little of the process whereby this might take place. Moreover, we suspect that the occasions of schema creation are not frequent. Reorganization of the memory system is not something that should be accomplished lightly. The new structure that should be formed is not easy to determine: The entire literature on "insightful" learning and problem solving, on creativity, on discovery learning, etc., can probably be considered as reports of studies of how new schemata get created. We do not believe that the human memory system simply reorganizes itself whenever new patterns are discovered:

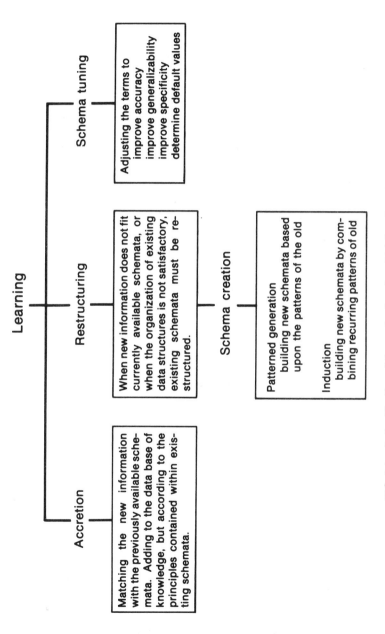

Learning

Accretion

Matching the new information with the previously available schemata. Adding to the data base of knowledge, but according to the principles contained within existing schemata.

Restructuring

When new information does not fit currently available schemata, or when the organization of existing data structures is not satisfactory, existing schemata must be restructured.

Schema tuning

Adjusting the terms to
improve accuracy
improve generalizability
improve specificity
determine default values

Schema creation

Patterned generation
building new schemata based upon the patterns of the old

Induction
building new schemata by combining recurring patterns of old

FIG. 2.1. A classification of the mechanisms by which learning might occur.

51

the discovery of patterns, the matching of analogous schemata to the current situation, must probably require considerable analysis. This is the area that we believe requires the most study in the future.

ACKNOWLEDGMENTS

This research was supported by the Advanced Research Projects Agency and the Office of Naval Research of the Department of Defense and was monitored by ONR under Contract No: N00014-76-C-0628.

REFERENCES

Bowerman, M. Semantic factors in the acquisition of rules for word use and sentence construction. In D. Morehead & A. Morehead (Eds.), *Language deficiency in children: Selected readings.* Baltimore: University Park Press, in press.

Clark, E. V. What's in a word: On the child's acquisition of semantics in his first language. In T. E. Moore (Ed.), *Cognitive development and the acquisition of language.* New York: Academic Press, 1973.

Crossman, E. R. F. W. A Theory of the acquisition of speed-skill. *Ergonomics,* 1959, *2,* 153–166.

Dale, P. S. *Language development: Structure and function.* New York: Holt, Rinehart & Winston, 1976.

Donaldson, M., & Wales, R. J. On the acquisition of some relational terms. In R. Hayes (Ed.), *Cognition and the development of language.* New York: Wiley, 1970.

Fitts, P. M. Perceptual-motor skill learning. In A. W. Melton (Ed.), *Categories of human learning.* New York: Academic Press, 1964.

Gentner, D. Evidence for the psychological reality of semantic components: The verbs of possession. In D. A. Norman, D. E. Rumelhart, & the LNR Research Group, *Explorations in cognition.* San Francisco: W. H. Freeman, 1975.

Hewitt, C., Bishop, P., & Steiger, R. *A universal modular ACTOR formalism for artificial intelligence.* Proceedings of the Third International Conference on Artificial Intelligence, Stanford, California, 1973.

Newell, A. Production systems: Models of control structures: In W. G. Chase (Ed.), *Visual information processing.* New York: Academic Press, 1973.

Norman, D. A. *Memory and attention* (2nd ed.). New York: Wiley, 1976.

Norman, D. A. Learning complex topics. *American Scientist,* in press.

Norman, D. A., & Bobrow, D. G. On the role of active memory processes in perception and cognition. In C. N. Cofer (Ed.), *The structure of human memory.* San Francisco: W. H. Freeman, 1976.

Norman, D. A., Rumelhart, D. E., & the LNR Research Group. *Explorations in cognition.* San Francisco: W. H. Freeman, 1975.

Reddy, R., & Newell, A. Knowledge and its representation in a speech understanding system. In L. W. Gregg (Ed.), *Knowledge and cognition.* Hillsdale, N.J.: Lawrence Erlbaum Associates, 1974.

Rumelhart, D. E. Toward an interactive model of reading. In S. Dornic (Ed.) *Attention and performance, VI.* Hillsdale, N.J.: Lawrence Erlbaum Associates, 1977.

Rumelhart, D. E., & Ortony, A. The representation of knowledge in memory. In R. C.

Anderson, R. J. Spiro, & W. E. Montague (Eds.) *Schooling and the acquisition of knowledge.* Hillsdale, N.J.: Lawrence Erlbaum Associates, 1977.

Seibel, R. Discrimination reaction time for a 1,023-alternative task. *Journal of Experimental Psychology,* 1963, *66,* 215–226.

Selfridge, O. G., & Neisser, U. Pattern recognition by machine. *Scientific American,* 1960, *203,* 60–68.

3
Comments on the Papers by Hunt and by Rumelhart and Norman

Douglas L. Hintzman

University of Oregon

Once, not many years ago, Psychology was ruled by a cruel Behaviorist regime that forced its underlings to conduct experiments and recite operational definitions. It forbade introspective observations and even outlawed the public use of mentalistic language (the Psychologists' native tongue). It is perhaps an indication of how much attitudes have changed since the tyrannical Behaviorists were overthrown that this morning we were able to hear two papers—one claiming to be "semi-rigorous" and the other making no claims to rigor of any degree—neither of which made much contact with data, either real or simulated. One might debate whether this represents an altogether healthy trend. But I don't want to be unfairly characterized as a "running dog of Behaviorism," so I will content myself with raising the question and will not attempt to answer it.

Let me discuss the two papers in reverse order—Rumelhart's first and then Hunt's.

Rumelhart and Norman, in their treatment of learning, use a concept similar to Minsky's (1975) "frame" and Schank and Abelson's (1975) "script." They prefer the word "schema," which they have borrowed from Bartlett and from Piaget. Bartlett (1932) himself had this to say about the word: "I strongly dislike the term 'schema'. It is at once too definite and too sketchy. The word is already widely used in controversial psychological writing to refer generally to any rather vaguely outlined theory [pp. 200–201]." Bartlett went on to use the definite-but-sketchy nature of this despised term to his best advantage. There has since been a great deal of thoroughly inconclusive debate over just what he intended the term to mean.

Having struggled with Bartlett's theory myself, I approach other theories that employ the term *schema* with dark suspicion. Fortunately, Rumelhart and Norman seem to have something more definite in mind than Bartlett had. Indeed, we may suppose that the schema notion has been refined to the point that it can be embodied in a computer program—an invaluable tool not available in Bartlett's day.

Rumelhart and Norman make an important point: that most memory research and therefore most memory theories are restricted to a particular kind of learning or memory. They call this the *accretion* or accumulation of memories, referring to the processing and retention of information about events that match our pre-existing concepts and expectations. It is contrasted with learning that requires changes in the schemata we use to understand the world—by either adjusting the parameters of schemata (*tuning*) or by creating new ones (*restructuring*).

One can see here the influence of Piaget, who distinguishes between *assimilation*, which does not require changes in schemata, and *accommodation*, which does. But the distinction Rumelhart and Norman make also seems to be related to another distinction that philosophers of memory have made for many years. Henri Bergson (1911) distinguished between what he called *true memory*, which involves memory for personal experiences, and *habit memory*, which involves general concepts and skills. In more recent work, philosophers have preferred the terms *personal memory* and *factual memory*. And Tulving (1972) introduced the distinction into current psychological theory using the terms *episodic memory* and *semantic memory*. A number of other labels have been used by other writers; but the distinction appears always to be the same: Memory for personal experiences—that is, particular events in one's past—is contrasted with memory for general concepts. Now, a general concept must be derived from a number of individual experiences, all of which have something in common. The concept is an abstract idea in which only the "something in common" is represented, and details of the individual instances are suppressed or lost. It is this process of constructing general concepts out of particular events to which Rumelhart and Norman direct our attention: How are semantic memories derived from episodic ones?

Unfortunately, their ideas about the specifics of this process seem very hazy. Some of the questions that arise are familiar to students of learning: Is schema formation incremental or all-or-none? Is contiguity sufficient for schema formation, as the authors say, or does feedback (i.e., reinforcement) play a role, as some of their examples suggest? How selective is schema formation—Are all the schemata activated by an input altered when learning occurs, or is change restricted to schemata that are relevant? As difficult as we know such questions are, they must be answered by any theory of human learning that pretends to be complete.

Some of Rumelhart and Norman's discussion suggests to me a rather complex "executive routine" that actively makes decisions about what changes are appropriate and when they should be made. If such a mechanism is intended, something should be said about its structure. Obviously, a great deal must be said about it if these ideas are to be realized in a computer program. One might suppose that such an executive routine would use special "learning schemata" that would apply each type of alteration—accretion, tuning, and restructuring—only when appropriate. This implies a highly sophisticated ability to identify abstract patterns of discrepancy, and it raises the question of how complex the executive routine must be. To some extent, these "learning schemata" would have to be innate (primitives)—although to some extent they must themselves be learned or "bootstrapped" in, through experience. One wonders how simple a system a person could start with and still end up with a sufficiently powerful executive routine.

Let me now turn to Professor Hunt's paper. Hunt proposes a theory of thinking that has some familiar components—the distinction between active and long-term memory, for example—and others that are unusual. To me, however, one feature of his theory stands out from all the others: his proposal that thinking consists of a succession of sensory images in active memory. A thought, Hunt proposes, is "a coherent sequence of internal events that we could perceive if the appropriate external events occurred." Representations in active memory have "isomorphic relations to some dimensions of conceivable physical stimuli." No thoughts are possible, then, that cannot be represented by sensory images.

Could it be that images—and only images—are the substance of thought? This idea goes back as far as Aristotle, and since Aristotle's time, several good reasons have emerged for doubting that it is so. These arguments have all been made by others—sometimes at great length—but it is perhaps a worthwhile exercise to rehearse them briefly here.

First, of course, there are the reports of imageless thought made by members of the Würzburg school at the beginning of this century (see Humphrey, 1963). History shows that one can interpret such reports in two ways. Either there *is* imageless thought, as the Würzburgers said, or anyone who reports imageless thought is an incompetent observer, as Titchener claimed. The demise of the introspective method, which was caught in the crossfire of these two warring factions, contributed to the rise of Behaviorism (lamented earlier in my remarks).

But even if Titchener were right in asserting that all thinking is accompanied by imagery, there would remain the logical problem of how the multifaceted content of thought could be represented by images. If complete, a visual image must contain more properties than the thought process is ordinarily concerned with. For example, if one constructs an image corresponding to the thought "Roger has black hair," it might serve just as well to represent "You can't see

Roger's scalp" or "Roger has two eyes." Hunt points out that images can be incomplete and therefore abstract. But an incomplete image is just as concrete as an abstract one. If one's image of "Roger has black hair" includes hair but no eyes, then it might as easily represent "Roger doesn't have eyes." (Indeed, it might not be recognizable as Roger at all.) The point is that thought can single out particular properties for examination in isolation. Sensory images are too concrete to be the sole medium in which this is carried out.

A related point concerns the problem of abstract ideas. The philosophers Berkeley and Hume debated whether generic images were possible—an image of the general concept "triangle," for example, or of the general concept "animal." Champions of the theory that images are the substance of thought have taken two positions: Either the general concept is represented by an image of a particular instance, or it is represented by a prototype image, which is a kind of average of the images of the individual exemplars of the category. The first of these positions will clearly not do, because it does not differentiate between the particular and the general. If one were to use his cocker spaniel image to stand for "animal," he might erroneously conclude that animals are things that bark, have floppy ears, and like to be petted. The second position will not do either. If the prototype image is vague enough to represent all members of the category, then it may not be possible to imagine it at all; if it is specific enough to be imagined, then it may not represent all members of the category. I may have a generic image for "animal" that is dark and furry and four-legged—but such an image cannot encompass an instance such as Moby Dick. I will not even discuss the problems of representing in images such concepts as "system," "contradiction," and "abstraction," because I have no idea where to begin. What would an image of "irrelevance" be like?

All of these problems, Hunt ignores. But he does mention abstract relations— two in particular: "opposite" and "class membership." He assumes that these relations are in long-term memory, but it is not clear just how they are supposed to have gotten there. The only way a new idea can get into long-term memory is for it to pass through active memory. But active memory only holds images, so the only concepts that can be learned are those that can be imaged. The problem of representing an abstract relation in an image may be even more difficult than that of representing a generic concept such as "animal." What would an image of "opposite" be like? Or "class membership," "has as parts," or "if then"? The only way around this problem would seem to be to postulate, as Kant did, that certain abstract relations are innate categories of the mind, or primitives, out of which all other concepts are built. But because of their abstract nature, such relations *still* would be impossible to image; and this means they could not enter into the active thought process as it has been conceptualized by Hunt.

Now I am not unaware that Hunt has built an escape hatch into his theory. Let me hasten to nail it shut. Abstract ideas, it turns out, can be represented by auditory images of *words*. Concepts such as "animal" and "irrelevance" cause no special problems. The sensory images representing them in active memory can be linguistic.

Apparently, Hunt is not alone in making this proposal—it has been particularly popular in the Soviet Union. Sokolov, in his book, *Inner Speech and Thought*, (1972), has reviewed the evidence regarding the role of speech in thinking, concluding that "thoughts are always associated with words, i.e., in the absence of words there are no thoughts [p. 40]." He cites a dramatic experiment by Mesmer, who made an unsuccessful attempt to think without words—"an attempt," Sokolov tells us, "that brought him to the brink of insanity [p. 48]."

Whatever the meaning of Mesmer's experience (NIMH regulations, of course, prohibit replication on college sophomores), the question of interest here is not whether thinking is always accompanied by inner speech—it is whether the imagery identified as inner speech could be, in itself, the substance of thought. This is what Hunt's theory seems to require. But this proposal seems indefensible, because the image of a word, with a few unimportant exceptions such as "meow," has no direct correspondence to the thing it represents.

If words themselves were the substance of thought, the facts of psychology would be quite different than they are. Phonemic confusions would not be peculiar phenomena restricted to certain short-term memory tasks—they would pervade human thought. We would forever be confusing imitation with innovation, anecdotes with antidotes, naming with maiming, referees with refugees, diaphragms with diagrams, and abstinence with accidents. Because only the word itself could be present in thought, no word could be said to have two meanings, and no meaning could have two words. The tip-of-the-tongue state and related experiences would never occur, because one could never be conscious of a meaning without knowing the precisely appropriate word. "Irrelevant" and "extraneous" would not be seen as similar concepts. Such a judgment is based on an abstract, semantic code, not on a concrete, sensory image.

Perhaps the best evidence that thinking does not consist entirely of word images comes from work on the problem of language understanding done first in linguistics and more recently in cognitive psychology. However language understanding occurs, it is abundantly clear that it does *not* take place at the level of word strings. This is illustrated by the complementary phenomena of ambiguity and paraphrase. The sentence,

1. The missionary is cooking.

is ambiguous; it has two meanings. The two sentences,

2. William showed that the hypothesis is false.

and

3. The conjecture was disproved by Bill.

are paraphrases; their meanings are essentially the same.

How are such judgments of ambiguity and paraphrase made? They might be made by the operator Hunt calls the *test for identity*. But the matches and mismatches underlying such judgments are certainly not made on the "surface structures" of the sentences. This is why a deeper level of language analysis is postulated: a "deep structure" of the sentence or an even "deeper" conceptual representation that combines the information in the sentence with that derived from the context in which it occurred. This underlying, *abstract* representation of the meaning of the sentence must be available to active memory in order for the appropriate *test for identity* to be performed.

What is Hunt's theory lacking? I think it is exactly what the Rumelhart and Norman proposal has: a general way of representing ideas, both abstract and concrete. A sensory image, I have argued, cannot adequately represent abstract information — even if the image is incomplete. This is because it is necessarily tied directly to dimensions of concrete, sensory experience. A schema, on the other hand, is not limited in this way. It can receive input from other schemata; thus it can be as specific as a particular image or as abstract as the concept "abstract" itself. The generality of the schema is essentially a matter of how precisely the variables are specified, or how many slots are filled in. In principle, there is no other difference between the schematic representations of concrete and abstract ideas. If one's theory permits all schemata (not just images) access to active memory, then abstract concepts need not be excluded from the processes of thought.

REFERENCES

Bartlett, F. C. *Remembering.* Cambridge: Cambridge University Press, 1932.

Bergson, H. [*Matter and memory*] (N. M. Paul & W. S. Palmer, Trans.). New York: MacMillan, 1911. (Originally published, 1896.)

Humphrey, G. *Thinking.* New York: Wiley, 1963.

Minsky, M. A framework for representing knowledge. In P. Winston (Ed.), *The psychology of computer vision.* New York: McGraw-Hill, 1975.

Sokolov, A. N. [*Inner speech and thought*] (G. T. Onischenko, Trans.). New York: Plenum Press, 1972.

Schank, R. C., & Abelson, R. P. *Scripts, plans, and knowledge.* Proceedings of the Fourth International Conference on Artificial Intelligence, 1975, *1,* 151–157.

Tulving, E. Episodic and semantic memory. In E. Tulving & W. D. Donaldson (Eds.), *Organization of memory.* New York: Academic Press, 1972.

4
A Seductive Paradigm

Howard H. Kendler

University of California, Santa Barbara

A general psychologist is confronted with special problems when serving as a discussant in a conference, such as this, in which the participants share a common language and orientation. He has the responsibility to discuss the issues within the conceptual framework of the conference, but he also has the obligation to perceive them in the larger context of all of psychology. I was willing to undertake this challenge for two reasons. First, I view my own research efforts (Kendler & Kendler, 1975) as a link between the learning theories of the past (Hull, 1952; Spence, 1950; Tolman, 1932) and the information-processing formulations of today. Secondly, I anticipated that my efforts as a discussant would be helpful in my quest, hopefully not quixotic, of trying to make sense out of psychology. If one is a general psychologist, he cannot avoid asking himself how can a community of apparently rational scholars draw so many conflicting conclusions about fundamental psychological principles? The easy answer for many psychologists to such a query, if not in print, at least in bars at meetings, is that the assumption of rationality is open to dispute. Interpretations of psychology that are at odds with one's own are misguided, an expression of ignorance or incompetence, or better yet, both.

I have never ascribed to this simple-minded, egocentric interpretation of the diversity of the broad models of psychology. Perhaps my resistance to this oversimplified view is the respect and admiration I had for my early teachers, each enunciating fundamentally conflicting views: Solomon Asch, a committed Gestalt psychologist, and Kenneth Spence, a missionary Neobehaviorist. But of greater importance is the realization that all experimental behavioral psychologists are not playing the game of science with the same set of rules. They employ different criteria for judging a conclusion as warranted and an empirical relationship as important. Most of the time, their theoretical hypotheses are not in direct conflict with others, because they are expressed within different epistemological frameworks and refer to different realms of empirical data. I am not suggesting a sugar-coated eclecticism, which suggests that everybody is right for different reasons and that a tolerant attitude by all will destroy the barriers that divide contemporary psychology into groups of warring factions, or at least, alienated strangers. If extreme characterizations are required, the one that would be closest to the truth is that everybody is wrong because their views of behavior are inevitably distorted by the narrowness of the empirical base from which they have sprung.

Let me terminate this sermon, at least for a moment, in order to deal with the assigned task of discussing the contributions of Earl Hunt and of David Rumelhart and Donald Norman.

Although the content of both papers are quite different, they share a common epistemological structure. This structure throws light on the information-processing approach, which has achieved the pinnacle of popularity among experimental behavioral psychologists, a position previously occupied by a host of orientations far too numerous to mention. The dominant impression that I had when reading the papers by Hunt and by Rumelhart and Norman was the boldness and breadth of their theorizing and the relatively small amount of empirical studies cited to support the conceptual edifice. This statement is purely descriptive and carries no critical implication. It is made to underline the changes in the methodological frame of reference for theorizing that has occurred over the past decades. Sigmund Koch (1964), the aging l'enfant terrible of American psychology, who unfortunately is ignored by most experimental psychologists and listened to too seriously by many clinicians, bemoaned the fact that psychologists adopted methodological positions about the nature of science that had been rejected by philosophers. He was referring mainly to the Neobehavioristic orientation of Hull and Spence but also to the cognitive behaviorism of Tolman, both positions being strongly influenced by logical positivism. This position, which made a sharp distinction between metaphysics and science, logical and factual truth, meaningful and meaningless statements, and theoretical and empirical concepts, had achieved dominance among philosophers of science during the first third of the twentieth century. Psychologists in their passionate search for scientific respectability accepted many of the tenets of logical positivism and used them to justify their empirical and theoretical style. While psychologists were shoring up their position with the methodological arguments of logical positivism, logical positivism itself was wilting under the onslaught of philosophical criticism that demonstrated that their sharp distinctions were at best blurred and at worst, nonexistent.

The decline of logical positivism does not however, in my opinion, justify Koch's position that psychologists should have ignored their methodological notions. It would be unfortunate if psychologists felt compelled to seek Good Housekeeping-type Seals of Approval for their methodological positions from philosophers of science who are currently in vogue. If they did, they would be forced to change thier methodological orientation and practices every decade or so. Psychologists would be better off to adopt methodological principles consistent with the needs of their discipline rather to have them imposed from the outside. In addition it should be noted that even though logical positivism died, or more properly disintegrated, many of its notions have been absorbed in a revised form in contemporary views of philosophy of science. Perhaps experimental psychologists have much to learn from the legacy of logical positivism as it relates to their activities as empiricists and theorists. Although these revised notions do not provide as clear a guide as the original conception, they nevertheless provide an appropriate direction. Perhaps the most that we can expect from the philosophy of science are ideals toward which we should strive rather than general methodological rules which can be employed to guide empirical and theoretical decisions.

My point in discussing the place of logical positivism in the psychology of the '40s and '50s leads up to the philosophical position that is dominating the contemporary scene in experimental behavioral psychology. That position is the one described in the widely read *The Structure of Scientific Revolutions* by Thomas Kuhn, originally published in 1962. Kuhn's major thesis was that scientific progress was not based on the accumulation of individual discoveries and conceptual insights but instead was an outgrowth of two markedly different enterprises: *normal science* and *revolution*. *Normal science* refers to the accumulation of knowledge within a widely adopted combined methodological–theoretical framework, labeled by Kuhn as a *paradigm*. A paradigm possesses two major characteristics. First, it attracts to its fold a group of adherents; second, it provides them with a number of unanswerable questions that keep them busy experimenting and publishing (and of course, getting raises and promotions). The paradigm provides an intellectual structure that integrates "important" facts and at the same time generates numerous research opportunities. Therefore Kuhn describes normal science as a "mopping-up" activity.

The second kind of historical development in science is the *revolution*, an event in which a prevailing paradigm is overthrown by a new one. Revolutions are not achieved in a simple objective fashion by the application of a clear-cut decision rule that reveals the superiority of a new paradigm over an old one. Rather, the historical process that replaces an old paradigm with a new one is complex, involving, in the last analysis, the subjective conviction that one is superior to the other. Empirical data are involved in the conflict between competing paradigms, and arguments are put forward that the evidence is consistent only with one of the competing paradigms. But these debates are not decisive, because the data do not have an independent existence of their own. All data are theory-laden and cannot be perceived independently of the theory. To support the notion of the conflation between fact and theory, Kuhn offers data from psychological experiments. He cites the evidence of Bruner and Postman (1949), who found that when an incongruous playing card such as a *black four of hearts* is briefly exposed to college students, most of them identify it as a *red four of hearts* or a *black four of spades*. Kuhn uses these results to support his contention that facts and theories are not independent; theoretical preconceptions determine what is observed. Kuhn, in my opinion, makes a fundamental error when considering the Bruner and Postman study as a proto-type of the scientific effort. He likens the task of the observing scientist to that of the subject in the Bruner–Postman study. The correct analogy is that the scientist is the experimenter, because it is he who makes the observations and reports them to his fellow scientists. It should be noted that Bruner and Postman experienced no difficulty in communicating the true characteristics of the anomalous card to the scientific community. Regardless of the readers' theoreti-cal preconceptions, no confusion occurred in the empirical meaning of a *black four of hearts*.

I do not wish to maintain that it is always easy to draw as sharp a distinction between data and theoretical languages as was done with the Bruner–Postman study. My position about this matter is neatly expressed by Nagel (1971):

> It would be idle to pretend . . . that there are no difficulties in drawing a distinction between observational and theoretical statements; and I certainly do not know how to make such a distinction precise. Nevertheless, I do not consider that this distinction is therefore otiose any more than I believe that the fact that no sharp line can be drawn to mark off day from night or living organisms from inanimate systems makes these distinctions empty and useless [p. 19] .

Nagel's attitude is at odds with the extreme subjectivity of Kuhn's position in regard to the decision rules that govern the selection of one paradigm over another. The significant point, however, is that Kuhn's position has been subjected to intense criticism (e.g., Lakatos & Musgrave, 1970), and he himself has backed off from his original conception by emphasizing evolutionary pro-cesses in the history of science as well as more objective indices (e.g., accuracy, scope) in selecting paradigms. Nevertheless, these revisions and modifications tend to be ignored in psychology, and the more extreme Kuhnian doctrine, in which a shift to a new paradigm possesses qualities of a religious conversion, is the one that is widely adopted, either consciously or unconsciously.

My reading of the current state of psychology is that most cognitive and information-processing psychologists assume the more extreme Kuhnian posi-tion. In support of this contention, I offer Weimer and Palermo's *Cognition and the Symbolic Processes* (1974), which is replete with proclamations of the infallibility of the cognitive paradigm. It is this kind of intuitive conviction, in my opinion, that encourages the ambitious theorizing that Hunt, and Rumelhart and Norman indulge in. The theorizing is not demanded by the force of ex-perimental data but rather by the conviction that intrinsic truth inheres in the information-processing paradigm.

In the most fundamental sense, a theory is some symbolic system that coherently organizes a factual domain. Although Hunt initially refers to his formulation as *semantic-image theory,* he admits soon thereafter that it "is not a theory, it is a theme underlying a theory." I would call it a pretheoretical model, because it represents an informal conception that operates an analogy in theory construction. Such tools cannot be rejected, not even criticized. Their implications are not capable of being falsified, and their value can only be ascertained by their achievements. One can express reservations, however, which could alert a theorist to potential weakness that might show up as he tries to convert his informal model into a formal theory.

I would express reservations upon the heavy emphasis Hunt places on concepts in computer science. The rationality of the computer may be a poor base to erect a psychology of human thinking. This is the position of Joseph Weizenbaum (1976), a distinguished computer scientist. Although I do not share all of his views, many of which are concerned with ethical issues, I resonate to the notion that computers and humans should not be viewed as members of the same genus. Although computer simulators of human behavior can deny making this assumption, the fact remains that there are fundamental processes that govern the actions of a computer, that there are processes that govern the behavior of humans, and that computers and humans may not be isomorphic in any fundamental way. In response to such a statement, a computer scientist can argue that *in principle* a suitably programmed computer can simulate any kind of behavior. I am not qualified to debate this logical issue, but I am willing to accept its validity. But, and this is a big *but,* one must distinguish between the logical truth of the argument and its practical implication. Although the *in-principle* argument can justify efforts at computer simulation of human behavior, success, it must be recognized, is not guaranteed.

If we shift from a logical to an empirical framework, we can evaluate the success of computer simulation by considering the claims that have been made in the past. The great expectations of machine translation have not been realized by computer science, and one can argue that if a computer cannot be made to "speak" like a human, it certainly will not be made to "think" like one. One can also evaluate the achievements of the General Problem Solver (Newell & Simon, 1972), which contains programmed instructions assumed to be equivalent to common problem-solving processes that guide human thought. Weizenbaum argues that this is an inflated claim because the GPS is not a general theory, because it requires entirely different memory structures when it is switched from one task to another — for example, from chess to a crypt-arithmetic puzzle. In essence, according to Weizenbaum (1976), "GPS is nothing more than a programming language in which it is possible to write programs from certain highly specialized tasks [p. 176] ."

In addition, one must also consider the problem of translating a computer program that is "successful" in simulating behavior into a theory with clearly stated premises. According to Smith (in press):

> Anyone who has tried to read a theory embedded in a program knows how difficult it is to arrive at the general principles of the theory. More likely than not, whatever general

principles there are, are buried in the mass of details needed to make the theory sufficient, i.e., needed to make the program run. More generally, as theories become increasingly sufficient they must by nature contain more details, and consequently their claims become less transparent.

As Smith later points out, a theory expressed in the form of a computer program may be so opaque that it is impossible to know what evidence could be inconsistent with the theory. Needless to say, a theory, the implications of which cannot be falsified, should be viewed with suspicion.

I don't know whether Hunt is saying too little or too much when he proclaims that *"cognition proceeds by an orderly sequence of sensory images."* Are images, one of his key concepts, a theoretical construct whose true meaning will only be achieved when his formulation makes the transition from a pretheoretical model to a theory with deductive capacity? Or does his image refer specifically to mental images, and if they do, how is he to handle the problem of imageless thought, a fairly well-documented phenomenological experience?

Rumelhart and Norman's effort can also be viewed, properly so, as a pretheoretical model. The judgment as to its value will also have to await its future development. I wish it did not represent such a sharp break with many of the learning theories of the past. I cannot help but feel that the development of Rumelhart's theoretical model could profit from considering some empirical evidence obtained within other paradigms. As one example, I mention the possible relationship between his interest in children's overgeneralization and overrestriction of conceptual terms and the Neobehavioristic dual-stage developmental theory of discrimination theory, which postulates an ontogenetic change from single-unit to mediational functioning (Kendler & Kendler, 1975).

In essence, both Hunt and Rumelhart and Norman are having an affair with the information-processing paradigm. That is understandable, because that paradigm has many attractive features. But, as in all affairs, one must be on guard to avoid being seduced for the wrong reasons. Is the paradigm's attractiveness a consequence of its heuristic value in generating research? If it is, then that is not enough. At this stage in the history of psychology, with an overabundance of data, it becomes difficult to defend a new paradigm, because it will encourage more research. What we badly need is a theoretical framework capable of integrating data from a wide variety of empirical areas. This, of course, is what Hunt, and Rumelhart and Norman are trying to do. My reservations are not about the goal they seek but the manner in which they are seeking it. Their conceptualizations are spun out of their imagination with little guidance being provided by systematic empirical relationships. A general theory must ultimately explain data, so why not be guided by data? Is it because the information-processing paradigm has been unsuccessful in providing systematic information upon which to erect a theoretical edifice? Is this why there is such a proliferation of models within the information-processing paradigm? Do psychologists have an affinity for the information-processing paradigm not because it reflects fundamental behavioral principles but rather because its terminology and flow charts provide an intuitive sense of understanding? These are easy questions to pose and difficult, if not impossible, ones to answer. But they must be entertained so that the psychological community will avoid dissipating an excessive amount of talent and effort on a paradigm of limited value. To avoid such a consequence, I urge Hunt, and Rumelhart and Norman, and other information processors, to take seriously Alfred North Whitehead's characterization of science: "the union of *passionate interest in the detailed facts* [author's italics] with equal devotion to abstract generalization."

REFERENCES

Bruner, J. S., & Postman, L. On the perception of incongruity: A paradigm. *Journal of Personality,* 1949, *18,* 206–223.

Hull, C. L. *A behavior system.* New Haven, Conn.: Yale University Press, 1952.

Kendler, H. H., & Kendler, T. S. From discrimination learning to cognitive development: A neobehavioristic odyssey. In W. K. Estes (Ed.), *Handbook of learning and cognitive processes* (Vol. 1). Hillsdale, N.J.: Lawrence Erlbaum Associates, 1975.

Koch, S. Psychology and emerging conceptions of knowledge as unitary. In T. W. Wann (Ed.), *Behaviorism and phenomenology.* Illinois: University of Chicago Press, 1964.

Kuhn, T. S. *The structure of scientific revolutions.* Chicago: University of Chicago Press, 1962.

Lakatos, I., & Musgrave, A. (Eds.). *Criticism and the growth of knowledge.* Cambridge: Cambridge University Press, 1970.

Nagel, E. Theory and observation. In E. Nagel, S. Bromburger, & A. Grünbaum (Eds.), *Observation and theory in science.* Baltimore: Johns Hopkins Press, 1971.

Newell, A., & Simon, H. A. *Human problem solving.* Englewood Cliffs, N.J.: Prentice-Hall, 1972.

Smith, E. E. Theories of semantic memory. In W. K. Estes (Ed.), *Handbook of learning and cognitive processes* (Vol. 6). Hillsdale, N.J.: Lawrence Erlbaum Associates, in press.

Spence, K. W. Cognitive versus stimulus response theories of learning. *Psychological Review,* 1950, *57,* 159–172.

Tolman, E. C. *Purposive behavior in animals and men.* New York: Appleton-Century-Crofts, 1932.

Weimer, W. B., & Palermo, D. S. (Eds.). *Cognition and the symbolic processes.* Hillsdale, N.J.: Lawrence Erlbaum Associates, 1974.

Weizenbaum, J. *Computer power and human reason.* San Francisco: W. H. Freeman, 1976.

Section II

5

Semantic Information and Visual Information Processing

Roberta L. Klatzky
Ann M. Stoy

University of California, Santa Barbara

The study of semantics can generally be viewed as the study of meaning, independent of form. At least, that is close to the definition one finds upon consulting a dictionary. But if that definition is adopted, it may seem inappropriate to even consider the subjects of semantics and visual information processing together. Because to speak of the processing of *visual* information suggests a representation that retains its physical form, and to speak of *semantics* implies independence from physical form.

It is the purpose of this paper to attempt a resolution of these apparently conflicting views. More specifically, we consider whether visual information is represented in the human processing system in some modality-specific form and to what extent such a representation can be considered semantic as well as visual. Our general conclusion can be foretold: It seems that there is little that the human processor performs with visually presented information that does not reflect knowledge of its meaning. As one follows a visual stimulus through the processing system, semantic knowledge plays an increasingly important role. And even at peripheral levels in this stream of processing, it is difficult to isolate a truly visual code.

This paper has two major sections. First, we follow visually presented information, verbal and nonverbal, through a hypothesized sequence of processing stages, beginning with sensory reception and concluding with long-term retention. At each point in the sequence, we consider what we know about the representation of the information in memory – the memory "code" – with particular focus on the extent to which it reflects semantic processing. Next, we present data that explore semantic effects in what seems to be a simple task that does not need semantics at all, namely, comparing briefly presented visual stimuli. Ultimately, we hope to convey the pervasive effects of semantic knowledge on visual cognition.

Before we begin our discussion of semantics and visual information processing, it is important to define such terms as *semantic* and *visual* in the sense that they will be used here. The label "visual information" can generally have two senses: The information can describe the physical appearance of some material, or it can be visual in the sense of some modality-specific format. The former sense of the term "visual information" does not require that it be in some format specific to pictorial data. Instead, the information could have a format like that used to represent any information conveyed by words or to represent meaning in general. The word "round," for example, describes a circle's appearance, but this information does not differ in form from the information conveying that the circle is a "coin." Visual information in a form that is not exclusive to visual properties we shall term *visual/semantic,* because it is a subset of semantic information in general.

The second sense of the term visual refers to information in modality-specific form. This sort of information could be a sensory trace, or it could be at a higher level, for example, an "image" or what Klatzky (1975) has called a *short-term visual code.* It might be tempting to call this sort of visual representation an *analog code,* a term suggesting that it has picture-like properties; however, to do so implies a stronger theoretical stance than that of this paper. We shall call it simply *visual* information (in contrast to visual/semantic). (For example, in a propositional system, information might be "visual" in the sense used here because the propositions describing it use relational terms exclusive to the visual modality. However, this information would not be analog.) We shall assume that visual information is distinct from visual/semantic because its code is specific to the visual modality and because it conveys the appearance of an item irrespective of its meaning. It is assumed by most theorists that semantic (including visual/semantic) representations are at a deeper, or more abstract, level than visual representations.

REVIEW OF LITERATURE

Sensory Reception

Let us now begin our review by considering the sensory reception of visually presented information. It might seem that with as peripheral a stage of processing as sensory intake, semantic effects cannot possibly play an important role. After all, before a visual stimulus has been recognized, when it simply registers on a receptive visual system, what do we know about its meaning, and what role can meaning play?

To a certain extent, this analysis is accurate. To illustrate the fact that at this stage the semantic system may not play a major role, we can consider the work of Sperling (1960), who developed a paradigm that verifies the existence of a visual sensory (as opposed to meaningful) memory. Briefly, Sperling showed that when a viewer receives too much visual information to be able to report all of it successfully, he can nevertheless report back some designated portion of it with total accuracy, as long as the relevant portion is cued within a quarter-second or so after presentation. This indicates that what is available immediately after a visual stimulus vanishes is much more than can be observed from a delayed report. The stimulus is assumed to be extended by a sensory information store for a brief time after its cessation.

That the sensory store demonstrated by Sperling does not itself convey the meaning of the visual stimulus is indicated by the differential effects of two kinds of report cues: In the experimental conditions showing sensory storage, the information cued for report is designated by its spatial location. When instead, the cue designates some meaningful dimension of the stimulus (e.g., reports all digits but not letters), there is no advantage of cued report over delayed report. Clearly, the fact that the report cue is ineffective when it designates stimuli by some aspect of meaning indicates that this sensory memory does not represent that meaning.

On the other hand, to find that there is a passive sensory memory where purely visual information is represented without reference to its meaning does not preclude the possibility that semantic properties influence inputs to the store or readouts from it. On the input side, there is much evidence that natural eye movements are directed to new information by the meaningful context in which it occurs (reviewed in Kahneman, 1973). Thus the eye is directed to apprehend, and the visual memory to store, information that is meaningful in the current context. This certainly represents a semantic determiner of inputs to sensory memory.

On the readout side of sensory memory, semantic effects have been demonstrated through several experiments. Generally, the purpose of sensory memory is assumed to be to extend a brief stimulus long enough for it to undergo analysis and pattern recognition. Several studies (Biederman, Glass, & Stacy, 1973; Palmer, 1975; Reicher, 1969) have shown that recognition of visual stimuli (letters or pictures) is markedly enhanced when those stimuli are embedded in a meaningful context. This suggests that semantic knowledge influences the identification of information in the sensory store. For example, Biederman et al. presented to subjects scenes in which they were to search for an object. When the "scenes" were constructed by cutting up normal scenes and putting them back together in incoherent, jumbled fashion, detection was much poorer than when the coherent scenes themselves were presented. The effect of jumbling is assumed to arise because it impairs the subject's ability to derive a topic or overall schema for the scene. Apparently, subjects viewing a scene use such an overall semantic schema to direct their identification of information in the sensory store; this proposal is supported by the fact that the likelihood of the object in the scene has a marked effect on its detection.

The influence of meaning on visual detection was also illustrated by Potter (1975). She presented a sequence of pictures of scenes and objects at so rapid a pace that the pictures could not be recognized in a subsequent test. Yet, subjects could detect when a particular object or scene occurred, given advance information about it. Most important for our present purposes is the fact that two kinds of advance information were equally useful: the name of the stimulus class (e.g., a boat) or a picture of the particular stimulus to be detected. What this means is that under conditions where detection must be very rapid, information about the meaning of a class is sufficient to detect one of its members. Further, because advance information about meaning (the stimulus class) is about as useful as information about specific visual properties (the picture), the implication is that "a scene is processed rapidly to an abstract level of meaning before intentional selection occurs" (Potter, 1975, p. 966). Apparently, semantics plays an important role even this early in the information-processing sequence.

Short-term Memory

In commonly proposed theories of human information processing, after patterns in the sensory store have been recognized (a process in which we have just seen that semantic organization plays a major role), some representation of the recognized stimuli is passed on to a temporary or "short-term" memory. One paradigm that has been used to investigate this store is the measure of memory span: A subject is presented with a brief list of items and is asked to recall them immediately. The maximum number of items that can be recalled is assumed to represent the limit of the short-term memory capacity, or its span.

The first thing to note about memory-span research is that the appropriate unit of measure for the span is what Miller (1956) has called the "chunk." Rather than some prespecified unit, a chunk is defined by the meaningful organization the subject imposes on the input material. Thus, the memory span for verbal material holds roughly constant at about five to nine chunks, but a chunk may correspond to a letter, a word, or even a phrase. Because the span of short-term memory is best measured in meaningful units, short-term retention, at least of verbal material, reflects rather obviously the effects of semantic encoding processes.

The memory span is little affected by the mode of presentation of the material, visual or auditory, which is another indication that short-term memory represents meaningfully coded material and not modality-specific information. On the other hand, there is much evidence that the information in this memory, however meaningfully it is packed into chunks and whatever its input format, is ultimately stored in acoustic form. For example, when subjects mistakenly report some word that was not on a given list, their error is frequently similar in sound to some list word (Conrad, 1963).

In the literature on short-term memory, the question has often been raised as to the possible storage of information in something other than a verbal–acoustic form. The idea is that in focusing on material that is readily encoded verbally, for subsequent verbal report, researchers have ignored the possibility that there might be nonsensory, short-term storage of visual information in a form closer to its input format. For example, visually presented letters might be held for some time with representation of their visual form rather than with acoustic encodings of their names.

Strong evidence for the possibility of such a visual short-term store comes from the work of Posner and his colleagues (reviewed in Posner, 1969). In their experiments, two letters were presented to a subject, who was instructed to respond according to whether or not the letters had the same name. The time required for a positive response was less when two identical letters were presented (e.g., A and A) than when the two letters differed in case (e.g., A and a). Posner argued that this is inconsistent with the idea that the letters must be encoded in terms of their names in order to respond, for the names match equally well in both the identical and different-case conditions. Instead, he proposed that identical letters are matched by the identity of their visual form, whereas nonidentical letters must be matched at the more abstract level of their names, leading to slower response times for the latter.

In other studies, Posner, Boies, Eichelman, and Taylor (1969) separated the two letters by an interstimulus interval. In this case, if an advantage is found for identical letters, there must be some representation of the physical form of the first letter in memory when the second appears and the two letters are compared. Such an advantage was found, indicating the existence of visual memory for the first letter. This result was obtained even when the interstimulus interval was filled with a masking field, ruling out the possibility that the operative visual memory was at a sensory level. Moreover, as the separation between the two letters was increased up to 2 seconds, the advantage of identical letters gradually decreased, suggesting that the visual memory for the first letter decayed in about that time.

The research reported later in this paper suggests that the apparent use of a short-term memory that retains visually presented items in a purely visual form is in fact an incomplete account. Our research implicates semantic effects even in the comparison of two identical visual stimuli, where the stimuli are pictures. At this point, however, we confine ourselves to a brief discussion of other research that modifies the interpretation of the same/different data in terms of a gradually decaying visual store; later, we expand on this discussion.

One additional characteristic of the demonstrated visual memory is that there can be generated, from information in long-term memory, a representation that resembles the memory code retained immediately after presentation of a visual stimulus. This is indicated by an experiment in which subjects were given either an auditory (i.e., spoken name) or visual presentation of the first letter, followed after an interval by a visual letter (Posner et al., 1969). With a 1-second interstimulus interval, response times were identical for two critical conditions: Two identical visual letters were matched no faster than when the first letter was auditory and the second visual. This seems to indicate that subjects used the auditory presentation to access long-term memory and to generate a visual representation of the corresponding letter. And this generated code seems comparable to the memorial representation of a letter 1 second after its visual presentation.

Kroll and his colleagures have conducted a series of experiments with paradigms like Posner's (Kroll, Kellicutt, Berrian, & Kreisler, 1974; Parks & Kroll, 1975). Their work suggests a picture of the task that is quite different from the original visual–verbal dichotomy. First, it appears that the gradual decline in the response-time advantage for identical letters reflects, rather than autonomous visual decay, a subjectively controlled, progressive abstraction of the memorial code of the first stimulus presented. Second, the matches supposedly based on names, those involving nonidentical letters from the same category, apparently do not involve names at all. Instead, the authors suggest that given the first letter in a trial, the subject accesses the corresponding category in long-term memory and generates the alternate letter. The second letter, when it appears, is compared to both the generated alternative and the visual-memory representation of the first letter.

Our own work to be described expands still further on this view of the same/different task. We suggest that not only is information in long-term memory accessed and compared, but this information may more appropriately be labeled semantic than visual.

Long-term Memory

Let us turn now from the immediate recall tasks that are assumed to tap short-term memory to paradigms that tap the more durable store termed *long-term memory*. It is this store that is assumed to be the permanent repository for semantic information, so it is no surprise to discover that semantics plays a critical role in long-term memory experiments. This is true even when those experiments use material that is supposed to be "meaningless."

Perhaps the first person to make the mistake of assuming that one could measure long-term retention of "meaningless" material was Ebbinghaus, when he invented the consonant–vowel–consonant combination called a "nonsense syllable," hoping to study the formation of new associations independent of prior knowledge. But we now know that to an imaginative subject presented with some arbitrary syllable, some meaning can always be discerned. And the more readily a syllable can be rendered with some semantic interpretation, the better it will be recalled. Going a step beyond arbitrary combinations of letters into syllables, we find that sets of words arbitrarily combined to form lists can be organized by semantic rules into units larger than the single word. And, the degree of organization correlates highly with ultimate recall. This whole trend of making arbitrary material meaningful and thus better remembered can be extended again, from syllables and words to sentences. This has been done, for example, in work by Bransford and Johnson (1972) and Dooling and Lachman (1971). They had subjects recall passages that were minimally interpretable. When such a passage was presented along with a picture or label that suddenly made it comprehensible, memory for the passage dramatically improved.

The point of the foregoing is that verbal material, even when thought to be minimally sensible, shows strong effects of semantic encoding for long-term retention. This is quite consistent with the idea that long-term memory is the store for semantic rules, of which a great many apply to the verbal domain. But what of the encoding of pictorial information into long-term memory? Do the same semantic rules apply, and if so, is the encoded representation the same as that of verbal information? Currently, the question of whether pictorial information is represented in the long-term store in the same form as verbal information or in contrast, in a unique nonverbal form, is a topic under much debate (see, e.g., Anderson & Bower, 1973; Paivio, 1971; Pylyshyn, 1973). Some theorists have advocated a "dual-coding" position, stating that there are separate but related memory systems for verbal and nonverbal (or imaginal) memories. Others advocate the position that all material, no matter what its original form or what information it conveys, is represented by the same underlying semantic code. We might better make this point with an analogy: It is as if the single-code theorist is saying, "Be it an art collection or a stock portfolio, any asset is ultimately represented in the same terms, its monetary value." The dual-coding advocate might maintain, "Artistic assets have an esthetic value that can never be represented by money."

The controversy over separate or unitary coding systems for pictorial and verbal stimuli has generated much more research than could be reviewed in this presentation. For example, some research supports the dual-coding view by examining effects of stimulus properties on a variety of learning tasks. Specifically, when pictures are used as stimuli, with instructions to remember their names, performance is superior to conditions where names alone are used. When the stimuli are all words, there are still strong effects of their concreteness or "imaginability," with more concrete words better learned and remembered. When subjects are trying to learn lists of words, instructions that elicit the formation of "mental images" also facilitate performance. These findings have been interpreted as evidence for the idea that information can be stored in either a verbal or imaginal mode, and its retrieval reflects the sum of storage in the two modes. Thus if a word has an imaginal representation as well as a verbal one (as would happen, for example, if it were presented with a picture), recall will be higher than if just the verbal code existed.

Much evidence favoring differential encoding for pictorial and verbal material has been obtained. However, in viewing this evidence, it is important to keep in mind just what the difference between dual and unitary coding might be. To speak of a common code for pictures and words does not mean that no difference between these two classes of items should be found in memory research. In fact, it is quite likely that the kind of information that is encoded differs according to the stimulus class, with more representation of physical properties in the case of pictures and perhaps with more verbally determined associations in the case of words. Similarly, to speak of dual coding does not mean that if pictorial information is stored in images, there is no representation of its meaning in memory, because the imaginal representation might convey meaning as well as a verbal encoding could (Paivio, 1971), and pictorial stimuli might also be represented in a verbal form, thus receiving a verbal–semantic coding.

Thus the critical question is not whether different information is derived from the presentation of pictures and words; undoubtedly it is. Nor does the key question concern whether pictures receive *any* semantic representation in long-term memory; undoubtedly they do. Instead, the question is whether the representation of information about pictures in memory may have a separate, structurally different format from the corresponding code for words, or whether both pictorial and verbal information are represented in memory with a common format that might best be labeled with a general term – *semantic*.

One way to investigate potential long-term coding differences between pictures and words is to determine the effect that verbal labeling has on pictorial retention. If pictures are encoded with an image of their visual features, then presenting verbal labels along with the pictures should not have much effect on picture retention. This was the general reasoning behind several studies in which the pictures to be shown were not readily interpretable. For example, when subjects are shown "Mooney" pictures, formed by deletion of contours from figures, later recognition of a picture occurs only when the subject can *interpret* it at the time of its presentation and reinterpret it when it appears on the recognition test (Freedman & Haber, 1974; Wiseman & Neisser, 1974). A similar phenomenon has been demonstrated by Bower, Karlin, and Dueck (1975), who showed subjects "nonsense" pictures, some with a label that rendered them interpretable and some with no label. The labels greatly facilitated subsequent reproduction of the pictures.

These findings are reminiscent of the previously cited work on recall of passages: If either a nonsensical passage or a nonsensical picture is provided with a semantic interpretation when it is studied, memory is facilitated. However, one question that might be raised with regard to the picture studies is whether the positive effect of labeling depends on the label being meaningful with respect to the corresponding picture. Conceivably labeling might simply increase the subject's motivation to study the picture, and thus might influence recall independently of its semantic content. Klatzky and Rafnel (1976) recently tested this question by repeating the Bower et al. study, but they presented subjects with either no labels for nonsense pictures, meaningful labels, or meaningless labels. With the meaningful labels, the pictures "made sense," just as a Mooney figure makes sense once an interpretation is found. The meaningless labels, in contrast, were simply paired arbitrarily with their pictures. Klatzky and Rafnel found that recall of the pictures given meaningless labels was no better than recall of those with no labels at all. Only a meaningful label, one which permitted a nonsense picture to be sensibly interpreted, led to an improvement in recall. Moreover, the meaningful label had its greatest effect when it was presented to a subject at the time the picture was presented, not if it was simply presented at the time of retrieval. Thus meaningful labeling in these studies seems to have facilitated the encoding of pictorial material for later pictorial reproduction. And this suggests that successful reproduction depended on a semantic interpretation of the picture as well as an analysis of its visual features. This is more consistent with the unitary-code view of picture memory than with the dual-code view.

The foregoing experiment strongly implicates semantic knowledge in the encoding of pictures, thus suggesting that pictures and words may ultimately be represented in memory in some common semantic format. Work by Guenther and Klatzky with "semantic memory" paradigms supports the same idea of a semantic commonality for pictures and words. This work makes use of techniques developed quite recently to reveal the structure of long-term memory for material other than experimental lists of words, namely the body of semantic knowledge we carry extra-experimentally (e.g., Collins & Quillian, 1969; Smith, Shoben, & Rips, 1974).

Like the vast majority of long-term memory studies, experiments on semantic memory typically use words as the stimulus material. A common technique is to present a subject with a statement about well-known concepts, for example, "A snail is an animal," and ask him to verify or reject it. The time for the subject's response is then determined. One of the most robust findings to come out of this work concerns the relationship between the concepts: The more semantically related they are, the faster is a positive response and the slower a negative response. Such findings place constraints on the structure of semantic knowledge.

Guenther and Klatzky conducted a semantic-memory study in which subjects were to indicate whether or not two simultaneous stimuli were both members of a given target category, for example, whether or not two sparrows were birds. In one experiment of this type, the stimuli were pictures; in another, words; and in a third, the stimuli were a mixture of pictures and words. One finding in these studies was that positive-response time was faster when two stimuli on a trial were semantically related. Interestingly, the magnitude of this effect was almost as large when one instance was a picture and the other a word as when both instances were pictures or both were words. Thus relatedness effects seemed to transcend the form of the stimuli that were related. This suggests that the locus of such effects may be a semantic representation in memory that is common to both pictures and words.

To sum up our review so far, we have found that semantic information plays an important role in all stages of visual information processing, from initial input to final storage. The analysis of the meaning of what has previously been seen affects inputs to the visual sense. The sensory input may be encoded in a specifically visual form, but its analysis and subsequent short-term encoding reflect the meaning that it imparts. Finally, when pictorial information is ultimately stored in long-term memory, its storage format reflects semantic processing. In short, it is difficult to isolate some specifically visual coding of information from the coding of nonpictorial information such as words. Instead, it seems that semantic knowledge is applied to the processing of both verbal and nonverbal material.

RESEARCH OF KLATZKY AND STOY

With the foregoing in mind, let us now turn to the considerations of research we have conducted on the role of semantics in short-term visual coding. The paradigm used in this research is basically the one developed by Posner and his associates, previously described, but with pictorial stimuli. At this point, we review the paradigm, discuss in more detail work indicating that it may reflect something other than a specifically visual memory, and finally, describe studies suggesting that in fact it is semantic information that is conveyed by the codes of items in this task.

Experimental Paradigm

First, to review briefly, Posner's task requires subjects, on each of a series of trials, to compare two stimuli (e.g., letters) and to indicate whether they have the same name (a positive response) or different names (a negative response). Two types of positive trials can occur: On some trials, the two stimuli can be identical; we call this an *identity match*. On others, they can be nonidentical but have the same name, such as an upper-and lower-case A; we call this a *category match*. The dependent variable in this task is reaction time, and it has been found that the time for an identity match is less than the time for a category match as long as the stimuli occur within a few seconds of one another. Moreover, as an interpolated interval between the two stimuli increases, identity-match reaction time gradually rises until it is the same as category-match time. Posner interpreted these results as indicating first that different codes are used for the two types of match – visual codes for the identity match and name codes for the category match. Moreover, when the two stimuli are separated in time, the matching process logically must utilize a memorial code of the first stimulus. This leads to the additional inference that identity matches, with short interstimulus intervals, rely on a visual-memory code of the first stimulus. The gradual increase in identity-match reaction time with increasing interstimulus intervals is attributed to gradual decay of this visual-memory code.

Other findings with this paradigm suggest that the memorial code of the first stimulus, used for identity matches, is relatively abstract. As has already been mentioned, the difference between category and identity matches is unaffected by the introduction of a masking field during the interstimulus interval, which would eliminate any sensory trace of the first stimulus. We have found further evidence for the abstract level of this memory code (Klatzky & Stoy, 1974). In a variant of the Posner task, using pictures of common objects as stimuli, we found that the time to match two identical pictures was no less than the time for matching two pictures that were mirror images of one another. This result suggests that the short-term code of the first picture was more abstract than some template-like form.

Kroll et al. (1974) found evidence that not only is the memory code of the first stimulus in this task quite abstract, but it appears to undergo a process of selective abstraction rather than visual decay. They conducted a letter-matching task with temporally separated letter pairs that might or might not differ in color on each trial. One group of subjects had to perform a same/different judgment of the letters on the basis of names; a second group not only performed such a judgment but also had to recall the color of the first letters on each trial. Under these conditions, subjects in the latter group were slower when the letter pairs on a given trial differed in color than when they were the same color. In contrast, reaction time of the subjects who did not have to recall stimulus color was unaffected by color differences, after the briefest inter-stimulus interval. These results (particularly for identity matches) imply that those subjects for whom color information was irrelevant could discard that information over time, retaining a more abstract stimulus representation that conveyed only data relevant to their decision. Thus it seems that rather than undergoing visual decay, the memorial code of the first stimulus became more abstract, with a process under the subject's control.

We have already described evidence that subjects can generate, from long-term memory, codes similar to the memory trace retained of the first stimulus on a trial of Posner's task. Other research by Klatzky and Stoy suggests a revised description of processing in the task, in which a process like the proposed generation plays a central role. Specifically, we propose the model depicted in Figure 5.1. This shows that after the first stimulus is presented during a trial, the subject accesses long-term memory and activates, or "generates," codes representing stimuli that might occur if the trial were positive. (For example, upon being shown a lower-case a, the subject would generate codes to represent this a and an upper-case A.) Thus the subject has two types of codes activated – a retained trace of the first stimulus presented, and generated codes representing both members of the category. When the second stimulus appears, it is compared to both types of codes, and if a match is found, a positive response is made. Otherwise, the subject makes a negative response.

The interpretation of a match between stimuli at the category level as based on a non-name code generated from long-term memory has also been proposed and supported by other theorists. Recently, Parks and Kroll (1975) conducted an experiment based on the assumption that the gradual decrease in the reaction-

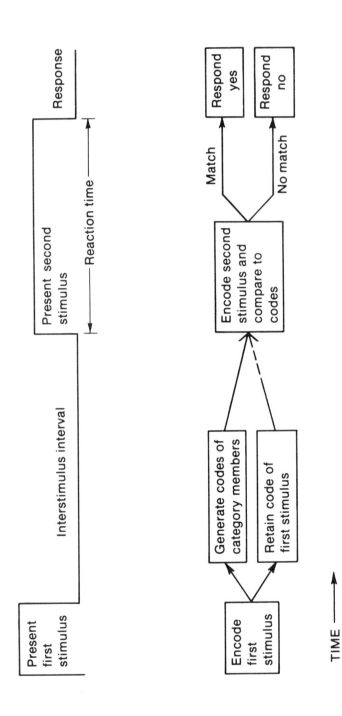

FIGURE 5.1 Events of a single trial of the matching task (top) and a model of the processing that occurs (bottom).

time advantage of identity matches over category matches is due to the fact that with time, the subject can generate a code for category matches that enables them to be performed as fast as identity matches. They therefore manipulated task variables that might make the generation of alternative stimuli in the category more difficult, proposing that this should lead to a longer-lasting advantage for identity matches over category matches. And in fact, this result was obtained. For example, when the number of stimuli in each category was increased, thus increasing the number of alternatives to generate, the identity-match advantage was retained for as long as 8 seconds. This occurred even when the subject had to rehearse the name of the first-stimulus category throughout the interstimulus interval, ensuring that a name code was available. These findings support the hypothesis that the category match is based on a generated code other than a name.

Our own work with a modified version of this paradigm using pictures as stimuli not only indicates that subjects generate from long-term memory a code to use for category matches; it also suggests that such a generated code can form the basis for identity matches. In our studies, subjects took part in a series of trials, in each of which they indicated whether or not two temporally separated pictures of common objects were from the same category (e.g., whether both were pictures of trees, both pipes, etc.). As in the Posner studies, there were various conditions under which a positive response — a match by category — could occur. They included: identity matches, in which the two pictures were identical, and category matches, in which the two pictures were nonidentical but were from the same category. There were also negative trials, in which the two pictures came from different categories. The measured variable in this task was reaction time, defined as the interval between the onset of the second picture and the subject's response.

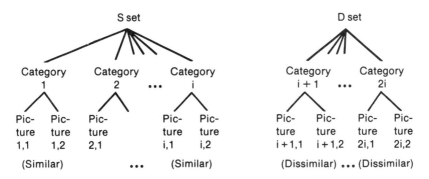

SUBJECT'S STIMULUS POOL

FIGURE 5.2 Structure of a subject's stimulus pool.

Besides varying the type of trial, we varied three additional factors—category structure, session type, and interstimulus interval. We first discuss the "category structure" factor. (See Figure 5.2.) Each stimulus in these experiments was a picture (i.e., black-and-white drawing) representing some category of common objects. Over a series of several experimental sessions, each subject had experience with a pool of about 12–24 of these pictures. The subject's stimulus pool consisted of two different pictures from each of several categories, for example, two pictures of a snake, two of a pipe, and so on. The category-structure variable refers to the fact that for half the categories, the two pictures representing the category were similar (this type of category is referred to as an *S category*), and for the other categories, the two pictures representing the category were dissimilar (this type of category is referred to as a *D category*). For example, the subject's stimulus pool might include two pictures representing a pipe, and these two pictures might be similar. The pool might also include two pictures representing a snake, and these might be dissimilar. In this case, the pipe pictures would compose an S category, and the snake pictures would compose a D category.

The differences between pairs of category exemplars in the subject's stimulus pool necessarily imply that each type of positive trial could be broken down according to the stimuli that occurred. An identity match could involve the repeated presentation of one of the pictures in an S category or one in a D category. A category match could involve the successive presentation of the two pictures in an S category or the pictures in a D category. Thus, in terms of the above example, an identity-match S trial might consist of a presentation of one of the pipes, followed by another presentation of the same pipe. A category-match S trial might consist of the presentation of one of the pipes, followed by the other. Similarly, an identity-match D trial might consist of two successive presentations of the same snake picture, whereas a category-match D trial might involve presentations of the two different snake pictures, successively. In summary, the category-structure variable refers to the fact that stimuli in the experiments fall into one of two types of categories (S or D) defined by the similarity between category members. The specific nature of the similarity manipulation varied over experiments.

As mentioned previously, subjects in these experiments took part in several sessions; each session included about 100 trials and lasted about an hour. The variable "session type" refers to the fact that there were three different kinds of sessions, defined according to the type of trials that could occur. In *mixed sessions,* any type of trial – identity match, category match, or negative – could occur; in *pure identity sessions,* only identity matches and negative trials occurred; and in *pure category sessions,* only category matches and negative trials occurred. The subject was instructed before each session as to what trials could occur.

Finally, the variable "interstimulus interval" (ISI) refers to the fact that within each experiment, several ISIs were used. The ISIs ranged from .05 to 4.0 seconds, and the ISI variable was crossed with all other factors in each experiment. The ISI was generally held constant over a block of about 10 trials and alternated between blocks within each session.

In summary, the principal independent variables were trial type (identity match, category match, and negative); session type (in mixed sessions, both types of positive trials could occur, and in pure sessions, just one type of positive trial could occur); interstimulus interval; and category structure (the two pictures in an S category were similar; pictures in a D category were dissimilar).

Previous Results and Model

In our first experiments with this paradigm (reported in Klatzky & Stoy, 1974), the category-structure factor varied the similarity of shape between pairs of pictures in the same category. Thus, each S category contained two visually similar pictures, and each D category contained two visually dissimilar pictures. We found that the category-structure variable had no effect in the pure sessions, but it had a pronounced effect in the mixed sessions. Specifically, both for identity matches and category matches in mixed sessions, reaction time was less when the pictures presented on the trial were members of an S category than when they were members of a D category.

The important implication of this category-structure effect (that is, a difference in reaction time according to whether the pictures used in a trial came from a category with similar or dissimilar members) is that the subject's processing of the stimuli on a given trial reflects his knowledge of the category from which they come. This is particularly indicated by the fact that the type of category from which the pictures come, S or D, affects reaction time even on identity trials. Because all identity trials are the same insofar as they involve presentation of two identical pictures, if the subjects were operating only within the context of the trial, there should be no effect of the stimulus category. That there is such an effect therefore indicates that subjects do not operate within the single-trial context but in the larger context of the stimulus pool.[1]

[1] In order to substantiate this interpretation of the stimulus-type effect, it is important to rule out the possibility that the effect might simply be due to inherent differences in stimuli from the two sets (as opposed to the given stimulus-type manipulation). The inherent-differences hypothesis cannot explain why the given effect does not occur in pure sessions. Moreover, in all experiments described here, we ruled out this possibility by constructing a pool of stimuli that was twice as large as the one seen by any one subject. The assignment of stimuli to subjects could then be counterbalanced so that across subjects, each picture was used as often in an S pair as in a D pair. This means that S-category vs. D-category differences in reaction time cannot be explained by inherent differences among pictures in the two sets, because across subjects, both sets used the very same pictures.

Another important implication of the category-structure effect in this experiment is that category matches are not based on names but on some other abstract code containing information about both members of the category. Because the category names matched equally well for S and D categories, a true "name" match would not lead to the category-structure effect. Instead, it seems that the code used for category matches must represent the members of the category in some way other than their name.

In general, the results of the experiment just described (specifically, for mixed sessions) indicate that the codes used in both identity and category matches reflect the relationship between the two members of the category. Only in this way could there be a category–structure effect on both types of matches. More specifically, the effect of category structure suggests that the codes the subject uses to represent pictures in the task reflect the extent to which both pictures have attributes in common. This idea, that the stimulus codes reflect similarities between category members, has led us to a more specific model of the picture-matching task. (See Figure 5.1.) First, we assume that early in the course of the experiment, the subject forms in long-term memory a representation of each picture in his stimulus pool. It is useful to think of such a representation as a set of features, similar to those proposed in certain models of semantic memory (Smith et al., 1974). We also assume that the memorial trace retained after presentation of the first picture on a trial is composed of features. However, this code is at first more concrete than the long-term code.

Given the idea of feature-based codes, the model of processing on a single trial of the task can now be expanded: The trial begins when the first picture is presented. This presentation is assumed to result in an "immediate-memory" code of the presented stimulus; this code is quite concrete but becomes more abstract with time (i.e., features are discarded from it). In addition, during the interval following presentation of the first stimulus, the subject is assumed to access long-term memory and "generate," or activate, codes representing the stimuli that might occur, assuming the trial were positive. Generating codes is assumed to draw on a limited capacity. Capacity limitations are particularly important in mixed sessions, in which the second picture to appear might be either member of the category of the first. In this case, the subject wishes to generate codes representing both category members, so to reduce demands for capacity, he emphasizes in the generated codes those features common to both category members.

More specifically, we can assume that the features in the generated codes are weighted relative to their importance in the task and that limited capacity is manifested by a limit on the number of features that can be given high weights at any one time. In this case, features common to both category members should be given high weights, because these features, when activated, represent both pictures that might appear. Note that because there are more common features when the pictures are from an S category than when they are from a D category, on the average the generated code of each S-category picture should have more highly weighted features than the code of a D-category picture.

Following the interstimulus interval, during which codes are assumed to be generated, the next event of the trial is the appearance of the second picture. It is assumed that the subject compares this picture to the codes he has in memory. Several events are possible: First, the second picture may be identical to the first. In this case, the subject may match that picture to the immediate-memory code of the first, resulting in a fast positive response. The probability of this event is assumed to decrease as the interstimulus interval increases, because the immediate-memory code is growing more abstract over time. Second, the second picture may be identical to the first, but the subject may match the pictures on the basis of the generated (rather than immediate) code representing the first stimulus; this process is slower than the first case, and the probability that this event underlies the response increases with interstimulus interval (because the immediate-memory code becomes less effective). Third, the second picture may be the alternate member of the same category as the first. This leads to a match between the second stimulus and the generated code representing this stimulus, again a relatively slow process (as slow as that of the second case described). Finally, if no matches are obtained, the subject responds negatively.

This model generally accounts for the pattern of results in our initial experiment (Klatzky & Stoy, 1974). It accounts for the initial advantage of identity matches over category matches by assuming that some percentage of the time, the former results from a faster process than that used for category matches. The decrease in the identity-match advantage over time is assumed to reflect progressive abstraction of the immediate-memory code used for fast identity matches, reducing the probability that such matches can be performed. Most importantly, this model can account for the category-structure effect on both types of positive trials in mixed sessions. It does so by assuming that category matches and some percentage of identity matches are based on codes generated from long-term memory.[2] Such codes consist of weighted features, and there are more highly weighted features in codes representing an S-category stimulus than those

[2] It might be thought that category matches could utilize the immediate-memory code, just as identity matches do. (That is, the second stimulus might be assumed to be compared directly to the trace of the first.) This would predict category matches slower than identity matches (because the former would be based on a partial match of the stimuli, whereas the latter would reflect a complete match) and could also predict a category-structure effect on category trials (because S-category pairs would match better than D-category pairs). However, this hypothesis is untenable for two reasons: It cannot account for the category-structure effect in identity matches, and it predicts (inaccurately) that category-match reaction time will increase with interstimulus interval just as identity-match time does (because both are based on the same "fading" trace). Because category-match time generally does not vary with interstimulus interval, it must be based on a code with different temporal characteristics than that of the immediate trace; such a code is assumed to be generated from long-term memory.

representing a D-category stimulus. And a greater number of highly weighted features can be predicted to lead to faster responses by postulating one of a number of comparison processes. (For example, features of the second stimulus and active memory code might be compared, and a counter might be given a weighted increment or decrement for each match or mismatch, respectively. The counter would yield a positive or negative response by passing some upper or lower criterion, respectively.)

This model predicts category-structure effects only when either member of a category can occur as the second stimulus of a trial; this is the case in mixed sessions. In pure sessions, however, the subject needs to generate a code representing just one category member, because the first stimulus on a trial of a pure session predicts just a single second stimulus (the same one as the first stimulus in pure identity sessions and the alternate member of the category in pure category sessions). There is therefore little reason to predict a category-structure effect in pure sessions, because with just one category member to generate, there is no need to give higher weights to features that represent both members. Thus the model is consistent with the finding in our initial experiment of no category-structure effects in pure sessions.

The Present Experiments

Rationale. The general implication of the category-structure effect in our initial experiment (i.e., faster reaction time on trials using stimuli from S categories than on those using stimuli from D categories) is that the codes the subject uses in the picture-matching task, particularly those generated from long-term memory, reflect features common to category members (in mixed sessions). This suggests that the occurrence of category-structure effects can be used to study the nature of the codes used in the task. That is, when we observe a category-structure effect, we can infer that the manipulation used to define the category-structure variable (e.g., physical similarity in the initial experiment) must be reflected in the codes in memory. If the manipulation defining a category-structure variable has no effect on reaction time, then we can infer that the characteristics that define the manipulation were not represented in memory. In this way, similarity manipulations can be used as a technique to define the nature of the codes generated and used by the subject in comparing pictures.

For example, suppose we were to manipulate category structure in the following way: In half the S categories, the two pictures both have a black dot above them; in the other S categories, both pictures have a green dot. In each D category, one picture has a black dot above it and the other a green dot. (Note that pooled over all categories within each type, S or D, the same number of pictures has dots of each color. Thus the effects of the dots per se on encoding and comparison processes are balanced.) Under these circumstances, if we observe a category-structure effect, we can assume that the fact that the color of the dot is consistent within S categories but not within D categories is represented in performing the task, producing a relative advantage for trials using S-category stimuli. (Note that the effect is expected even on identity trials, in which both pictures presented have the same color dot, even for D categories.) However, if subjects ignored the dots, we would not find a category-structure effect.

We would probably not expect to find a category-structure effect simply by manipulating an easily ignored dot. However, if we conducted a series of such studies, gradually increasing the extent to which the manipulated characteristics are essential to the category, we might find that at some point in the series a category-structure effect appears and that it appears at all manipulations beyond this point. We can infer that at this critical point, we have manipulated a set of features that the subject uses in representing the pictures in memory. Below this point, the manipulated features are too obscure to be represented in long-term memory. Thus the point in the series at which category-structure effects appear approximates a "lower bound" on the specificity of the codes generated and used in the task.

In our initial experiment (Klatzky & Stoy, 1974), we manipulated visual similarity in terms of the shapes of pictures in a given category. By the foregoing reasoning, we initially interpreted our results as indicating that the codes used by the subject reflected visual features common to both members of the category. However, in manipulating shape similarity, we inevitably manipulated the semantic similarity of category members as well. For example, in one D category were two pictures representing the concept of ZEBRA. One depicted a zebra's head; the other a whole zebra. This undoubtedly constitutes a semantic dissimilarity as well as a visual one, especially relative to the relationship between stimuli in an S category (e.g., two similarly shaped PIPEs). This led to the possibility that it may not have been similarity of visual features, but of semantic features, that was represented in the subject's memorial codes in this task.

To explore this possibility and to attempt to identify the level of coding in the picture-matching task, we next conducted a series of experiments in which the category-structure variable reflected a range of similarities, from specific visual features to abstract semantic features. These studies used the same design as that previously described, with minor differences (noted in Table 5.1). The principal factors were trial type (positive identity match, positive category match, and negative), interstimulus interval (ranging from .05 to 4.0 seconds), session type (pure identity, pure category, and mixed), and category structure. As before, the last factor referred to the fact that the experimental stimuli were pictures, two representing each of several categories. For half the categories (S categories), the two pictures were similar in some respect. The remaining categories (D categories) each comprised two pictures that were dissimilar in that respect. The principal concern of each study was whether there would be a

TABLE 5.1

Details of Method for the Four Studies

	Visual Features	Subordinate/Basic	Basic/Superordinate	Synonym/Homonym
Total # of Categories[a]	12	6[b]	6[b]	10[c]
# of Sessions (Excluding Practice)	3 mixed, 2 pure[d]	2 mixed, 2 pure[d]	2 mixed, 2 pure[d]	2 pure identity, 2 pure category, 3 mixed
# of trials per block (Block by ISI)	11–12 in pure sessions, 8 in mixed	10	10	10
# of trials per season	96: pure sessions, 128: mixed	120	120	120
Interstimulus Intervals (Seconds)	.05, 4.0	.25, 3.0	.25, 3.0	.25, 1.75, 4.0
Proportion of positive trials to negative trials	50:50	60:40	60:40	50:50

[a] Although this variable might be thought to affect the degree of picture learning, it apparently has little effect, because the category-structure effect occurs over a range of 6 to 12 categories in our studies.

[b] These were taken from the nonbiological taxonomies of Rosch et al. (1976). The 6 categories were: VEHICLE, FRUIT, CLOTHING, MUSICAL INSTRUMENT, FURNITURE, TOOL.

[c] The categories were: EYE, GLASSES, HANDS, HORN, KEYS, NAIL, NUT, PIPE, TRAIN, TRUNK.

[d] Each pure session was split so that half the session was a Pure Identity session and half was a Pure Category session.

Experiment	S Category		D Category	
Visual Features (House)	4-Attribute House # 1	4-Attribute House # 2 (2 Attributes Same)	4-Attribute House # 1'	4-Attribute House # 2' (No Attributes Same)
Subordinate/Basic (Vehicle)	Sports Car #1	Sports Car #2	Sports Car	Sedan
Basic/Superordinate (Vehicle)	Sports Car	Sedan	Sedan	Pickup Truck
Synonym/Homonym (Pipe)	Smoking Pipe #1	Smoking Pipe #2	Smoking Pipe	Plumbing Pipe

FIGURE 5.3 Examples of the category-structure manipulations of the four experiments. Each row shows for a given experiment and a given category (the name of which is in parentheses at left) the nature of the two category members if they were in a subject's S category or a D category.

category-structure effect in the identity and category matches of mixed sessions, showing faster reaction time for trials involving stimuli from S categories.

In these studies, four similarity manipulations were used to define category structure (see Figure 5.3). These reflected four levels of visual and semantic similarity. To reiterate, our reasoning is that the most concrete manipulation to produce the stimulus-type effect approximates a lower bound on the level of specificity of the codes used in this same/different task with pictorial stimuli.

The category-structure manipulations. We now describe the similarity manipulations used to define category structure in the four studies. The first study was called the "visual features" study. Here, the category-structure variable was defined by the number of specific, well-defined features that differed between stimuli. The word "features" is used here in the sense of physical attribute. Each stimulus picture was formed by selecting values of several variable attributes to impose on a basic shape. For example, one stimulus category was HOUSE. The two houses in this category were each formed by taking a basic house shape and then assigning one of several possible roofs, chimneys, windows, and doors to the house. The category-structure variable was then defined in terms of the number of such attributes the two members of a category had in common.

Each subject was assigned a stimulus pool of multi-attribute pictures consisting of two pictures representing each of several categories. (There were two or four variable attributes in each picture; however, the results were essentially the same for both numbers of attributes, so data were pooled over this variable.) The set of categories actually contained two subsets. In one subset (S categories), the two pictures in each category were identical with respect to *half* their variable attributes (e.g., there might be two HOUSE pictures, with identical windows and chimneys but different doors and roofs). For the remaining (D) categories, the two pictures differed with respect to *all* of their variable attributes. A final stimulus characteristic to note is that in order to discourage subjects from attempting to ignore the attributes and compare pictures on the basis of their outlines, each category was matched with one other for similarity of basic outline. This was intended to optimize the possibility that the subject would encode the specific features of the pictures.

In the next two studies, the category-structure variable was defined in terms of a distinction made by Rosch and her associates (Rosch, Mervis, Gray, Johnson, & Boyes–Braem, 1976) among different levels in categorical hierarchies. For several such hierarchies, for example, SPORTS CAR/CAR/VEHICLE, Rosch et al. have distinguished three levels: subordinate (in the example above, SPORTS CAR), basic (CAR), and superordinate (VEHICLE). According to Rosch et al., the basic level in a hierarchy is the level at which members have many attributes in common (according to reports from a large population). Because these attributes include not only physical features but also semantic attributes and associated motor movements, it seems appropriate to label them "semantic features," in the sense defined earlier in this paper. The members of super-ordinate-level categories, those above the basic level in the hierarchy, have many fewer such semantic features in common. And the members of subordinate categories, those below the basic level in the hierarchy, have hardly any more such semantic features in common than basic-level members.

Rosch's categorical distinctions provided the basis for the category-structure manipulations that were used in our next two studies. The first of these two was the "subordinate vs. basic" study. As usual, it used several categories of pictures, half S and half D, for each subject. All categories were named for the subject with labels at Rosch's superordinate levels (e.g., the name of one category was VEHICLE). However, for half the categories in this study, the two pictures were both members of the same subordinate-level category (e.g., both members of the VEHICLE category depicted sports cars); these were the S categories. In con-trast, the remaining categories were represented by pictures from different subordinate but the same basic-level categories (e.g., within the category named VEHICLE, one picture depicted a sports car and the other a sedan; the basic-level category in this hierarchy is CAR); these were the D categories. (Of course, each single subject had just one pair of pictures — same subordinate level or same basic level — for a given name such as VEHICLE, but across subjects, each picture was paired with others so as to occur in both S and D categories.) Thus the category-structure manipulation in this study pitted S categories containing same-subordinate-level pictures against D categories containing same-basic-level pictures. In theory, this difference between the S and D categories must be principally defined by features more concrete than the semantic features de-scribed by Rosch et al. (e.g., by features of the specific exemplars used), because two members of the same subordinate category supposedly have hardly any such semantic features in common that are not also common to members of the same basic level from different subordinate categories.

The next study in this series was the "basic vs. superordinate" study. It used a category-structure manipulation defined by a larger number of semantic features than the previous one. This study again used names from Rosch's superordinate-level categories. For each stubject, half the categories were represented by two pictures from the same basic level but different subordinate levels (e.g., a sports car and a sedan for the category VEHICLE); these were the S categories. The remaining categories were represented by two pictures from different basic levels but the same superordinate (e.g., a sports car and a trailer truck for the category VEHICLE); these were the D categories. In this case, pairs of pictures from an S category, coming from the same basic level, are assumed to have many more semantic features in common than pairs from a D category, which are from different basic levels. Thus this category-structure manipulation represents a difference of a relatively large number of semantic features.

Our final study manipulated category structure with an even larger difference than previously used. It was the "synonym vs. homonym" study. In some cases, the two pictures in a given category, although they were called by the same name, actually had different meanings (as represented by two different diction-ary entries). For example, representing the category PIPE might be a picture of a smoking pipe and one of a plumbing pipe. Pictures of this sort formed a D category. In contrast, an S category was formed by a pair of visually distinct pictures representing the same meaning of their name (e.g., two pictures of a smoking-type pipe). In other words, the S categories contained synonym pairs and the D categories homonym pairs. This category-structure manipulation should represent an even greater difference in semantic features than the basic-vs.-superordinate study represented, because in this case, the two pictures in a D category have few properties in common except their name. In contrast, the pairs of pictures in S categories appear to be at a common level somewhat analogous to Rosch et al.'s basic level. This is supported by the finding that when the pictures used in this study were shown, one at a time, to raters, the raters tended to give both pictures in an S category the same name. (If two pictures represent different basic-level categories, they should spontaneously be given different names, e.g., "car" and "truck.") But pictures in a D category that have the same name cannot be considered as at the same basic level, because they represent different meanings of the name.

Results and discussion. In this series of four studies, the stimulus-type manip-ulation was used to vary the differential similarity of members of S and D categories in four ways. In all four studies, members of an S category were more similar to one another than members of a D category. But more importantly, these four manipulations fell along a continuum, representing the extent of this differential similarity between S and D category members. That is, the difference between S and D categories corresponds to the properties S-category members share but D-category members do not, and this difference increased over the four studies. This increase involves both the level in a categorical hierarchy at which the difference obtains, and the number of features that can be assumed to differ.

In the first study, the difference between S and D categories that defines the category-structure variable was one of properties specific to the particular pictures used. In the second study, the category-structure variable manipulated not particular visual features (although members of S categories were visually more similar, in general, than members of D categories) but rather more general properties that items from the same subordinate-level class share but that items from different subordinate-level classes do not. Because this manipulation occurs within classes at a more concrete level than the basic level, it can be presumed that the features manipulated are generally more concrete than the semantic features noted by Rosch et al. to be common to all category members. In the third study, the category-structure variable manipulated features common to basic-level items but not superordinate-level items; these include many of the more abstract semantic features studied by Rosch. In the fourth study, the category-structure variable manipulated features that items at the same basic (and superordinate) level share but that items from completely different classes do not; this includes virtually all the features studied by Rosch. Taken as a series, then, the category-structure manipulations of the four studies differentiate between S and D categories with respect to increasingly higher levels in a hierarchy, from visually similar pictures of objects within a class, to sub-basic levels, to sub-superordinate levels, to manipulations at a level above superordinate classes.

The principal question in these studies was at what point along this dimension would the category-structure effect first be observed. It is assumed that if a category-structure effect on reaction time is observed in a study, then the generated codes used in the task must contain information corresponding to the given category-structure manipulation. The most refined manipulation (that is, the lowest point on the above dimension) that leads to a category-structure effect thus represents a lower boundary on the degree of specificity represented in those codes. For example, if a manipulation of the number of specific visual features common to members of the S vs. D categories affects reaction time, then the codes of the stimuli used in the task must be at least concrete enough to represent such specific visual features.

The data of principal interest here are the reaction times for positive responses in mixed sessions. These data are shown in Figures 5.4 and 5.5. In addition, Tables 5.2 and 5.3 present the data for negative trials and pure sessions. (These data exclude error trials and practice sessions.) Figure 5.4 is a summary graph, showing the magnitude of the category-structure effect in mixed sessions for each study. This graph is pooled over positive match type (identity, category) and interstimulus interval; it represents the overall extent to which stimuli in S

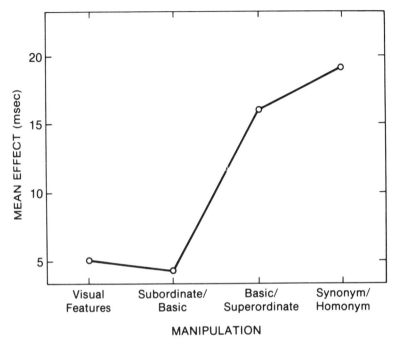

FIGURE 5.4 Magnitude of the category-structure effect in mixed sessions (that is, reaction time for trials using stimuli from D categories, minus the corresponding reaction time for S categories, averaged over both positive match types and all interstimulus intervals) for the manipulation used in each of the four studies.

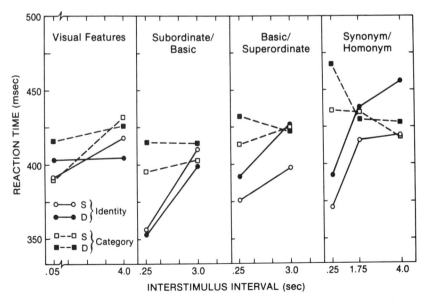

FIGURE 5.5 Mean reaction time (in milliseconds) for each interstimulus interval, each positive match type (identity and category), and each category type (S and D), for mixed sessions in each of the four studies.

TABLE 5.2

Mean Reaction Time for Positive Responses (in Msec.) of Pure Sessions, for Each Interstimulus Interval, Each Session Type, and Each Category Type (S, D), for Each of the Four Studies

Interstimulus Interval (Sec.)	Visual Features		Subordinate/Basic		Basic/Superordinate		Synonym/Homonym		
	.05	4.0	.25	3.0	.25	3.0	.25	1.75	4.0
S Categories									
Identity Session	358	415	352	395	353	383	347	388	418
Category Session	420	449	395	402	393	388	411	418	417
D Categories									
Identity Session	394	389	355	375	360	396	349	371	387
Category Session	470	443	391	400	389	402	414	407	390

TABLE 5.3

Mean Reaction Time for Negative Responses (in Msec.) for Each Interstimulus Interval and Each Session Type, for Each of the Four Studies

	Visual Features		Subordinate/Basic		Basic/Superordinate		Synonym/Homonym		
Interstimulus Interval (Sec.)	.05	4.0	.25	3.0	.25	3.0	.25	1.75	4.0
Pure Category Sessions	444	498	431	477	438	482	451	446	452
Pure Identity Sessions	433	474	423	453	444	452	410	416	436
Mixed Sessions	439	480	439	478	452	469	468	475	470

and D categories led to different reaction times in mixed sessions. Figure 5.5 shows the mixed-session data broken down by interstimulus interval, positive match type, and category structure, for each study.

In general, the data from these studies show the usual effects of match type and interstimulus interval, with identity-match reaction time faster than category-match time at short interstimulus intervals and gradually rising to meet category-match reaction time. More central to our interests are the results of the various category-structure manipulations.

In the first study, in which the manipulation was one of specific visual features, there was no category-structure effect. Although caution must be used when interpreting a null effect, according to the view of the task previously given, this suggests that the codes generated from long-term memory were not specific enough to convey such visual details. However, it is important to note that there was an identity-match advantage at the shortest interstimulus interval (.05 sec., the shortest used over all studies). This indicates that the immediate-memory code assumed to form the basis for at least some identity matches was concrete enough to represent specific visual features, because the mismatch of these features on category-match trials constituted their only difference from identity-match trials.

The results of the second study (subordinate vs. basic) similarly fail to show an overall category-structure effect in mixed sessions. (There appears to be a tendency for category structure to affect category matches, but tests at each ISI do not show significance.) Again, it is important to treat such null results with caution, but these data suggest that at least under the experimental conditions, subjects were generally not representing the features manipulated by this category-structure variable when making their picture comparisons. Because this study used a category-structure manipulation at a rather refined semantic level (pitting the commonalities among same-subordinate-level categories against those of same-basic-level categories), we can infer that the codes the subject generates are not specific enough to convey, for example, the attributes that are shared by two desk lamps but differ between desk and floor lamps. According to Rosch et al., these attributes include few semantic features (in the sense previously described), because people tend to list the same properties for both kinds of lamps. The principal differences between S and D categories in this study, then, are more concrete than these semantic features, and the study suggests that picture comparisons do not involve such concrete details.

The third study (basic vs. superordinate), in which "category structure" referred to larger semantic differences (such as the attributes shared by two cars but not by a car and a truck), was the first along the continuum to show a category-structure effect.[3] The finding of category-structure effects in this study indicates that the features manipulated in the category-structure variable are represented in the codes used in the task. Thus these codes seem to be at a level that conveys such abstract semantic features.

The data of the fourth (synonym vs. homonym) study support this inference. Again, a category-structure effect is obtained (with a category/identity trade-off like that of the previous study). We can infer that the codes used in comparing pictures reflect the semantic commonalities of synonyms and not homonyms.

The graph of Figure 5.4 provides a summary of the four studies. It is discontinuous, showing no category-structure effects in studies with concrete manipulations, but showing the appearance of such effects when "semantic features" form the basis of the category-structure variable. This pattern of results suggests that the codes used in picture matching are at an abstract semantic level.

In summary, our investigation of the picture-matching task suggests that semantic information plays an important role. In order to compare two temporally separated pictures, we propose that a subject accesses a representation of the picture category and generates a set of features to use for the comparison. The data presented here suggest that these features are more abstract than specific visual attributes. Instead, they seem to be at a semantic level, because the most refined category-structure manipulation to affect reaction time involved a relatively large number of semantic features. Although a more specifically visual code may be available shortly after the first picture is presented, this code soon becomes no more effective than the generated one. Thus it seems appropriate to say that codes can be used in the task that represent semantic features above a specifically visual level, although at least some of these semantic features quite probably pertain to visual characteristics. This view of the matching task for pictures is quite different from the original depiction based on letters, which assumed that the operative stimulus codes were representations of purely visual form and names.

Our finding that semantic knowledge plays a central part in so simple a visual process as comparing two identical pictures is but on aspect of a more general rule. In reviewing the literature on visual information processing, we consistently

[3] Before interpreting these results, several points are noteworthy about this study. First, the category-structure manipulation may involve names as well as semantic features: Because people tend to name objects at the basic level ("car," "truck"), S categories have same-name objects, and D categories do not. The fourth study, and the initial study of Klatzky & Stoy (1974), do not share this problem and still yield category-structure effects, so the name-correspondence confounding does not appear to be a critical one. Second, category-structure effects are found at both interstimulus intervals for the identity matches but not at the longer one in category matches. Instead, at the longer interstimulus interval, the effect is particularly strong for identity matches. Our model offers a post hoc explanation for the finding that where category matches do not show the category-structure effect, it is enhanced in identity matches: After viewing the first stimulus, subjects may adopt a strategy of emphasizing the alternate member of the category in the generation process, giving some of its features high weights at the expense of features exclusive to the first stimulus. This would result in a trade-off of the category-structure effect between identity and category matches like that observed. For this reason, it seems the category-structure effect is best measured with an average over both positive match types.

find semantics of crucial importance. Truly visual coding, in the sense of visual and not semantic, appears to be a rare event, one that occurs only at peripheral stages in the processing system.

ACKNOWLEDGMENTS

This research was supported by Grant No. MH25090, awarded to the first author by the National Institute of Mental Health.

REFERENCES

Anderson, J. R., & Bower, G. H. *Human associative memory.* V. H. Winston & Sons, 1973.

Biederman, I., Glass, A. L., & Stacy, E. W., Jr. Searching for objects in real-world scenes. *Journal of Experimental Psychology, 1973, 97,* 22–27.

Bower, G. H., Karlin, M. B., & Dueck, A. Comprehension and memory for pictures. *Memory & Cognition, 1975, 3,* 216–220.

Bransford, J. D., & Johnson, M. K. Contextual prerequisities for understanding: Some investigations of comprehension and recall. *Journal of Verbal Learning and Verbal Behavior, 1972, 11,* 717–726.

Collins, A. M., & Quillian, M. R. Retrieval time from semantic memory. *Journal of Verbal Learning and Verbal Behavior, 1969, 8,* 240–247.

Conrad, R. Acoustic confusions and memory span for words. *Nature,* 1963, *197,* 1029–1030.

Dooling, D. J., & Lachman, R. Effects of comprehension on retention of prose. *Journal of Experimental Psychology,* 1971, *88,* 216–222.

Freedman, J., & Haber, R. N. One reason why we rarely forget a face. *Bulletin of the Psychonomic Society, 1974, 3,* 107–109.

Kahneman, D. *Attention and effort.* Prentice-Hall, 1973.

Klatzky, R. L. *Human memory: Structures and processes.* W. H. Freeman, 1975.

Klatzky, R. L., & Rafnel, K. Labeling effects on memory for nonsense pictures. *Memory & Cognition, 1976, 4,* 717–720.

Klatzky, R. L., & Stoy, A. M. Using visual codes for comparisons of pictures. *Memory & Cognition, 1974, 2,* 727–736.

Kroll, N. E. A., Kellicutt, M. H., Berrian, R. W., & Kreisler, A. F. Effects of irrelevant color changes on speed of visual recognition following short retention intervals. *Journal of Experimental Psychology, 1974, 103,* 97–106.

Miller, G. A. The magical number seven, plus or minus two: Some limits on our capacity for processing information. *Psychological Review, 1956, 63,* 81–97.

Paivio, A. *Imagery and verbal processes.* Holt, Rinehart & Winston, 1971.

Palmer, S. E. The effects of contextual scenes on the identification of objects. *Memory & Cognition, 1975, 3,* 519–526.

Parks, T. E., & Kroll, N. E. A. Enduring visual memory despite forced verbal rehearsal. *Journal of Experimental Psychology: Human Learning and Memory, 1975, 1,* 648–654.

Posner, M. I. Abstraction and the process of recognition. In J. T. Spence & G. H. Bower (Eds.), *Advances in learning and motivation* (Vol. 3). Academic Press, 1969.

Posner, M. I., Boies, S. J., Eichelman, W. H., & Taylor, R. L. Retention of visual and name codes of single letters. *Journal of Experimental Psychology, 1969, 79*(1, Pt. 2).

Potter, M. C. Meaning in visual search. *Science,* 1975, *187,* 965–966.

Pylyshyn, Z. W. What the mind's eye tells the mind's brain: A critique of mental imagery. *Psychological Bulletin,* 1973, *80,* 1–24.

Reicher, G. M. Perceptual recognition as a function of meaningfulness of stimulus material. *Journal of Experimental Psychology,* 1969, *81,* 275–280.

Rosch, E., Mervis, C. B., Gray, W., Johnson, D., & Boyes-Braem, P. Basic objects in natural categories. *Cognitive Psychology,* 1976, *8,* 382–439.

Smith, E. E., Shoben, E. J., & Rips, L. J. Structure and process in semantic memory: A featural model for semantic decision. *Psychological Review,* 1974, *81,* 214–241.

Sperling, G. The information available in brief visual presentations. *Psychological Monographs,* 1960, *74*(11, Whole No. 498).

Wiseman, G., & Neisser, U. Perceptual organization as a determinant of visual recognition memory. *American Journal of Psychology,* 1974, *87,* 675–681.

6
Some Factors Involved in the Recognition of Words

Carol Conrad

University of New Mexico

Most current models of semantic memory have as their goal the specification of how we, as humans, process language information. In doing so, they attempt to describe the available information that we use in speaking, listening, reading, and writing; how that information is represented and organized in memory; and the mental operations we perform on that information during comprehension and production. The models differ in the extent to which they specify each of these factors, as well as the manner in which they specify them. One aspect of a model of language comprehension that is often not specified in detail is that of word recognition (e.g., Norman et al., 1975). Clearly, however, word recognition is an important early step in understanding what we hear or read. The present paper discusses some current research on word recognition within the framework of a model that specifies several independent but interrelated memory subsystems for storing available information about words. The subsystems of interest are those in which orthographic, phonemic, and semantic information are represented. Retrieval of information from these subsystems is assumed to proceed in parallel and to involve a process of spreading activation within subsystems. In addition, the possible effect of an attentional mechanism on retrieval of word information is discussed. The ideas presented, particularly the notion of isolable subsystems in memory, are somewhat speculative; they represent my attempt to integrate a fairly large corpus of data and ideas on word recognition.

ISOLABLE SUBSYSTEMS IN SEMANTIC MEMORY

Studies of word recognition in semantic memory have dealt primarily with the activation or retrieval of semantic information – information about the meanings of words. However, it is quite apparent that we know a great deal more about words than just what they mean. We know what they look like and how they are spelled, we know what they sound like, and we know how to pronounce them and how to write or type them. The notion of isolable subsystems, then, suggests that each of these kinds of information about words — semantic, visual or orthographic, phonemic or name, and motor — is abstractly represented in separate but interrelated memory systems and may be retrieved independently.¹ The assumption that information about words may be stored in several different subsystems of memory is not a new one, nor is the idea that the information represented in these systems is abstract in the sense that it is not isomorphic to the input words that we see or hear. Thus the word "cat," whether typed or printed or handwritten, will have the same representation in a visual memory system. Similarly, the word "run" has a single name representation that is independent of the voice in which the word is spoken. However, the idea that word information in the subsystems may be retrieved independently and in parallel is not well established and is counter to the prevailing ideas in the experimental literature on information processing. Specifically, models of information processing in general, and language comprehension in particular, have postulated serial stages of processing in which the execution of one stage must depend on the outcome of a previous stage. For example, to recognize a visually presented word, it has been hypothesized that one must first retrieve a visual representation or code for the word. Through association we then retrieve the name of the word, and finally, having the name allows us to retrieve the meaning of that word. To identify a spoken word, it is not necessary to access a visual representation or code for the word, but we must retrieve its name in order to access the semantic representation of the word. This idea of serial dependent stages of retrieval is implicit in the levels of processing theory proposed by Craik and Lockhart (1972) and in the model of reading proposed by LaBerge and Samuels (1974), among others, and is diagrammed in Figure 6.1(a). In contrast, the notion of independent access suggests that the successive and additive assumptions of serial models are not properties of adult word recognition. Rather, it suggests that the retrieval of visual, name, and lexical information occurs independently and in parallel for each type of code. Thus, this hypothesis predicts that we may retrieve the meaning of a word without first retrieving its name or that we may retrieve the name of a visually presented word *before* fully accessing a visual code for that word. This model is illustrated in Figure 6.1(b).

To establish the isolability of several systems, it must be shown that factors that influence retrieval time for one system do not influence the time to retrieve information from other systems as well. Unlike a serial model, which predicts that increasing the time for recognizing the visual form of a word will also increase the time to recognize the word's meaning, a model that proposes independent retrieval of each type of representation must predict that increasing time for the retrieval of visual information will not affect the time needed to retrieve the word's meaning. Similar predictions hold for visual and name codes

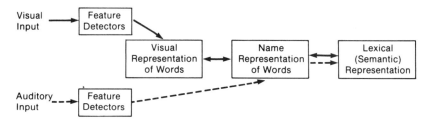

a. A Serial Model

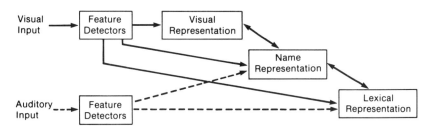

b. The Isolable Subsystems Model

FIGURE 6.1   Two models of retrieval during word recognition.

and for name and semantic codes. Posner et al. (1972) have reviewed some evidence that supports the isolable subsystems model. Briefly, Posner has shown that factors that increase the time to judge two letters visually the same (e.g., AA) by making them less discriminable does not affect the time to judge that both have the same name (e.g., Aa) or that both are vowels (E,a) or consonants (B,C). In addition, Posner (1970) has demonstrated that Ss can access semantic information about a visually presented letter without first activating the internal units related to the letter name. Clearly these findings are consistent with the isolable subsystems model of Figure 6.1(b) but not with the serial model shown in Figure 6.1(a).

There is, however, a problem in using the data cited by Posner et al. to argue strongly for a model of word recognition that postulates the independent retrieval of codes in isolable subsystems. That is, the data came from experiments that used letters rather than words as stimuli, with no clear indication that the data can be generalized to words. However, a recent series of experiments by Meyer et al. (Meyer, Schvaneveldt, & Ruddy, 1974) does suggest that a model of recognition that includes the notion of isolable subsystems may be a viable one for words as well as letters. The studies used a lexical decision task in which Ss were sequentially presented with either two words or one word and one nonword; then the studies asked for a word–nonword response immediately following each stimulus. Reaction times (RT) were the dependent variable, with those for the word–word pairs being the ones of interest. In the first experiment, the second words in the pairs were manipulated in two ways: (a) they were either visually clear or visually degraded, and (b) they were either semantically related (e.g., BREAD–BUTTER) or were unrelated (FENCE–BUTTER). Of interest was the extent to which visually degrading the second word increased RTs to this word and the extent to which having just retrieved related lexical information in responding to the first word facilitated responding to the second word. The results indicated a significant main affect of both visual clarity and semantic relatedness. More importantly, there was also a significant interaction between these two factors, with a greater semantic facilitation effect for visually degraded words than for visually clear words. Such an interaction cannot be predicted by the serial model shown in Figure 6.1(a), although it can predict both main effects. The isolable subsystems model with independent parallel access does predict interactions of this type.

At first glance, the main effect of visual clarity might appear to be contrary to Posner's results with letters. However, an analysis of the lexical decision task requirements suggests that this is not necessarily the case. To decide that a string of letters is a word, one could use either stored visual information, name information, semantic information, or any combination of these. For situations in which a visual input is clearly discriminable, we know that Ss will perform fastest on a visual-matching task, slower on a name-matching task, and even slower yet on a semantic-matching task, suggesting a time ordering from fast to slow for the retrieval of visual, name, and semantic information. Thus an optimal strategy in the lexical-decision task is to make a decision based primarily on retrieved visual information, as long as the visual input is clear. However, when the input is degraded, it would make sense to rely more on name and/or semantic information to make a decision, because this information would be available as soon or sooner than the visual information. One might then assume that in the lexical-decision task, Ss make a decision based on at least partial information from visual, name, and semantic systems but that the amount of information required from each system may vary. This strategy-switching interpretation is consistent with the Meyer et al. results and with the notion of isolable subsystems that may be accessed independently. That is, for clear stimuli, Ss rely more heavily on retrieved visual information, and for degraded stimuli, they rely more heavily on retrieved name and semantic information. Thus one would expect a larger semantic priming effect for a degraded visual image. However, for this interpretation to be acceptable, one would like to know that Ss were in fact using all three types of information to make a lexical decision; this is precisely what Meyer et al.'s second experiment indicates. That is, it shows an effect of both visual and name similarities between the first and second words on RTs to the second word. Thus RTs in the lexical-decision task are affected by visual and by name factors (Experiment II) and by semantic factors (Experiment I). Although this is not the only possible interpretation of these results (see Meyer et al., 1974, for another), it is consistent with their data and with the idea that information about words is stored in several different but interrelated systems that may be accessed in parallel.

Data like those of Meyer et al. (see also Herrmann et al., 1975; Kolers, 1975), which show interactions between visual, name, and/or semantic factors on word recognition tasks are consistent with the idea that there are isolable subsystems that may be accessed independently and in parallel. Although they are in no sense conclusive, the data do suggest that this is a reasonable framework for describing the organization and retrieval of word information.

Organization of Information within Subsystems

The second aspect of the word recognition model that I discuss is that of organization of information within the isolable subsystems discussed in the preceding section and retrieval of this information when a word is seen or heard. In the past few years, there has been a great deal of research that attempts to determine how information is organized in the semantic system. In general, this research suggests that meanings are organized on the basis of their semantic similarity. Thus two meanings that share many semantic properties (e.g., the meanings of the words BEAR and DEER) will be more closely associated in the system than two meanings that do not have common semantic properties (e.g., BEAR and PARE). I would like to suggest that the other subsystems of semantic memory are organized on basically the same principle; that is, information in the visual system is organized in such a way that words that have a high degree of orthographic similarity — i.e., look very much alike — are closely related in the system, whereas those that are orthographically dissimilar will be less closely related. For example, the visual representations of the words BEAR and DEAR will be highly associated, whereas those of BEAR and JUMP will not. Similarly, in the name system, the names of words are organized on the basis of their sound similarities. Thus the representations of words that sound similar, such as BEAR and PAIR, will be more highly associated within this system than words that sound very different, such as DOG and CAT. Support for this proposal comes from memory studies that show confusions among, and intrusions of, similar sounding words, those that show clustering on the basis of sound similarities, and those that show priming affects for words that sound similar.[1]

---

[1] It should be pointed out that we cannot presently specify a precise degree of semantic similarity, name similarity, or visual similarity except by assessing S's performance on a variety of converging tasks with different dependent measures. That is, we have no single list of, say, semantic features that allow us to rate words on the basis of number of shared features and then to predict subject performance. In fact, it is still unclear whether semantic representations can be best described as lists of semantic features or lists of properties, or in some cases, even as visual images. However, it seems to me that the multidimensional scaling work of Smith and his colleagues (Rips, Shoben, & Smith, 1973; Smith, Rips, & Shoben, 1974) is a promising start in this direction.

SPREADING ACTIVATION

A basic mechanism of retrieval proposed to account for the above data is that of spreading activation or excitation. When a single word is presented, the visual, name, and semantic representations for that word are activated in memory. In addition, highly associated visual, name, and semantic representations for other words are also activated although perhaps less strongly than those of the presented word. This produces the phenomenon of priming, where having just seen or heard one word reduces the time to recognize a second, related word. If recognition depends on a representation being activated to a threshold level (Morton, 1969), then the activation of the representation for the second word receives a head start, because this representation has already been partially activated when the first word was presented. Less additional activation is needed to reach threshold, and recognition time for the second word is decreased. The degree of activation of the representation of a second word seems to depend on how highly associated that word is to the presented word (Warren, 1974). In addition, activation appears to decay or decrease over time (Meyer et al., 1972; Warren, 1972) so that the magnitude of the priming effect decreases as the interval between words increases.[2] In general, then, this explanation proposes that word recognition involves both the activation of memory representations for words actually seen or heard and the activation of representations for words that are similar to the input words.

I have recently been doing some studies to determine the extent of spreading activation within the semantic system under conditions that require sufficient comprehension of a sentence to permit accurate paraphrase. The task used is a modification of the Stroop technique. Subjects hear a sentence followed by the visual presentation of a single word printed in colored ink that is either related or unrelated to the last word in the sentence. Their task is to listen to the sentence, name the color of the ink as quickly as possible, and then recall or paraphrase the sentence aloud. Color-naming reaction times are the dependent measure and are used to assess the types of information that have been activated at the time Ss recognize the last word in the sentence. That is, printed words whose representations have received prior activation from hearing the last word in the sentence should be recognized more quickly than those whose representations have not been previously activated. This faster recognition time increases color-naming RTs by producing an increased tendency to respond with the name of the word rather than with the color of the ink in which it is printed. The size of the difference in RTs when the printed word is unrelated to the last word

[2]It is presently unclear whether decay rates are the same in each of the subsystems being discussed and whether these rates are task-determined. That is, activation may decay more quickly in the visual and name systems than in the semantic system, and this may be particularly true when the task requires comprehension of meaning.

heard and when it is related provides a measure of what information was activated at the time the last word in the sentence was heard. As such, the technique is useful in evaluating several current models of semantic memory that make differing predictions about what semantic information is retrieved during the comprehension of sentences. More specifically, Smith and his colleagues (1973; 1974) have proposed a two-stage comparison model of sentence verification. During the first and obligatory stage, all of the semantic features of the subject and predicate of a sentence are retrieved and compared for overlap of features. During the second and optional stage, only the defining features of the words are compared. The important point, however, is that initially both defining and characteristic features are activated. Similarly, the spreading activation model of Collins and Loftus (1975) proposes that, at the time when the words of a sentence are heard, activation spreads through the semantic system in a decreasing gradient until an intersection of activation between the subject and predicate of the sentence occurs. Because the semantic properties that specify the meaning of the words presented will be activated most quickly and most strongly, this model also seems to strongly imply that all or at least most of the semantic features or properties of a presented word will be activated. In contrast to these models, the so-called constructive theories of sentence comprehension (c.f. Bransford & Johnson, 1972) hypothesize that retrieval of information from semantic memory is context-determined. That is, only those semantic properties appropriate to the context in which a word is embedded will be activated. Thus for a sentence like

1. The man attempted to lift the piano.

the constructive theories predict that the semantic property expressed as "pianos are heavy" will be activated but that properties like "pianos have strings" or "pianos produce music" will not be activated. The models of Smith and of Collins and Loftus, on the other hand, predict that all of these properties will be activated at the time one hears or reads the word PIANO in sentence 1.

I recently attempted to test these predictions using the aforementioned color-naming task. In the experimental conditions, aurally presented sentences like

2. The man tuned the piano.
3. The man lifted the piano.

were followed by colored words that reflected context-appropriate properties of the last word in the sentence (e.g., STRINGS for sentence 2 and HEAVY for sentence 3) or context-inappropriate properties of the last word (HEAVY for sentence 2 and STRINGS for sentence 3). In the control conditions, the same colored words were preceded by sentences that contained no words phonemically, orthographically, or semantically similar to the colored words. For each property, the degree of prior activation attributable to hearing the related last word in the sentence was determined by subtracting the RT for color naming in

TABLE 6.1

Mean RTs and The Difference Between These for Experimental and Control Conditions, Obtained in Experiment That Assessed the Effects of Context on the Retrieval of Semantic Properties of Words

	Experimental	Control	Difference
Frequently Mentioned Properties			
Context-Appropriate	708	649	+59
Context-Inappropriate	686	637	+49
Infrequently Mentioned Properties			
Context-Appropriate	663	621	+42
Context-Inappropriate	634	630	+4

the appropriate control condition from the RT in the experimental condition. The results were decidedly not clear-cut. For some of the properties, activation appeared to be context-determined, as the constructive theories would predict, and for other properties, activation appeared to occur independent of context, as the theories of Smith and of Collins and Loftus would predict. Thus, in the foregoing example, STRINGS appeared to be activated at the time Ss heard the word "piano" in both sentences 2 and 3, but HEAVY was activated only when Ss heard the word "piano" in the context of sentence 3. The data, then, did not provide unequivocable support for any of the models. A subsequent analysis of the data suggested that one good predictor of whether or not a semantic property will be activated at the time Ss hear a word that can be described as possessing a certain property is the frequency with which Ss who are asked to describe or define a word include the property in their description.[3] For example, when asked to describe a piano, one of the most frequent properties mentioned is that it has strings. That it is heavy is mentioned infrequently.

A replication of the above experiment, using the same methodology but independently manipulating whether the properties were frequently or infrequently mentioned, confirms the importance of frequency-of-mention of properties in determining whether or not these properties will be retrieved when a word is heard. Means of the mean RT for each S in each condition are shown in Table 6.1. Color-naming RTs were longer for both context-appropriate and context-inappropriate conditions when the colored words were frequently mentioned properties of the last word in the sentences used in the experimental conditions. For infrequently mentioned properties, the color-naming RTs were longer than those in the appropriate control condition only when the colored word was a property implied by the sentence context. Thus Ss show color-

[3]It should be noted that in my data, which assess frequency of mention of properties, there appears to be a fairly high positive correlation between whether a property is frequent or infrequent and whether it fits Smith's definition of a defining feature, or of a characteristic feature. I do not know whether the defining-characteristic distinction is a better predictor of the RT data than is the high–low frequency distinction.

naming interference for both context-appropriate and context-inappropriate properties when these properties are frequently mentioned but show interference in only the context-appropriate condition when the properties are infrequently mentioned. This suggests that the retrieval of frequently mentioned properties of words does not depend on the context in which the word is heard but that the retrieval of infrequently mentioned properties is context-determined.

This interpretation would suggest that this inference process requires more than just semantic information. This interpretation may have some appeal to those who maintain that words do not have clearly specifiable meanings. However, it seems particularly difficult to test in that it requires an experimental technique that does not confound storage with retrieval.

Another interpretation is that all learned semantic properties of words are stored in the semantic system but that there are two different types of retrieval processes that people use to access this information − automatic retrieval processes and attention-requiring retrieval processes (LaBerge & Samuels, 1974; Posner & Snyder, 1975). Either process may be used to retrieve highly associated (frequently mentioned) properties, but less highly associated properties can be retrieved only with the aid of an attentional mechanism. Because we generally focus our attention on integrating information during sentence comprehension rather than focusing on the meanings of individual words, low frequency properties of these words are generally not activated. This will be discussed further in the next section.

A third possible interpretation is that, in the color-naming experiments, all properties were in fact activated to varying degrees but that the experimental task is not sensitive enough to detect low levels of activation. If interpreted in this way, the results would not wholly support any of the theories, because none of them can account for a context effect only with low frequency properties. In fact, none of these interpretations are consistent with either the theories of Smith or of Collins and Loftus or with the constructive theories. Rather, they suggest that word recognition, at the meaning level, is more complex than any of the theories suggest, either because only partial information about word meanings is stored in the semantic system or because, frequently, only partial information is retrieved.

THE ROLE OF ATTENTION IN WORD RECOGNITION

In the preceding section, an interpretation of the color-naming experiment was suggested that postulated two different ways of activating or retrieving information from a memory system. One, which requires input from an attentional system, is referred to as *attended retrieval;* the other, which does not require input from the attentional system, is called *automatic retrieval.* I believe there are differences between these two types of retrieval as a result of the nature of the attentional system that appear to be important for understanding word recognition. The first is that in attended retrieval, we are consciously aware of what is retrieved; in automatic retrieval, there is no conscious awareness. This is equivalent to saying that the attentional system is a mechanism of consciousness. To demonstrate automatic retrieval in word recognition, then, we must be able to show that we retrieve information of which we are not aware. The second implication is that in attended retrieval but not automatic retrieval, there is subject control over what information is retrieved. This suggests, then, that the attentional system is a control mechanism that has direct influence on the way in which we process information. It permits the use of strategies that guide or control how we utilize information stored in memory. In the absence of attentional control (automatic retrieval), what is retrieved is determined by situational and long-term frequency variables that affect the degree of association between representations both within and across systems. Thus, for word recognition, in the absence of attentional control, we automatically activate all well-established representations – visual, name, and semantic – that are related to the input. In addition, through the mechanism of spreading activation, other highly related representations in each system are also activated. It should be noted that this distinction between automatic and attended processes is similar to those suggested by LaBerge and Samuels (1974) and Posner and Snyder (1975). It differs primarily in that it does not equate the attentional system with a limited capacity processing system, as do the other models. The models are similar in that all view the attentional system as a control mechanism and as a mechanism of consciousness and, importantly, that retrieval may be either attended or automatic for highly learned information. For information that is not well-learned, only attended retrieval is possible. Like Posner and Snyder's model, the present model also assumes that automatic processes may proceed in parallel.

The distinction between attended and automatic processes clearly implies that there are two different senses in which we can talk about word recognition. In the attended sense, a word is recognized when we are able to report its name or what it means. In the automatic sense, recognition implies that we have activated representations related to a word in the visual, name, or semantic systems without being aware of the information contained in those representations. I would like to suggest that recognition in the automatic sense more closely approximates what actually occurs in normal listening or reading situations. To demonstrate this, it must be shown that when we are not actively attending to the individual words in an input, all well-learned representations of those words are activated in memory, and it must be shown that we are unaware of that activation. The evidence to support this suggestion is somewhat sketchy but does suggest that this is a reasonable possibility.

TABLE 6.2
Three Types of Stimuli Used in Earlier
Stroop-Related Tasks[a]

A	B	C
RED (blue)	RED (red)	TABLE (green)
GREEN (red)	GREEN (green)	CAR (blue)
BLACK (green)	BLACK (black)	DRUG (red)
BLUE (black)	BLUE (blue)	HEAVY (black)

[a]In A, which is the standard stroop condition, the name of the word and the name of the ink color differ, but both designate colors; in B they are the same. In C (see Keele, 1973), the names of the words do not designate colors. Ink colors are indicated in parentheses.

Control

Perhaps the best demonstration of our inability to control the retrieval of information is the Stroop task and variants thereof. It is clear that when Ss are asked to name the ink color of the words in Table 6.2(a), the most efficient way to proceed is to avoid recognizing the name of the words. However, for most Ss, this is impossible unless they adopt a strategy such as squinting their eyes. Rather, they appear to simultaneously retrieve both the name of the word and the name of the color of the ink, resulting in a response competition that produces long ink-naming latencies. Support for this interpretation is provided by a study (Hintzman et al., 1972) that demonstrates response facilitation when the color of the ink and the name of the word are both the same [Table 6.2(b)] and by a study (Keele, 1973) showing that vocal color-naming interference can be eliminated for stimuli like those in Table 6.2(c) but not for stimuli like those in Table 6.2(a) by using a keypress response rather than a vocal response. Thus there is no response interference when a keypress corresponds to the name of the ink but not the name of the word; the interference remains when there does exist a keypress response for both the name of the word and the name of the ink. The important point is that this response competition could be eliminated by simply not retrieving the name of the word. However, in the Stroop situation, most Ss seem unable to exert this kind of control over what they retrieve. Rather, they appear to activate the name of the printed word while attending to the color of the ink in which the word is printed.

One of the implications of automatic retrieval as it has been described for word recognition is that for experienced language users, all highly-learned representations for a word will be retrieved at the time that word is seen or heard. A somewhat counter-intuitive prediction of this hypothesis is that when

TABLE 6.3

Examples of Stimuli Used in Rhyming Experiment[a]

	Experimental	Control
Visual Similarity	"HUNT, PUNT, RUNT" – AUNT (red) "NOSE, HOSE, POSE" – LOSE (green)	"STICK, CLICK, BRICK" – AUNT (red) "GROWL, PROWL, HOWL" – LOSE (green)
Phonemic Similarity	"WHY, FLY, TRY" – SIGH (black) "FAIL, JAIL, NAIL" – WHALE (red)	"JUMP, PUMP, DUMP" – SIGH (black) "CHANCE, DANCE, TRANCE" – WHALE (red)

[a]Ink colors are indicated in parentheses.

one hears a word, its visual representation as well as its name and semantic representations will be retrieved. This seems to me to be an interesting prediction with respect to the issue of control, in part because, by itself, retrieving visual information during speech recognition would seem to have little or no functional value. If control of what is retrieved were possible during automatic retrieval, then it seems likely that visual information would not be retrieved given a spoken input.

I have conducted one experiment that attempts to test this hypothesis, using the color-naming procedure discussed earlier. Subjects heard a series of three spoken words that rhymed with one another and were visually similar. The spoken words were followed by a single, visually presented word that was printed in colored ink. The printed word was either orthographically or phonemically similar to the three spoken words that preceded it or, in the control condition, was visually, phonemically, and semantically dissimilar to the preceding words. Examples of the different types of stimuli are given in Table 6.3. Subjects were required to listen to the spoken words, name the color of the ink for the printed words, and then repeat the spoken words. Color-naming RTs were recorded.

Earlier it was suggested that, through the mechanism of spreading activation, retrieval of a name representation for a word would also result in activation of representations of similar sounding words and that retrieval of a visual representation would result in the activation of representations for visually similar words as well. Thus, in this experiment, one would clearly predict interference in the color-naming task for words similar in sound to those just heard. In addition, if the visual representations of the spoken words are retrieved at the time the words are heard, one would also predict interference in color-naming for words visually similar to those heard.

Means of the mean RTs for the ten *S*s are shown in Table 6.4. All *S*s had difference scores (experimental condition minus control condition) in the predicted direction for both the visually similar and phonemically similar conditions. Thus the RT data for this study suggests that hearing the spoken words served to facilitate the retrieval of both visually and phonemically similar word representations, because there was interference in the color-naming task for both visually and phonemically similar words. Moreover, the size of the interference effect was not different for the two types of relationships. These results provide

TABLE 6.4
Mean RTs and Differences Between These for Experimental
and Control Conditions, Obtained in Rhyming Experiment

	Experimental	Control	Difference
Visually Similar	850	816	+34
Phonemically Similar	848	811	+37

support for the notion that spreading activation occurs in both the visual and name systems. In addition, they suggest that, in this situation, Ss were retrieving visual representations of words that they had just heard. It is certainly possible, however, that this latter effect is situation-specific, and in a more natural situation (e.g., listening to connected discourse), visual representations of heard words are not retrieved. That is, listening to a series of rhyming words may have created a set in which Ss deliberately attended to visual as well as name aspects of the words. However, Ss' reports suggest that this is unlikely. Most did not recognize that some of the printed words were visually similar to those just heard; of those who did notice this relationship, all reported that they did not attempt to "think about" what the words looked like as they heard them. This suggests that Ss were processing the spoken words automatically and that the visual retrieval effect is not due to a conscious set to retrieve visual information. Even so, I am presently attempting to replicate the experiment using connected discourse instead of a series of rhyming words.

Both the Stroop task and this experiment suggest that there are at least some circumstances in which word recognition involves a retrieval process over which we have no control. However, there also appear to be clear individual differences with respect to being able to control what information we retrieve. For example, not all Ss show interference effects in the Stroop task.

For quite some time I have been interested in the cognitive processes involved in highly skilled adult reading. In particular, I was interested in assessing the hypothesis that highly skilled readers, unlike most of us, do not automatically retrieve name representations of words as they read (Bower, 1970; Smith, 1971; and Meyer, Schvaneveldt, & Ruddy, 1974). If this hypothesis were correct, then highly skilled readers should not show interference in the Stroop task or its variants, because they would be able to inhibit retrieval of the word name, and thus there would be no response competition. However, in trying to test this hypothesis, one encounters an immediate difficulty — highly skilled readers are not easy to find. So far, I have located four Ss who meet my criteria of a highly skilled reader. All read unfamiliar technical material at over 1000 words per minute with excellent comprehension. For example, one person who knew little about car engines, read a manual on how to rebuild a Porsche engine at approximately 1200 wpm and demonstrated a clear understanding, in both an oral and a practical test, of how the engine operated and what was involved in taking it apart. A control S read the same manual at approximately 200 wpm with lesser comprehension. Each of the four skilled readers was given the standard Stroop task and also served as an S in a color-naming experiment similar to that described in the section on spreading activation. None of the Ss showed color-naming interference on either task, i.e., there were no RT differences for experimental and control conditions. In addition, on the second task, Ss could not recall the names of the words they had seen, unlike control Ss who were not highly skilled readers. These results suggest that for these Ss, it was possible to inhibit retrieval of name information for visually presented words. The highly skilled readers, then, unlike many college students, demonstrated a degree of control over what was retrieved during word recognition. Thus, with respect to individual control over what information is retrieved, there appear to be clear individual differences, even within the same tasks.

Awareness

The second important aspect of automatic retrieval is that of nonawareness. That is, we may not be aware of information that is retrieved. Most of the data that supports retrieval without awareness comes from dichotic listening studies that demonstrate the effects of unattended inputs on attended ones in situations where *S*s are unable to report any knowledge of the unattended input. Similar studies by MacKay (1973) and by Lachner and Garrett (1973) have shown that the interpretation given attended lexically ambiguous sentences can be influenced by presenting biasing information that is unattended. In these studies, *S*s heard sentences like

5. The boys were throwing stones at the bank.

in one ear and were instructed to attend to and paraphrase the sentence. In the unattended ear, *S*s were presented biasing sentences like

6a. There's not much water in the river.
6b. That is the new savings and loan building.

The interpretation given the ambiguous sentence was clearly influenced by the content of the unattended sentence. Thus *S*s were retrieving semantic information for the unattended words even though they could not report anything about the meanings of the unattended sentences.

Similarly, in a series of dichotic listening experiments, Corteen and his colleagues (Corteen & Wood, 1972; Corteen & Dunn, 1974) conditioned *S*s to produce a GSR to a series of city names. These names, along with other city names, were then embedded in an unattended message in a dichotic listening task in which *S*s were required to shadow an attended message. GSRs to the unattended words were recorded and were clearly elevated both in response to the already conditioned city names and in response to new city names as well, suggesting that semantic information for the unattended words was being retrieved at input. Awareness of the unattended input was assessed both by verbal recall and by using a keypress task, in which *S*s were asked to produce a keypress response whenever they heard a city name in either ear. Both measures indicated that *S*s were not aware of having heard the unattended input. Again, these experiments appear to demonstrate retrieval of semantic information without awareness.

Experiments using a variant of the Stroop task also support the notion of retrieval of semantic information without awareness. In one study (Conrad, 1974), Ss listened to an unambiguous sentence that ended in a homonym such as

7. The men were drinking port.

Immediately following the sentence they saw a single word, printed in colored ink, which reflected one of the two common meanings of the homonyms (e.g., for sentence 7, either wine or harbor). Color-naming RTs showed clear interference effects for both meanings of the homonym, independent of the context of the sentence in which the homonym was embedded, suggesting that Ss retrieved both meanings of the homonym at the time it was heard. However, Ss were aware only of retrieving the context-appropriate meaning of the homonym and did not even recognize that the sentences frequently ended in homonyms. Thus the context-inappropriate meanings were being retrieved but without the S's conscious awareness.

These studies, then, support the notion that under some circumstances, word recognition involves the automatic retrieval of information in memory without awareness or without S's control over what information is retrieved. Although one must be cautious in generalizing the results of studies that use isolated words as stimuli to the comprehension of sentences or connected discourse, I do believe that the data suggest that normal language comprehension may usually involve automatic rather than attended retrieval as long as the words are familiar.

SUMMARY

As rather sophisticated and highly practiced users of language, we appear to have several different types of information about words stored in memory. There is data to suggest that each type of information is coded in an independently accessible system and is organized within that system according to the degree of commonality of features or properties of the words represented in the system. Word recognition, then, involves both the parallel retrieval of multiple codes for a particular input and, through the mechanism of spreading activation, the retrieval of other, related word codes in each system. However, precisely what information is retrieved may vary both across people, as a result of practice, and across situations, depending on whether or not an attentional control mechanism is used. That is, the attentional system may permit us to exert some control over which of the representational systems are accessed when a word is presented. However, when we are not exerting this control, recognition involves the automatic activation of a series of stable, well-learned pathways in memory, resulting in the retrieval of all available information about the input. Individual differences, such as those observed between average and very fast readers, may be a consequence of long-term practice in using the attentional system to inhibit the activation of selected pathways.

REFERENCES

Bower, T. G. R. Reading by eye. In H. Levin & J. P. Williams (Eds.), *Basic studies on reading*. New York: Basic Books, 1970.

Bransford, J. D., & Johnson, M. K. Contextual prerequisites for understanding: Some investigations of comprehension and recall. *Journal of Verbal Learning and Verbal Behavior*, 1972, *11*, 717–726.

Collins, A., & Loftus, E. F. A spreading activation theory of semantic processing. *Psychological Review*, 1975, *82*, 407–428.

Conrad, C. Context effects in sentence comprehension: A study of the subjective lexicon. *Memory and Cognition*, 1974, *2*, 130–138.

Corteen, R. S., & Dunn, D. Shock associated words in a non-attended message: A test for momentary awareness. *Journal of Experimental Psychology*, 1974, *102*, 1143–1144.

Corteen, R. S., & Wood, B. Automatic responses to shock associated words in an unattended channel. *Journal of Experimental Psychology*, 1972, *97*, 308–313.

Craik, F. I. M., & Lockhart, R. S. Levels of processing: A model for memory research. *Journal of Verbal Learning and Verbal Behavior*, 1972, *11*, 671–684.

Herrmann, D. J., McLaughlin, J. P., & Nelson, B. C. Visual and semantic factors in recognition from long term memory. *Memory and Cognition*, 1975, *3*, 381–384.

Hintzman, D. L., Carre, F. A., Eskridge, V. L., Owens, A. M., Shaff, S. S., & Sparks, E. M. "Stroop" effect: Input or output phenomenon. *Journal of Experimental Psychology*, 1972, *95*, 458–459.

Keele, S. W. *Attention and human performance*. Pacific Palisades, Cal.: Goodyear, 1973.

Kolers, P. Specificity of operations in sentence recognition. *Cognitive Psychology*, 1975, *7*, 289–306.

LaBerge, D., & Samuels, S. J. Toward a theory of automatic information processing in reading. *Cognitive Psychology*, 1974, *6*, 293–323.

Lachner, J. R., & Garrett, M. F. Resolving ambiguity effects of biasing context in the unattended ear. *Cognition*, 1973, *1*, 359–372.

MacKay, D. G. Aspects of the theory of comprehension, memory and attention. *Quarterly Journal of Experimental Psychology*, 1973, *25*, 22–40.

Meyer, D. E., Schvaneveldt, R. W., & Ruddy, M. G. *Activation of lexical memory*. Paper presented at meeting of the Psychonomic Society, St. Louis, Mo., November, 1972.

Meyer, D. E., Schvaneveldt, R. W., & Ruddy, M. G. Loci of contextual effects on visual word recognition. In P. Rabbitt & S. Dornic (Eds.), *Attention and performance V*. New York: Academic Press, 1974.

Morton, J. Interaction of information in word recognition. *Psychological Review*, 1969, *76*, 165–178.

Norman, D. A., Rumelhart, D. E., & the LNR Research Group. *Explorations in cognition*. San Francisco: W. H. Freeman, 1975.

Posner, M. I. On the relationship between letter names and superordinate categories. *Quarterly Journal of Experimental Psychology*, 1970, *22*, 179–287.

Posner, M. I., Lewis, J. L., & Conrad, C. Component processes in reading: A performance analysis. In J. F. Kavanagh & I. G. Mattingly (Eds.), *Language by ear and by eye*. Cambridge: MIT Press, 1972.

Posner, M. I., & Snyder, C. R. R. Attention and cognitive control. In R. Solso (Ed.), *Information processing and cognition: The Loyola Symposium*. Hillsdale, N. J.: Lawrence Erlbaum Associates, 1975.

Rips, L. J., Shoben, E. J., & Smith, E. E. Semantic distance and the vertification of semantic relations. *Journal of Verbal Learning and Verbal Behavior*, 1973, *12*, 1–20.

Smith, F. *Understanding reading*. New York: Holt, Rinehart & Winston, 1971.

Smith, E. E., Rips, L. J., & Shoben, E. J. Semantic memory and psychological semantics. In G. H. Bower (Ed.), *The psychology of learning and motivation* (Vol. 8). New York: Holt, Rinehart & Winston, 1974.

Warren, R. E. Stimulus encoding and memory. *Journal of Experimental Psychology,* 1972, *94,* 90–100.

Warren, R. E. Association, directionality, and stimulus encoding. *Journal of Experimental Psychology,* 1974, *102,* 151–158.

7

Processes in Classifying Pictures and Words: Parallel? Independent? Obligatory?

Janice M. Keenan

University of Denver

Think of what it is like to dribble a basketball. When you are first learning, you always look at the ball. In one obvious sense you *must* look at the ball. However, when you attain the proficiency of, say, a Pete Maravich, you never look at the ball. Now then, imagine an intermediate case. You *can* dribble the ball without looking at it, but, as a matter of fact, you do for the most part look at the ball.

We are in this case imagining an output function, a motor function — bouncing a ball with a hand. The output function is correlated with two input functions: seeing the ball's motion and feeling the ball's motion. For the beginner, the output function really depends on the two input functions. Without the inputs the ball simply will not dependably go up and down. For the middle case, the output still can be said to depend on both inputs in the sense that we do always use information from both hand and eye; but in another sense, the output function does not depend on the eye because we can, at least sometimes, dribble the ball without looking at it. The professional dribbler is merely one who is the worse for looking at the ball. So he learns not to look at it. The middling dribbler is merely one who does not find himself under any pressure to unlearn a bad habit.

So we can ask of these input functions whether they are parallel, whether they are independent, and whether they are obligatory or automatic. I see reading or recognizing words and pictures as similar to the middle case. The output behavior (that is, understanding or recognizing) is correlated with multiple input processes. These might include visual sensory processes, orthographic or pictorial coding, phonemic coding, and semantic interpretive processes, as well as semantic elaborative processes. It is plausible to say that our reading and recognizing experiences have brought to pass a typical configuration of these

121

input processes. But like the middling dribbler, it is not clear that all of the input processes are obligatory for performance; perhaps most of us have yet to unlearn bad habits. Nor is it clear that the processes are independent. We can ask, then, of these component processes in what sense they are parallel, independent, and automatic. Conrad and Klatzky, among others, have asked these questions, and I wish to consider their answers.

Note the problems involved in answering these questions. The criteria for establishing independence have yet to be specified. Both in the case of the middling dribbler and in the case of reading and recognizing pictures and words, we have two or more processes occurring together. Because it is possible to arrange matters such that one process operates in the absence of the other, should we therefore consider these processes independent? Or shall we say that because the processes almost always occur together, i.e., without special circumstances, that the processes are therefore dependent? And if we base our decision on the latter, the typical case, what evidence do we use for identifying separate processes? In other words, how do we know whether we are dealing with two processes that are dependent or just one process?

In the case of dribbling, we distinguish two processes on the basis of two separate input channels: the eye and the hand. With psychological processes, it is not so simple; but for our purposes we often just assign different processes to the different types of information we identify. Or rather, we *hypothesize* different processes for different types of information.

The distinction between different types of information is clear enough. The psychologist allows his distinctions to vary according to the nature of the known object; thus, distinctions that apply to knowledge of a word do not necessarily apply to knowledge of a picture or knowledge of a sentence. Most psychologists decompose knowledge of a word into (a) knowledge of how it appears to the auditory and visual senses; (b) knowledge of how it is produced, either written or orally; and (c) knowledge about its referent. Knowledge of a sentence requires further distinctions. It is decomposed into knowledge of its words, plus knowledge of its word-order structure (syntactic information) and knowledge of the sentence meaning (semantic or propositional information). Because the ultimate goal of the cognitive psychologist is to specify the mental processes and structures underlying behavior, he needs to show that there are behavioral criteria for making these various distinctions. In view of this statement, it is interesting to note that the distinction between syntactic and semantic knowledge-structures was borrowed from linguistics. Because the goal of the linguist is not that of the psychologist, it may turn out that this distinction is ill-suited to the goal of describing language behavior. In fact, Clark and Haviland (1974) have argued quite convincingly that, with respect to psychological processes, syntax cannot be divorced from semantics.

The question, then, is this: Is there behavioral evidence for distinctions such as those between visual information, phonemic information, and semantic information? Conrad argues affirmatively on this point. The logic of her argument is to demonstrate that the different types of information *can* operate independently. Klatzky, on the other hand, concludes from her studies that "truly visual coding is a rare event," occuring only at the periphery. Her conclusions imply that for any cognitive task, it is impossible to separate knowledge of visual form from knowledge of referent.

Let's examine the arguments in some detail. In arguing for isolable subsystems, Conrad is really attacking two separate issues concerning process models of word recognition. One is the serial versus parallel issue; the other is the question of dependence or independence of processes. She correctly argues against a serial characterization of the processes involved; results from Posner (1969), Meyer, Schvaneveldt, and Ruddy (1974), and Marslen–Wilson (1975) all support her argument. But to show that various processes are operating in parallel is not to show that these processes are independent. And unless it can be shown that these processes are independent, it cannot be argued that the distinctions between types of information are valid.

Conrad presents three lines of evidence to support her argument for different types of knowledge or independent processes. Her first line of evidence follows the reasoning of the additive factor logic of Sternberg (1969). If a variable is found to affect one process but not another, then this is evidence for the independence of these processes. She cites evidence from Posner showing that visual degradation affects identity matches but not name matches. Such evidence clearly supports the notion of independent processes, but it seems to be limited to very simple visual displays. For example, if the visual display is made slightly more complex by employing letters of different orientations, very different results obtain. This was shown by Buggie (1970). He used the same paradigm as Posner with letters of different orientations and found that it takes longer to respond "different" to stimuli having the same name, e.g., ∀ and a, than to stimuli having different names, e.g., ∀ and b. Thus, in a task that does not even require the use of names, processing at the name level is affecting processing at the visual level.

The additive factor logic would lead one to conclude that Conrad's second line of evidence, the lexical-decision studies of Meyer, Schvaneveldt, & Ruddy (1974), fails to support her argument. These authors find that visual degradation interacts with semantic context, suggesting that both factors are affecting the same process. Conrad renders this result amenable to the notion of isolable sybsystems by proposing a switching strategy between the two subsystems. But a switching strategy allows the results of one process to become available to the other process, thus rendering the two processes nonindependent.

Finally, Conrad argues that the ability of speed readers to inhibit processing of irrelevant information supports the notion of isolable subsystems. This is certainly the most intriguing line of evidence. It does not, however, tell us whether these processes are independent in the normal individual, just as the independence of Pete Maravich's eye and hand does not allow us to make conclusions about the independence of these input processes in the middling dribbler. But it does show that a particular set of learning experiences can result in a separation of these processes.

It appears then that Klatzky may be right: beyond peripheral processing, there is no behavioral evidence concerning the normal individual to support a distinction between semantic information and any other type of information. There are, however, two problems with this conclusion. First, Klatzky's results may be limited by the nature of the task she employed. Second, it is not clear what is meant by peripheral processing.

There are three aspects of the task Klatzky employed that deserve consideration. First of all, semantic processing could have been induced by the basis on which the subject was to respond – category membership. Is semantic information also involved when the task requires physical identity matches? Klatzky's data do not answer this question. Second, the small number of stimuli and the large number of practice trials guaranteed that the subject knew the stimuli quite well. But suppose in the visual features study that the subject also had to respond to new examples of the categories, e.g., a new house similar to the exemplars in the S and D categories; would the same results obtain? Finally, the results may depend on the use of relatively complex visual displays of highly familiar objects. Posner (1969) has shown that both of these factors alter the nature of short-term visual processing. If the stimuli in a physical matching task are simple enough, such as letters (familiar) and Gibson figures (unfamiliar), there is no advantage of familiarity. However, if the figures are complex, judgments become faster with increased familiarity. If familiarity can be equated with having a semantic representation, then perhaps semantic information only plays a role in the processing of complex stimuli.

Klatzky does find an identity-match advantage at the shortest interstimulus intervals (ISI), 50 msec., but does not find the advantage at an ISI of 250 msec. Physical identity matches in the Posner paradigm with letters show an advantage for ISIs of at least a second; however, his stimuli are much simpler. The question is whether this brief storage is what is meant by peripheral processing. Also, can we take this as evidence for visual storage independent of semantics? We must await answers to the questions raised earlier concerning task variables before we can answer this question.

Having considered Conrad's and Klatzky's answers to the questions of parallel and independent processes in recognizing pictures and words, we turn now to the third question: To what extent are these processes obligatory? The discovery of obligatory processing of irrelevant information is not a recent one; Stroop reported his findings in 1935. What is new, however, is the evidence demonstrating the generality of the phenomenon. Klatzky finds that semantic knowledge always plays a central part in a task which only requires matching of visual features. Conrad claims that the orthographic representation of a word is always primed by an auditory presentation, although her interpretation is open to question.[1] Furthermore, she finds that what distinguishes a speed reader from the rest of the literate population is the extent to which various processes are obligatory. To these findings let me add another — a recent finding by one of my graduate students at the University of Denver, Rob Guttentag. He used stimuli such as those in Figure 7.1 in a Posner matching paradigm. The subject first saw either a picture or a word, followed either by a picture with a word inside it or a control probe — just a picture or just a word. The basis for matching was a between-subjects factor. In other words, a given subject either always matched the standard to the word part of the probe or always responded on the basis of the picture part of the probe. Thus one might expect that after several practice trials, the subject would adopt a strategy of ignoring the irrelevant information because it was always a picture or always a word. However, it appears that subjects are not able to adopt such a strategy. The results of the experiment are depicted in Table 7.1. For both types of matches, it is clear that the irrelevant information is having some effect on processing, because the presence of irrelevant information generally results in longer response times. It appears also that the irrelevant information is being processed to a semantic level, because response times are consistently faster when the picture and word of the probe are correlated. So, not only does there seem to be obligatory visual and semantic processing, but these results suggest that the two processes are interdependent. Furthermore, the locus of interdependence seems to be in encoding the probe; a response-competition hypothesis would predict longer response times to say "different" when the irrelevant information is correlated with the standard, but no such effect was observed.

The notion of obligatory processes has important implications for information-processing models. Most theorists construct process models in which the only processing steps considered are those deemed relevant to the task. The finding that seemingly irrelevant processing is consuming processing capacity and resources throws a wrench in current process models. Certainly, the task for the

---

[1] Conrad finds increased color-naming latencies for words that are visually similar to those heard. On the basis of this finding, she concludes that "subjects were retrieving visual representations of words they had just heard." Unfortunately, all of the visually similar words are also phonemically dissimilar to those heard. Meyer et al. (1974) have shown that phonemic dissimilarity between target and prime results in longer latencies than unrelated, control pairs. Because Conrad shows that subjects are processing the colored words at a phonemic level, it follows that the longer latency for visually similar, phonemically dissimilar words could be due to phonemic interference. Furthermore, this explanation accommodates the fact that "the size of the interference effect was not different for the two types of relationships" (visually similar and phonemically similar); according to this explanation, both effects arise from the same phonemic system.

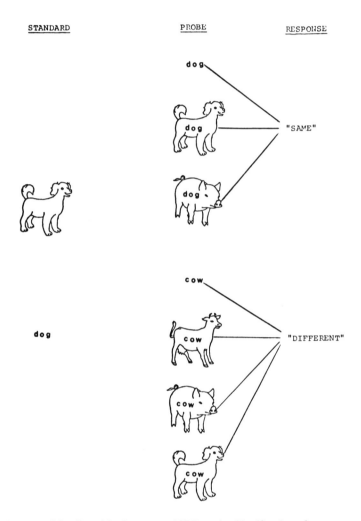

FIGURE 7.1 Stimuli used in Guttentag (1976) study. Classification of responses pertains to the case where the *S* must respond on the basis of the word.

immediate future is to discover: (a) what types of processing are obligatory, (b) at what level do they play a role – encoding? response competition?, (c) under what conditions do they play a role, and (d) how does one learn to inhibit these processes?

I would like to conclude my discussion with a comment concerning the notion of spreading activation discussed by Conrad. This notion is becoming widely accepted in the semantic-memory literature, seemingly without any reservation or criticisms. The spreading activation concept echoes Pavlov's pseudoneurological model of spreading cortical excitation, and I seriously doubt that it advances

TABLE 7.1
Mean Response Times (msec) for "Same" and "Different" Responses as a Function of Type
of Match and Nature of Irrelevant Information (from Guttentag, 1976)

	No Irrelevant Information	Correlated Irrelevant Information	Uncorrelated Irrelevant Information	Uncorrelated Irrelevant Information[a]
"Same" Responses				
Picture-Match	597	600	632	
Word-Match	597	620	653	
"Different" Responses				
Picture-Match	631	637	656	648
Word-Match	627	648	670	661

[a]Here the irrelevant information was correlated with the standard.

us any further than his model. The problem with the notion is that it implies a static memory structure, i.e., one with a fixed organization. In order to account for priming effects at various levels of analysis, Conrad elaborates the notion to include four or five fixed organizations — one for each type of information. Now, it seems to me that if we should have learned anything by changing our stimuli from single words to sentences, it would be that the semantic interpretation of most words is not fixed. Conrad's own experiments on spreading activations show that there is not a fixed organization at the semantic level. In fact, a recent encoding specificity experiment by Reder, Anderson, and Bjork (1974) makes the same point using high- and low-frequency words. What is primed or activated in reading a word cannot be predicted on the basis of the word's meaning but depends to a large extent on the context in which the word occurs as well as the demands of the task.

As an alternative to a spreading activation explanation of priming, I propose that we take account of the dynamics of the information-processing system and that we consider the nature of its operations. If we allow memory for encoding operations, not necessarily in terms of a record of operations, but simply in terms of the likelihood of employing one operation rather than another, then we can account for priming by the notion of overlap in encoding operations. To the extent that two stimuli share encoding operations, there will be priming effects.

Such a framework does not require a fixed organization of memory and can easily account for all existing data on priming effects. It differs from the spreading activation model in that, for instance, it yields the counterintuitive prediction that a given stimulus may not always be its best prime. If task demands on two occurrences of a stimulus are such that they require very different encoding operations, then some other stimulus that involves more similar encoding operations may yield greater priming effects. This stands as an exciting area for future research.

REFERENCES

Buggie, S. W. *Stimulus preprocessing and abstraction in the recognition of disoriented forms.* Unpublished masters thesis, University of Oregon, 1970.

Clark, H. H., & Haviland, S. E. Psychological processes as linguistic explanation. In D. Cohen (Ed.), *Explaining linguistic phenomena.* Washington, D. C.: Hemisphere Publishing Corporation, 1974.

Guttentag, R. *Interference effects in the naming and matching of pictures and words.* Unpublished manuscript, University of Denver, 1976.

Marslen–Wilson, W. D. Sentence perception as an interactive parallel process. *Science,* 1975, *189,* 226–228.

Meyer, D. E., Schvaneveldt, R. W., & Ruddy, M. G. Loci of contextual effects on visual word recognition. In P. Rabbitt & S. Dornic (Eds.), *Attention and performance V.* New York: Academic Press, 1974.

Posner, M. I. Abstraction and the process of recognition. In G. H. Bower & J. T. Spence (Eds.), *The psychology of learning and motivation* (Vol. 3). New York: Academic Press, 1969.

Reder, L. M., Anderson, J. R., & Bjork, R. A. A semantic interpretation of encoding specificity. *Journal of Experimental Psychology,* 1974, *102,* 648–656.

Sternberg, S. Memory scanning: Mental processes revealed by reaction-time experiments. *American Scientist,* 1969, *57,* 421–457.

Stroop, J. R. Studies of interference in serial verbal reaction. *Journal of Experimental Psychology,* 1935, *18,* 643–662.

8
The Distributed Memory Model Revisited: Discussion of the Papers by Conrad and by Klatzky and Stoy

Russell Revlin

University of California, Santa Barbara

The chapters by Conrad and by Klatzky and Stoy seem to take different approaches to the study of semantics; that this difference is only apparent is clear when you place them within the context of a general model of memory. The "context" that I would like to work from was provided a few years ago by Hunt (1971) when he asked the question, "What kind of computer is man [p. 57];" In this paper, Hunt sketched a distribution memory model, incorporating diverse memory components that appear to account for tasks such as those before us. Of primary interest is the portion of the distributed-memory model that details the functioning of the intermediate-memory buffers, as shown in Figure 8.1.

Briefly, the model claims that after pictures or words enter the sensory buffers, their physically coded representations are analyzed in the intermediate buffers where they are recoded by means of relatively automatic programs and data stored in long-term memory (LTM). Of course, one need not assume that there are actually such things as intermediate buffers; assume only that the processes so described operate in a sequential fashion from sensory input to long-term storage (i.e., there are different levels of processing). Figure 8.1 shows that the LTM codes and programs are accessed by STORE and FETCH components of the intermediate buffers and that LTM contains semantic relations (among other components) used in making decisions in conscious memory.

The system's functioning fits nicely with the paradigm used by Klatzky and Stoy. In their experiments, the input figures enter the appropriate intermediate-memory buffer; category codes in LTM are then automatically accessed; finally,

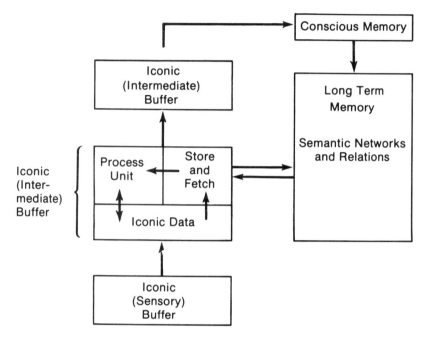

FIGURE 8.1   Hunt's distributed memory model (after Hunt, 1971).

the abstract codes of the "highly weighted (common) features" are added to the already stored information in conscious memory. Here, physical features are deleted over time, and the code becomes progressively composed of abstract features. This differential decay function occurs because while LTM can continue to refresh the abstract codes, only the physical presence of the stimuli can refresh the concrete features.

The distributed-memory model permits task constraints to determine the nature of the codes that are added to conscious memory. This property of the system is borrowed freely by both chapters reviewed here. For example, in Klatzky and Stoy, in pure identity sessions, the subject need not operate the FETCH mechanism, because he will only be required to make a *physical* match on the probe stimulus. In contrast, in mixed sessions, more elaborated codes must be accessed, because the subject might be required to perform category matches in addition to identity matches. Here, the subject is claimed to access semantic codes in LTM (namely, those highly weighted features that are important to the identification of elements in the same category). The distributed-memory model therefore predicts that there should not be a category-structure effect in pure sessions but only in mixed sessions. This is exactly what the results show: (a) no category-structure effect on identity matches for pure sessions in Experiment III (Basic/Superordinate) and Experiment IV (Synonym/

Homonym); (b) a category-structure effect for identity matches in the same experiments in mixed sessions.

This finding shows that the selection of representations in memory ("progressive recoding" in Hunt's terms) is not automatic and is under strategy control determined at least by the task constraints and the idiosyncratic trade-offs of the subjects (see Chapter 5). This is a crucial aspect of the work of Conrad as well, and I return to it shortly.

The category-structure effect of Klatzky and Stoy shows that LTM codes are called into play not only when what is traditionally termed "name" matching occurs (Posner, 1969) but also when identity matches are called for (in mixed sessions). Of course, one might argue that in Experiments III and IV (Klatzky and Stoy), in which the category structure affects the identity matches, the information has already been in memory for 750 msec (500 msec presentation time plus at least a 250 msec ISI). Although it will certainly be important to examine the presence of a category-structure effect at short display and ISI times, the present findings cannot be solely attributable to the effects of timing. For example, there was no category-structure effect in Experiment II, which had the same time parameters as Experiments III and IV. These experiments do differ, however, on the semantic features that characterize the elements in the sets.

Exploring the nature of these features is a major contribution of the Klatzky and Stoy study. The data show clearly that category matches are not made simply on the basis of "name" matches (see especially Experiment IV) but must entail information about the category from whence the stimuli are selected. The use of highly weighted features and the independent control over the selection of features in Klatzky and Stoy directly parallel the recognition mechanism of Hunt's (1971) where veridical and contrasting features are both assessed from semantic memory and processed in the intermediate buffers. These features are employed in different ways in higher-level decisions and in recognizing subsequently presented stimuli.

Both in Hunt and in Klatzky and Stoy, the selection of features and their processing is related to task constraints. As I mentioned earlier, Klatzky and Stoy argue that the retrieval processes of their subjects are under conscious (i.e., attentional) control: Subjects select FETCH strategies as a function of pure vs. mixed sessions and can even optimize retrieval by selecting different weights of features. Acknowledging the use of *strategies* not only provides the models with some flexibility but also facilitates the interpretation of data. However, such mechanisms can be abused if the models do not specify beforehand the conditions that evoke the strategies. This is not only a problem for the present research on elementary information processing, but it also poses difficulties for memory and problem-solving studies in which the subjects are said to employ mnemonics and chunking routines and to organize material "subjectively" (e.g., Bower & Winzenz, 1970; or Tulving, 1962). The problem for the development of psychological models has been succinctly expressed by Gerritsen, Gregg, and Simon (1975):

> If different strategies are used for a particular task, then no single information processing model will capture all the methods of organizing the performance of that task. Different strategies will usually call upon different elementary information processes; and even if the same processes are used, they will be used with different relative frequencies. Under these circumstances, chronometric studies cannot be expected to reveal basic time constants associated with underlying psychological processes, nor will the parameters that are measured be the same from one subject to another. The investigator is in danger of discovering facts only about the "sociology" of information processing — that is to say, about the knowledge and predispositions that subjects having particular backgrounds will bring to the laboratory, or that will be evoked from them by the conditions of the experiment — and not about the fundamental characteristics of the information processor that set the bounds within which the strategy can vary [p. 2].

Although the present contributors do not aim to isolate basic information-processing parameters, the ad hoc quality of the strategems to which they appeal can only foreshorten the extent to which their findings support more general models of semantic processing. Certainly, such obstacles are to be avoided if at all possible though they are often the consequence of breaking new ground.

Although the foregoing discussion has concentrated on the study by Klatzky and Stoy, it should be clear that the distributed-memory model provides a common format for comparing both chapters reviewed here. Both Klatzky and Stoy and Conrad study the nature of the FETCH mechanism and its reliance on semantic codes. Conrad assesses the nature of the LTM codes in word recognition and tests two hypotheses. First, that there are separable subsystems to which the recoding FETCH operations have access. Second, that these subsystems in LTM are scanned in parallel by means of spreading activation. This last hypothesis is related to the strong assumption that these subsystems are organized as networks of similarity relations. With respect to the distributed-memory model, this means that rather than a serial recoding of information from one buffer to the next higher buffer (which again FETCHES new information from LTM), the FETCH routines themselves operate in parallel.

The plausibility of this approach is argued by analogy from Posner's work on same—different tasks (e.g., Posner, 1969) with letter-matching identification. Conrad points out that it may be quite tenuous to extend the letter-identification findings to word recognition. Her suspicions are well founded in light of Klatzky's data for meaningful material. Although the work of Klatzky and Stoy does not argue against parallel physical and name searches in letter identification, it certainly contests the simple dichotomy of physical and nominal matches when the material being matched has elaborate semantic relations.

The weight of the memory system that Conrad describes is borne by the organization of the system: similarity, determined by feature proximities in a network, with accessing determined by spreading activation. This reduces retrieval processes to a single mechanism rather than different computational schemes for each type of data to be retrieved. The memory system is based on a traditional associationistic analysis that has gained new currency with the work of Collins and Quillian (1969; 1972) and most recently by Collins and Loftus (1975).

Although Conrad's analysis relies on the Collins and Loftus memory model, she does not fully appreciate one implication of that model: namely, that each node in the lexical network is connected to one or more concept nodes in the semantic network (and vice versa). The consequence of this is that there are ways of getting from the lexical features to the appropriate semantic features or to the phonological or orthographic features without engaging in parallel searches.

Of course, the distributed-memory model embodies many of the features of a parallel search. For example, one might conjecture that there are a host of search (FETCH) operations that are looking for either semantic, orthographic, or name features. These FETCH operations function in parallel (e.g., analogous to a horse race). When one finds its target, it facilitates retrieval on the other dimensions, because the initial stimulus is now recoded in the intermediate-term buffer, and a new operator is selected to retrieve the missing information. In this way, interfering with one FETCH operator need not interfere with others (because they function in parallel until one "hits"); however, facilitating one should facilitate the remainder of the search, because it will be curtailed immediately when a direct link from the new information to the searched-for code has been found. Hunt's description of the distributed-memory model would claim that when any dimension is found by the FETCH mechanism, an INTERRUPT signal stops processing (in the case of Conrad, the naming process), thereby producing Conrad's effect.

Conrad relies heavily on subject-initiated strategies. This is true, for example, of her explanation for the findings of Meyer, Schvaneveldt, and Ruddy (1974) and of her notion of automatic vs. attention-requiring retrieval. Although these notions have merit on independent grounds, their post-experiment applications detract from the strengths of the explanations of the data. Be that as it may, the flexibility that such notions possess helps us to see an important commonality in the work of Conrad and of Klatzky and Stoy: Both would agree that the perception and storage of information immediately accesses the semantic system — sometimes at the behest of the subject and sometimes without his awareness. Both papers provide new insights into the importance of semantic structures in all facets of the basic processing of meaningful material.

REFERENCES

Bower, G. H., & Winzenz, D. Comparison of associative learning strategies. *Psychonomic Science*, 1970, *20*, 119–120.

Collins, A. M., & Loftus, E. F. A spreading-activation theory of semantic processing. *Psychological Review*, 1975, *82*, 407–428.

Collins, A. M., & Quillian, M. R. Retrieval time from semantic memory. *Journal of Verbal Learning and Verbal Behavior,* 1969, *8,* 240–247.

Collins, A. M., & Quillian, M. R. How to make a language user. In E. Tulving & W. Donaldson (Eds.), *Organization and memory.* New York: Academic Press, 1972.

Gerritsen, R., Gregg, L. W., & Simon, H. A. *Task structure and subject strategies as determinants of latencies.* Carnegie-Mellon University, CIP Working Paper, 292, 1975.

Hunt, E. What kind of computer is man? *Cognitive Psychology,* 1971, *2,* 57–98.

Meyer, D. E., Schvaneveldt, R. W., & Ruddy, M. G. Loci of contextual effects on visual word recognition. In P. Rabbitt & S. Dornic (Eds.), *Attention and performance V.* New York: Academic Press, 1974.

Posner, M. I. Abstraction and the process of recognition. In J. T. Spence & G. H. Bower (Eds.), *Advances in learning and motivation* (Vol. 3). New York: Academic Press, 1969.

Tulving, E. Subjective organization in free recall of unrelated words. *Psychological Review,* 1962, *69,* 344–354.

Section III

"

9
Nominal, Perceptual, and Semantic Codes in Picture Categorization

Edward E. Smith
Gerald J. Balzano
Janet Walker

Stanford University

INTRODUCTION

Possible Interfaces Between Perception and Language

One function of language is to describe perceptual experience, but to decide that some linguistic description adequately captures a perceptual experience, one must have a procedure for relating the description and the perception. There appear to be two classes of such procedures. The first includes what we call *common-code* procedures. The essential idea is that one translates both the perception and the linguistic description into a common code, and then determines if the experience and description are congruent (e.g., Clark & Chase, 1972; Pylyshyn, 1973). The second class of procedures utilizes a *translation* approach. Here it is assumed that a perceptual experience and a description are kept in different codes, and that one relates the two by determining if one code can be translated into the other (e.g., Kosslyn & Pomerantz, 1977). To illustrate this approach, one could form a perceptual code for the experience and a semantic code for the description, and then see if the former in some way instantiates the latter.

We would like to consider these two classes of procedures in depth, but before we can do so, we need to make some comment about the codes upon which these procedures operate.

Possible codes. To make explicit the coding possibilities for perceptions and descriptions, let us take as our paradigm case the situation in which one must decide whether a single word is a true or false description of a picture of a familiar object, e.g., whether or not the word *fruit* correctly describes a pictured apple. What kinds of codes might one use for the word or picture? For the word, one possibility is to code it as an object name qua name, i.e., an orthographic or acoustic representation of the word itself. Another possibility is to code the word at a deeper level, one that highlights its meaning. Here we might have a visual image of the word's referent, or a semantic representation of the word, where the latter contains abstract components that both describe its referent and specify its relation to other words in the lexicon. Thus we have noted three possible codes for a word in our paradigm case: (a) name qua name (hereafter referred to as *nominal*), (b) referential image (hereafter, *imaginal*), and (c) semantic.

Roughly the same three kinds of codes may be used to represent the picture in our paradigm. The nominal code of a picture would again be an orthographic or acoustic representation of the name of the picture. Instead of an imaginal code for a picture, we can talk about its perceptual representation, which would be some sort of visual description in terms of primitive perceptual components. And lastly, the semantic code for a picture would again be a set of abstract components that describe it as well as specify its relation to other entities.

There are just two other aspects about codes or representations that should be noted. First, for a word, it is possible that the nominal and semantic codes are derived first and then used to develop the imaginal representation; in contrast, for a picture, the perceptual representation must be derived first and can then be used to access the nominal and semantic codes. Second, semantic and perceptual codes for an item differ not only in that the former is more abstract but also in that the two codes may have different contents. Thus a semantic code for a picture presumably contains information not perceptually available (e.g., the fact that an apple may contain a worm) and lacks some information that may have been part of a perceptual code (e.g., the fact that a particular apple had a small stem).

Common-code procedures. With the foregoing as background, we are ready to discuss common-code procedures for interfacing perceptions and descriptions. There are three possibilities to be considered, corresponding to whether the common code is nominal, imaginal—perceptual, or semantic.

The idea of a nominal code seems reasonable in our paradigm case. Intuitively, when one sees a pictured object, its name appears to be readily available (though it must have been derived from the perceptual code), and it seems plausible that the picture's name might be compared directly to the word to determine if the latter adequately describes the picture. Unfortunately, there is little in the way of prior research to back up this intuition. Although there is a rich literature on the naming of pictures, no one has related this work to the questions we are concerned with.

Although a common nominal code is a likely possibility for our paradigm, a common imaginal—perceptual code is less plausible, because the latter implies that the word has been coded imaginally, and this assumption can get us into trouble. The problem stems from having to form an image of an abstract word like *fruit*. What would be the attributes of such an image? That is, what perceptual properties characterize fruits in general? This is an old problem and one that won't go away. Berkeley stated it nicely a few hundred years ago, and Rosch, Mervis, Gray, Johnson, and Boyes—Braem (1976) have recently updated the case against abstract images. They took the pains to show that there is very little consensus on the perceptual properties attributed to a generic category like fruit. Given this, we do not pursue the imaginal—perceptual variant of the common-code procedure.

The last possible common code to consider is a semantic one. This possible interface between a perception and a linguistic description is clearly plausible, and is the one most favored in previous literature. Perhaps the best case for it can be found in the work of Clark and Chase (e.g., 1972). They presented perceptual displays of a star either above or below a plus and asked people to decide whether a sentence like *The star is above (below) the plus* was a true or false description of the display. Two aspects of their results implicated a semantic common code. Decision times were affected by the semantic complexity of the relational term (*below* is more complex than *above*), and the detailed pattern of the results could be precisely fit by models positing a semantic common code. (Trabasso, Rollins, & Shaughnessy, 1971, have independently provided similar results and similar models.)

Although these findings are impressive, how relevant are they to our paradigm case of relating a single word to a familiar object? For one thing, the Clark and Chase displays depicted locative relations between two separable entities, but we are concerned with displays that contain only a single entity. Perhaps the kind of common code needed for comparing representations of the relations between objects is different from that needed to compare representations of the objects themselves. A second point is that the Clark and Chase displays were such that no single-word description sufficed for an entire display, but the familiar objects we are concerned with can be encoded by a one-word description, i.e., their name. Conceivably, when a single word can describe a display, one may use only a surface code like the name itself. These factors make us cautious about generalizing Clark and Chase's conclusion to our paradigm.

There is, however, other research that is closer to our paradigm and that also suggests the use of a semantic common code. We are referring to the work of Seymour (e.g., 1973). In several experiments, Seymour asked people to decide whether a picture of a geometric form, like a circle, and a single word, say *square*, both belonged to the same category. He found that decisions that the two items were not from the same category were made more rapidly when there were fewer features shared by the picture and the concept designated by the word. For example, subjects responded "no" more rapidly to a pictured circle paired with the word *square* than to the same picture paired with the word *ellipse.* There is a problem, though, in taking this as evidence for a semantic code. The features involved may have been perceptual rather than semantic, i.e., subjects may have coded the word imaginally and the picture perceptually, because no abstract words were used. Furthermore, even if the common code involved was in fact semantic, there are reasons to question whether Seymour's findings would generalize to our paradigm. The semantic representations for simple geometric forms may be quite unlike those for common objects (the former may contain fewer and more clear-cut features), and few geometric forms are as readily nameable as common objects like apples. All in all, previous research makes a semantic common code a plausible candidate for our paradigm, but the issue is still an open one.

Translation procedures. Now let us deal with cases where the word and picture in our paradigm are coded differently, and a translation is required between them. All told, there are six such cases: The word may be coded nominally, imaginally, or semantically, and for each of the three possibilities, the picture may be represented in either of the two codes that differ from that of the word.

In the first case, one might code the word nominally and the picture perceptually, and try and relate the two. This won't work. Given the arbitrariness with which names are assigned to objects in various cultures, there is simply no meaningful way one can relate the properties of a name qua name with the perceptual properties of the name's referent. The arbitrariness of naming will also prohibit a translation in the second possible case, in which the word is coded nominally and the picture semantically.

The next two possibilities assume that in trying to relate a word like *fruit* to a pictured apple, one forms an imaginal code for the word. If one then codes the picture by its name, the arbitrariness of naming will again block any translation procedure. If, however, one codes the word imaginally and the picture semantically, then a translation is at least conceivable, because there should be some sets of corresponding components in the perceptual and semantic representations of the same class of objects (apples, in our example). Although this translation procedure is possible, it is not very plausible. Specifically, it requires an imaginal code for the word, and we have already noted the problem of forming an image for an abstract term like *fruit.*

Thus far we have argued that, for our paradigm case, translation is impossible when the word is coded nominally and unlikely when it is coded imaginally. What about a translation procedure when the word is coded semantically? For the case where the picture is coded nominally, we are again thwarted by the arbitrariness of naming. But if the picture is coded perceptually, then a translation procedure is finally viable. Thus a semantic code for *fruit* may contain components that can be instantiated by the perceptual components of a pictured apple. But, one might ask, why is this procedure plausible when the "converse" procedure involving an imaginal word-code and a semantic picture-code was considered implausible? Recall that in the latter case we had to make the troublesome assumption that one could generate a reliable image for abstract terms, whereas for the present procedure we need only postulate that one accesses a semantic representation of the word and then tests perceptual attributes of the picture to determine if these realize or *instantiate* the semantic components. Note that in the present case, we do not assume that one accesses a semantic code for the picture, because this would make it a common-code procedure.

It is in fact instructive to compare the semantic common-code procedure with our translation between a semantically coded word and a perceptually coded picture. The critical difference between the two is that the translation procedure involves the search for a mapping that will project a perceptual attribute into a semantic one, whereas the common-code procedure presupposes the existence and occurrence of such a mapping and operates on its results (mainly, or even solely, by testing for identity; see Clark & Chase, 1972). An example of the translation procedure should clarify this, so let's go back to our old standby of deciding that *fruit* correctly describes a pictured apple. Part of the semantic code for *fruit* may be the component, "edibility." In instantiating this, the perceptual attribute of nonrigidity may be a necessary condition, and the presence or absence of rigidity may be discernible directly from certain visual–texture information (Gibson, 1966). Thus we have come up with a mapping that projects perceptual information about rigidity into a semantic component concerned with edibility. And note that it was not necessary to assume that nonrigidity was part of the semantic code for the word *fruit,* that edibility was a perceptual attribute of a pictured apple, or that nonrigidity and edibility were in any sense identical or equivalent. The latter assumptions might, however, be required in a common-code procedure.

Let's try another example of our translation procedure. Consider the semantic component of the term *clothing* that can best be described as "wearableness." Because this entails that some part of the body be placed through a portion of the clothing-object and because most external body parts are cylindrical in cross section, the presence of circular or nearly circular apertures within the form of the clothing-object would seem to be a necessary perceptual attribute for instantiating wearableness. (A scarf is the only major exception we can think of, and even a scarf *as worn* encircles the head–neck area.) Here, then, perceptual information about circular apertures is projected onto the semantic component of wearableness.

In both of the preceding examples, we can invoke Gibson (1966) to support the assumption that the appropriate perceptual information is contained in the object (or picture). This is what makes the translation possible. Furthermore, there is no need to assume (as we might have to with a perceptual–imaginal common code) that an image could be formed of overall visual–texture information or of aperture-specifying information or that such information would ever figure prominently in an image of a fruit or of an article of clothing. Thus our translation procedure between a semantically coded word and a perceptually coded picture is manifestly different from any common-code procedure. Although such a translation procedure seems eminently plausible, we know of no evidence or argument that explicitly documents it.

To summarize, we have argued at some length that decisions in our paradigm could be accomplished by a translation procedure in which the word is coded semantically and the picture perceptually. In addition, we previously identified two common-code procedures that could be used in our paradigm, corresponding to nominal and semantic common-codes. We have therefore three possible procedures for interfacing perceptions and descriptions in our paradigm, and a major purpose of our studies was to provide data that would discriminate among them. In trying to do so, we found it convenient to group together the two procedures that involve any semantic coding and to contrast them with the procedure that relies only on nominal codes. As the reader will see, this kind of contrast can readily be studied experimentally.

Levels of Categorization

All of the foregoing dealt with the type of codes used in categorizing pictures with respect to words. There is, however, another fundamental question that one may ask about such categorizations. Is there a preferred *level* of abstractness for picture categorization? To illustrate, a pictured apple may be categorized as either an apple or, more abstractly, as a fruit. Is one of these levels preferable, and if so, why?

Basic levels. Intuition and everyday experience suggest that there is indeed a preferred level of categorization, and Rosch et al. (1976) have recently documented this. The idea is that the preferred level is the most abstract level of classification at which the class members share a substantial number of attributes. For example, we may classify certain entities as Washington state Delicious apples, or as apples, or as fruit. Although the first two classifications are such that their members share many attributes, the category of apples is the most abstract one at which many common perceptual attributes appear. Hence it is said to be the basic level. The basic level of classification, then, is a compromise between a wealth of information content (e.g., Washington state Delicious apples) and an economical, abstract description (e.g., fruit).

This notion seems to have a direct implication for our paradigm. One may be able to decide that a word is an adequate description of a picture faster when the word is at a basic level (*apple*) than at a nonbasic level (*fruit*). Note that this prediction is, on an a priori basis, independent of the question of what kinds of codes are used to interrelate words and pictures. Thus basic-level nominal codes may be compared faster than nonbasic codes, and similarly, basic-level semantic codes may be compared faster than nonbasic ones. Regardless of the codes used, the basic-levels hypothesis predicts that, for example, a pictured apple can be correctly classified faster when paired with *apple* (a basic-level term) than when paired with *fruit* (a nonbasic-level term).

Coding dependence. There is another way to look at this business of levels, one that leads to very different predictions than the basic-levels hypothesis. Suppose in our paradigm (in which the word precedes the picture) that the word affects the coding of the picture. Suppose in particular that the level of the word determines the level of abstractness at which the picture is coded, with pictures being coded at the same level as the word. To illustrate this coding-dependence hypothesis, assume that a picture of an apple is paired with either *fruit* or *apple*. When the word is *fruit,* one may code the picture perceptually at a level appropriate to the abstractness of the term and may thus inspect a certain (small) number of the picture's attributes. In contrast, when the word is *apple,* one would have to code the picture at a more specific level, and presumably this requires inspecting more attributes of the picture. So the less generic the word, the more pictorial attributes that have to be coded. This suggests that a picture may be categorized faster when paired with a generic than a specific word. Because generic words tend to be nonbasic terms and specific words tend to be basic terms [as determined by inspection of the Rosch et al. (1976) norms], our coding-dependence hypothesis leads to a prediction opposite to that of the basic-levels hypothesis. This contrast was tested explicitly in our experiments.[1]

EXPERIMENT 1: PICTURE–WORD CATEGORIZATIONS

Overview and Rationale

The experimental paradigm we used was as follows. Each trial started with the presentation of a one-word question, e.g., *fruit.* The experimenter spoke the word to the subjects, who repeated it back to insure they had heard it correctly. Then a picture was presented, and subjects indicated whether the question was true or false of the picture by pushing either a button labeled True or one labeled False as quickly as possible.

We wanted to use this paradigm to tell us something about the issues of type and level of code. To get at the latter, we simply varied the level of the

---

[1]Clearly there are other possible versions of a coding-dependence hypothesis, and we return to this point at the end of the paper.

question – it could be either a generic (high-level) term like *fruit* or a specific (low-level) term like *apple*. To get at the question of the type of code used took a little more doing. We were most interested in the possibility that the code used was at least partly semantic, as would be the case if subjects translated a perceptual code for the picture into a semantic code for the word or used a semantic common code. Thus we needed some indicators of a semantic comparison process. The literature on semantic memory provides such indicators. In numerous studies in this literature, subjects must rapidly decide on the truth or falsity of sentences like *An apple is a fruit.* Here it is generally acknowledged that only a semantic code is used, so we may take the effects obtained in these experiments as a kind of signature of this code. The two major effects in these semantic-memory studies seem to be: (a) True decisions are more rapid when the instance is considered a typical member of the category than when it is considered an atypical one; and (b) False decisions are more rapid when the two terms are judged to be semantically unrelated than when they are semantically related (see, e.g., Smith, Shoben, & Rips, 1974). With regard to the present work, the question is whether word–picture comparisons will also show typicality and relatedness effects. If they do, we have some evidence that a semantic code is involved.

Materials and Design

Experimental variations. The words used as questions in our paradigm are shown in Table 9.1. There were six high-level terms – *birds, fruits, vegetables, tools, furniture,* and *clothing.* According to Rosch et al. (1976), *birds* would be considered a basic-level term, whereas the other five terms would be considered nonbasic. For each of these six high-level categories, we used the names of six members of the category, and these are also shown in Table 9.1. In each column the first three low-level terms designate typical members of the high-level category, and the second three designate atypical members. [Typical items were of roughly the same frequency as atypical items, as determined by the Kucera & Francis (1967) norms.] Typicality was determined by Rosch's (1975)

TABLE 9.1
Question Used in Experiment 1

	Birds	Fruits	Vegetables	Tools	Furniture	Clothing
Typical	robin	orange	corn	saw	chair	pants
	bluejay	apple	carrot	hammer	sofa	shirt
	pigeon	banana	lettuce	drill	dresser	jacket
Atypical	swan	raisin	garlic	soldering iron	stool	hat
	flamingo	lime	mushroom	paintbrush	mirror	gloves
	chicken	coconut	pepper	wrench	bookcase	apron

norms and corroborated by our own norms when a separate group of subjects rated pairs consisting of a high-level word like *fruit* and a picture of an appropriate low-level concept like a pictured apple. Both sets of norms yielded virtually the identical partition of low-level terms into typical and atypical (the only major exception being that, in our norms, *wrench* replaced *drill* as a typical tool). All told, there were 42 different words, 36 low-level and 6 high-level, that could serve as questions. Each of them required a True response half the time and a False response the other half of the time.

Now consider the pictures. For each low-level term, we used two pictorical instantiations of it. Thus there were pictures of two different apples, two different robins, and so on. The pictures were naturalistic ones (we took them ourselves), and an effort was made to insure that pictures of atypical terms were as good instantiations of their concepts as pictures of typical terms were of their concepts. Let us explicate by means of an example. It was essential that a picture of a coconut (an atypical fruit) be as good an example of coconuts as a picture of an apple (a typical fruit) was a good example of apples. If this equivalence did not hold, then any typicality effect we obtained could be attributed to a confounding of typicality with goodness of pictures. To insure the equivalence in question, we had an independent group of subjects rate each picture for how good an example it was of its appropriate low-level category. Although these ratings showed some variations among our pictures, there was no overall difference between typical and atypical items.[2]

In all, there was a total of 72 different pictures, 2 for each of the 36 low-level categories. Each occurred twice on True trials, once with a high-level question and once with a low-level question, and twice on False trials, once with a high- and once with a low-level question. Thus for both True and False trials, typicality and question level were factorially combined. The other variable of major interest concerned False trials, and it was the semantic relatedness between the pictured category and the category of the question. A False trial was considered to be related if the picture and the question were either both drawn from biological categories (birds, fruits, and vegetables) or both drawn from nonbiological categories (tools, furniture, and clothing); otherwise the False trial was classified as unrelated.

With so many variables, it is helpful to have a schematic description of the overall design. Table 9.2 offers such a description. The possible trial types are

---

[2] Another reason for collecting these ratings was to allow us to look for typicality effects at the level of particular pictures. For example, if one picture of an apple was considered a better example of apples than another picture, then the former could be said to be more typical of apples, and we would expect faster responses to it. We did not find such an effect on the reaction items, although we did on the error rates. We strongly suspect that such a typicality effect would have appeared in the reaction times had we had more variability in the items. This kind of typicality effect is particularly interesting, because both typical and atypical items can have the same name.

TABLE 9.2

Design of Experiment 1: The Entries are Illustrative Questions (with the Number of Possible Observations per Trial Type Being Given in Parentheses)

Pictures	Trues		Falses			
	Low-Level	High-Level	Low-Level Same Category (Related)	Low-Level Different Category (Related/Unrelated)	High-Level (Related)	High-Level (Unrelated)
Robin_a	robin (1152)	bird (1152)	bluejay (576)			tool (576)
Robin_b	robin (1152)	bird (1152)		orange (288)	vegetable (576)	
Flamingo_a	flamingo (1152)	bird (1152)	chicken (576)		fruit (576)	furniture (576)
Flamingo_b	flamingo (1152)	bird (1152)		hat (288)		

146

listed along the top row of the table. The left-most column designates four sample bird pictures that were used, with the first pair representing typical instances and the second pair representing atypical instances. The entries in the table are questions that could occur on these trials.

The variations for the trials requiring a True response are very simple. Half the questions here are low-level terms (*robin* and *flamingo*), and the rest are high-level terms (*bird*). Things get more complicated when we look at the False trials. In addition to the variation in the typicality of the picture, these trials could involve either a low-level question (*bluejay, orange, chicken,* or *hat*) or a high-level question (*vegetable, tool, fruit,* and *furniture*). There are also two other factors that vary among these trial types. First, when the question was a low-level one, the pictured concept and the word concept could both belong to the same category, as when the picture is of a robin and the question is *bluejay* (low-level, same category), or the two concepts could be members of different categories, as when the picture is of a robin and the question is *orange* (low-level, different category). Second, the picture concept and question concept could be semantically related or unrelated. These two factors are partially confounded for low-level questions, because same-category trials cannot be semantically unrelated, whereas different-category trials can be either related or unrelated. The latter fact is shown in Table 9.2 by dividing the low-level, different-category trials into related and unrelated trials. In contrast to these complications at the low level, the high-level trials manifest a simple variation. Here the picture concept and question concept must be drawn from different categories, and the only variation is whether the two concepts are related or unrelated. Perhaps the simplest way to interpret all this is to treat the low-level, same-category trials as related trials; then, aside from the variation in typicality of the picture, there are basically four types of False trials corresponding to whether the question is low- or high-level and whether the two concepts are related or not. This is the way we interpret things when we present our results.

There are only a few other experimental details that we need to mention. We tested 32 subjects for 288 trials each (the number of possible observations per type of trial is given in parentheses in Table 9.2). The 288 trials were divided into 4 blocks of 72 each, and every block contained all of the types of trials of interest. The various conditions were randomized within a block, and although every subject experienced the same four blocks, the order of blocks was counterbalanced over subjects. Lastly, the experimental trials were preceded by 16 practice trials in which the pictures and questions concerned flowers and buildings.

Summary.   Before turning to our results, it is helpful to point out how our experimental variations relate to the substantive issues motivating this study. With regard to the levels variable, the coding dependence hypothesis predicts that for both True and False decisions, high-level questions should be answered faster than low-level questions. In contrast, the basic-levels hypothesis predicts

TABLE 9.3
Mean True RTs (in msec) for Experiment 1 as a Function
of Levels and Typicality (Sample Items Are Given in
Parentheses, with the Question Listed First)

	High-Level Question	Low-Level Question
Typical	616	571
	(fruit–apple)	(apple–apple)
Atypical	689	596
	(fruit–lime)	(lime–lime)

that for True decisions, low-level questions should be responded to faster than high-level questions except for the case of birds, for which the levels effect should reverse (*birds* is the only high-level term that is at the basic level). It is unclear whether the notion of a basic level has any implications for False decisions, because this notion was developed only with regard to valid categorizations. Now let's turn to the semantic factors — typicality and relatedness. The hypothesis that the code used is at least partly semantic predicts that relatedness effects should occur at both levels, but a typicality effect should occur only at the high-level. (The reason for the latter restriction is that typicality is defined as a relation between a low-level and a high-level category, e.g., an apple is a typical fruit, and seems to have little meaning when both concepts are at the low level, as when comparing a pictured apple to the word *apple*.) In contrast, the hypothesis that the code is a nominal one offers no grounds for predicting any relatedness effects or any effect of typicality at the high level.

Results

Errors. The error rates for the various conditions ranged from 2 to 14% and always showed the same effects as the reaction times (RTs). In fact, many of the significant effects that we report for the RTs were mirrored by significant effects on error rates. For ease of exposition, we present only the RT data.

True RTs. The mean RTs for the various conditions are shown in Table 9.3. There it can be seen that low-level questions produced faster RTs than high-level questions, thus supporting the basic-levels hypothesis over the coding-dependence notion.[3] We also found faster RTs to pictures of typical than atypical instances. The typicality effect was 73 msec for high-level questions but only 25 msec for low-level questions. This interaction between typicality and levels was most significant, as were the two main effects mentioned earlier. We had

---

[3] After completing this study, we discovered that Rosch et al. (1976) had performed a comparable study and had also obtained faster RTs to basic-level questions.

TABLE 9.4

Mean True RTs (in msec) for Experiment 1 as a Function of Levels and Categories

	High-Level Question	Low-Level Question	High–Low
Birds	598	631	−33
Fruits	675	531	144
Vegetables	724	571	153
Tools	627	642	−15
Furniture	654	568	86
Clothing	636	559	77

expected such an interaction because we thought typicality would only operate at the high level, but to our surprise the typicality effect was significant even at the low level.[4]

Let's take a further look at the levels effect. Table 9.4 shows this effect for each of the six generic categories we used. Following the basic levels hypothesis, we would expect faster RTs to the low-level question for all categories but birds, for which we would expect the opposite. As Table 9.4 indicates, five of our six predictions are correct. There are, however, two problems for the basic-levels hypothesis. First, there is a small reversal for the tools category, though the magnitude of this reversal is a nonsignificant 15 msec. Second, even for those five cases that show a basic-levels effect, there is a great deal of variability in its magnitude. The effect is large for fruits and vegetables, about 150 msec, moderate for furniture and clothing, about 80 msec, and small for birds, 30 msec. This variability was manifested by a significant interaction between levels and categories and is obviously one of the healthiest effects in the data.

False RTs. The mean RTs for the various conditions are shown in Table 9.5. The main four cells of the table give the data for trials in which the categories of the picture and the question were different; the lone cell at the extreme right gives the data for trials in which the same category furnished both the picture and question. For now we will ignore the latter cell.

The first thing to note is that the data are not broken down by typicality of the pictured concept. And for good reason. There was absolutely no hint of a typicality effect on False RT. With regard to significant findings, low-level questions again resulted in shorter RTs than high-level questions. Also, RTs were faster when the picture and question concepts were semantically unrelated. These two factors interacted, as the relatedness effect is 52 msec for high-level questions and a trivial 8 msec for low-level questions.

---

[4]The typicality effect at the low level was significant even when we removed the data for birds (the only category in which the low-level terms were not basic-level terms). Thus the effect in question can not be attributed to our inclusion of some nonbasic terms among low-level items.

TABLE 9.5

Mean False RTs (in msec) for Experiment 1 as a Function of Levels and Relatedness
(Sample Items Are Given in Parentheses, with the Question Listed First)

	High-Level Question	Low-Level Question	Low-Level Question (Same Category)
Related	657 (3.21)	577 (2.94)	665 (5.83)
	(vegetable–apple)	(corn–apple)	(lime–apple)
Unrelated	605 (1.55)	569 (1.50)	
	(tool–apple)	(hammer–apple)	

These results raise a couple of issues. First, it is unclear why there should be a relatedness effect at the high level and not at the low level. At first we thought this was due to the fact that we had done a relatively crude job of varying relatedness in this study; possibly the variation in relatedness at the low level was less than that at the high level. To check this, we had an independent group of 24 subjects rate each of our False pairs for semantic relatedness on a scale running from 0 (totally unrelated) to 7 (very related). The mean ratings for each of the types of trials are given in parentheses in Table 9.5. Contrary to our expectation, the variation in relatedness at the low level (1.50–2.94) was approximately the same as that at the high level (1.55–3.21).

Although we have thus far failed to turn up any evidence for a relatedness effect at a low level, remember that we have looked only at different-category Falses. The situation changes when we consider the data for low-level questions on same-category trials, which are presented in the cell at the extreme right of the table. Here, the picture and question were judged to be very related semantically, and this cell has the longest RT of any condition (665 msec.). In particular, it is much longer than the RT for the low-level unrelated trials (569 msec), thus demonstrating a relatedness effect for low-level questions. We should also point out that two very recent studies by other investigators (Gellatly & Gregg, 1975; Kosslyn, 1976) have also found a low-level relatedness effect with same-category pairs.

The second issue raised by the results in Table 9.5 is whether the relatedness effect at the high-level really reflects semantic relatedness or instead is due to perceptual relatedness. Although these notions can be hard to pull apart, we think we can argue that pure semantic relatedness is at least partly involved. The argument goes like this. Among the related trials that contained a question and a picture from different categories, only those that included a fruit and a vegetable seemed to seriously confound semantic and perceptual relatedness. In other related trials (e.g., a fruit and a bird, a tool and a piece of clothing), the relatedness seemed to be mainly semantic (e.g., both denote living entities, or both denote human artifacts). Thus, if our relatedness effect at the high-level really had a perceptual origin, it should disappear if we discard the fruit–vege-

TABLE 9.6

Mean False RTs (in msec) for Experiment 1 as a Function of Levels and Categories
(Different-Category Items Only)

Category of Pictures	High-Level Question	Low-Level Question	High–Low
Birds	620	584	36
Fruits	637	570	67
Vegetables	664	589	75
Tools	615	573	42
Furniture	585	554	31
Clothing	637	569	68

table pairings. We tried this and found that a significant relatedness effect was still present at the high level. Hence the effect in question appears to be at least partly semantic.

Thus far we have established that False RT was affected by both semantic relatedness and levels. We now want to examine further the levels effect, and it is again instructive to examine its magnitude across categories. The relevant data are given in Table 9.6. First some explanatory notes are in order. The categories given in the first column refer to the pictures rather than to the questions (analyzing by the categories of the questions does not change any of our results). Also, all of the data in the table are from trials where the question and picture were drawn from different categories. We could not possibly include same-category trials in this analysis, because such trials can be False at the low level but never at the high level.

Now for the results themselves. In contrast to the data for Trues, the False RTs in Table 9.6 were always longer for high-level terms, regardless of their basic-level status. Furthermore, there is comparatively little variability here, as the magnitude of the levels effect is of roughly the same size for all categories. This is in striking opposition to what we found for Trues, and an overall analysis of variance showed that there was a very significant interaction between levels, categories, and True-vs.-False responses.

Summary. With regard to the True RTs, we have two expected results — an overall basic-levels effect and a typicality effect for high-level questions. We also found three unexpected results —a low level typicality effect, a reversal of the basic-levels effect for tools, and a striking variability in the magnitude of the levels effect across categories. For False RTs, we found an overall basic levels effect and a relatedness effect at both levels (though only the high-level effect was clearly shown to be semantic). But we also found a reversal of the basic-levels effect for birds and comparatively little variability in the magnitude of the levels effect across categories. Any adequate theoretical account of this experiment must handle all of these results.

Possible Theoretical Accounts

Some preliminary considerations. We would like to account for our results with a relatively explicit model, something more than just a statement that there appears to be a semantic code involved in picture–word categorizations. In thinking about different models for our findings, the most critical concern was what the model assumed about the type of coding procedure used. In the Introduction, we argued for the feasibility of three types of procedures: translation between a semantically coded word and a coded picture, a semantic common code, and a nominal common code. The latter, taken alone, seems most unlikely in view of all the semantic effects we obtained, although it is possible to devise a model that postulates both nominal and semantic common codes. So there are still three possible coding procedures on which to base a model. We have in fact constructed three simple, sequential models for our results – one that posits a translation procedure, one that uses a semantic common code, and one that involves both nominal and semantic common codes. Because all three fail to handle all our results, and all fail in similar ways, we present only one of these serial models in detail – the model that posits both nominal and semantic common codes.

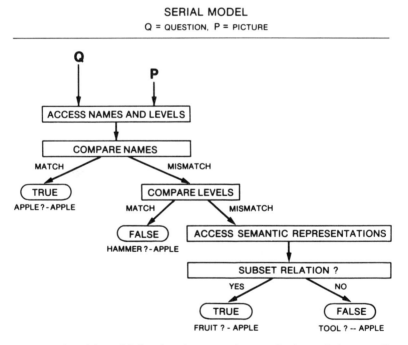

FIGURE 9.1 A serial model for the picture–word categorization task (see text for explanation).

A Serial model. The model is sketched in Figure 9.1. It postulates several stages, but the general idea is quite simple. The subject first tries to compare the nominal codes of the question and picture, and if this fails to yield a clear cut answer, he/she reports to a comparison of semantic codes.

Now let us go through the model step by step. First the subject accesses the names of the question and picture, as well as the levels of the two names (e.g., basic nonbasic). Presumably the name for the picture is always the basic-level name (as indicated by the data of Segui & Fraisse, 1968). Next the name of the question is compared to that of the picture. Should a match occur, the subject responds True. Because the picture's name is a basic-level term, one can only get a True response here when the name of the question is also at the basic level. This explains why subjects were generally faster in making True decisions to low-level questions than to high-level questions (the former were usually basic-level terms).

If the names of the question and picture mismatch, then the subject must determine why they mismatch. It could be because the question was a false description of the picture (e.g., the question was *hammer* and the picture was of an apple), or because the question was a true description at the nonbasic level (e.g., the question was *fruit* and the picture was of an apple). So what the subject must do is compare the levels of the question and picture names. If they match, then the question could not have been a true description of the picture, and the subject can now respond False. This will happen only when the question is a basic-level term (such terms tend to be basic level ones). If the levels of the question and picture mismatch, then the question must be a nonbasic-level term, and more processing is needed.

At this point, the subject accesses semantic representations from the name of the picture and the name of the question. Presumably our subject still has access to the levels of the picture and question and can now ask whether the low-level semantic representation is a subset of the high-level one. This is exactly what subjects do in semantic-memory studies – they use words to access semantic representations and then check for a subset relation. In such studies, researchers have consistently found typicality and relatedness effects. Thus for the box in Figure 9.1 labeled *Subset Relation,* we may fill in any known semantic-memory model that accounts for typicality and relatedness effects (e.g., Collins & Loftus, 1975; Smith et al., 1974). This gives us an explanation of typicality and relatedness effects for high-level questions, because the semantic mechanism operates only on high-level questions except for birds. (Note that this leaves us without any account of the typicality and relatedness effects that occurred when the question term was *bird.*) Of course the True and False responses that come off this semantic stage will take longer than those that came off the first or nominal stage.

The Serial model thus gives us a way of accounting for some of our most important findings. The levels effect arises because low-level questions, generally being basic-level terms, are processed in an early stage that considers only names, whereas high-level questions are usually for the high-level typicality effect at the low level, since Rosch (1975) has shown that the names of typical items can be compared faster than those of atypical items.[5]

The Serial model, however, also has many serious weaknesses. There are at least two critical problems in accounting for the True RTs. One was already mentioned—there is no way of dealing with typicality effects that occur when the question is *bird*. The second problem is that the model cannot account for the marked variation in the levels effect across categories. Other serious problems arise when we consider some of our results for False RTs. One difficulty here is that the model has no natural way of accounting for a relatedness effect at the low level. This problem arises because the model's representations for low-level terms (other than birds) are names, yet the effect occurring at this level is a perceptual or semantic one. Also with regard to False RTs, the model offers no apparent explanation of the reversal of a basic-levels effect for birds and no insights into why there was so little variation in the levels effect across categories. Finally, the Serial model leads to a prediction about the relative speeds of True and False decisions that is simply disconfirmed by the data. Trues should be faster than Falses at the low level, because True decisions do not require a comparison of levels (see Figure 9.1); in fact, Falses were slightly faster than Trues at the low level (573 vs. 583), respectively. This is a rather impressive list of failures, impressive enough to start thinking about other models.

We mentioned earlier that we had constructed two other sequential models and that these fail in the same way as the one we have just discussed. To appreciate this, we can briefly consider a sequential model that posits a semantic common code. This model has essentially the same structure as the one just presented. In fact, there are only two major changes: (a) Instead of accessing names plus levels initially, the subject now accesses semantic representations plus levels; and (b) Instead of comparing two names in the first comparison stage, the subject now compares two semantic representations to see if they are *identical*. This version of the serial model is no longer blatantly incompatible with a relatedness effect at the low level (because semantic representations of low-level terms are now being considered), but it does little better than its predecessor in handling most of the other problematic results for True and False RTs mentioned above. In particular, it cannot explain the variabiltiy of the levels effect

---

[5] Rosch (1975) pointed out that this effect was probably due to atypical names being longer than typical names in her study. This same confounding was also present in our study; in fact, we found a correlation of .42 between the difference in name lengths for typical and atypical items and the magnitude of the typicality effect at the low level. However, we have some reservations about this name-length explanation, because our second experiment, which required subjects to name the pictures, failed to show any typicality effect at the low level. If a variation in name length per se was really the cause of a typicality effect, we would have expected to find such an effect in a naming study.

for Trues and the absence of this variability for Falses, which we have come to believe is one of our most salient findings.

A critical question, then, is how to account for the differential variability in the levels effect. Our problem in answering this question is that we do not really understand the source of the variability. If we take seriously our notion that both nominal and semantic codes may be involved in picture—word categorizations, then the source for the variability could be in either type of code. The purpose of Experiment 2 was to isolate the operation of the naming code in order to determine whether it was giving rise to the variability in the levels effect.[6]

EXPERIMENT 2: NAMING ITEMS

Materials and Design

The same set of pictures was again presented, but now on each trial, the subject was required to name the picture as quickly as possible. There were four blocks of trials with all 72 pictures being presented in each block (again giving a total of 288 trials). On two of the blocks, the subject had to name the pictures at a specific or low level, and on the remaining blocks, the subjects used generic or high-level names. Prior to the trial—blocks requiring low-level names, subjects were given a list of the 36 relevant low-level names and were instructed to use them in naming the pictures for the next two blocks of trials. Similarly, prior to the blocks requiring high-level names, subjects were familiarized with the appropriate six high-level terms they were to use. The order of the low- vs. high-level blocks was counterbalanced over 20 subjects.

The critical variables, then, were the typicality of the pictured concept and the level of the required name. Of course the categories of the pictures also varied, and we were particularly interested in the variability of any levels effect over these categories.

Results

Error rates. Error frequency was again positively correlated with RTs. The error rates ranged from .3 to 5%, with a mean of 4%. All together, a total of 197 errors were committed, with the majority (121) occurring when a low-level name

[6]It is possible that the variability in the levels effect was due to a semantic code rather than a nominal code. Although this possibility must eventually be dealt with experimentally, it seems unlikely, because detailed studies of semantic memory suggest that the variability of semantic comparisons across categories is manifested equally in Trues and Falses (e.g., Smith et al., 1974).

TABLE 9.7
Mean Naming Times (in msec) for Experiment 2 as a
Function of Levels and Typicality

	High-Level Name	Low-Level Name
Typical	822	858
Atypical	866	849

was required. Among these low-level errors, the modal mistake was to give the name of another item in that category (e.g., calling a pictured apple an *orange*). For the 76 errors that occurred when a high-level name was required, the dominant mistake was to call fruits *vegetables,* and vice versa.

Naming times. The mean naming times are presented in Table 9.7 as a function of typicality and levels. There is a significant typicality effect here, but it interacts with levels. When a high-level name was required, pictures of typical instances were named faster than pictures of atypical ones. However, when low-level names were used, there was no effect at all of typicality.

The levels factor failed to produce a significant main effect here. But, for two reasons, it would be misleading to make much of this. First, there were 36 relevant responses in the low-level conditions and only 6 relevant ones in the high-level conditions; this difference in the number of possible responses would have benefited the high-level conditions (Oldfield, 1966), thereby obscuring any possible superiority of the low- over the high-level names. Second, the fact that there was no advantage of low- over high-level names does not mean that there was no advantage of basic over nonbasic names, because *birds* is a high-level but also a basic-level name. To check this, the data in Table 9.7 were regrouped according to their basic-level status and collapsed over typicality. The average latency for basic-level names was 813 msec, and that for nonbasic names was 884 msec. This difference was significant. It replicates the basic-levels effect on naming times that is evident in the data of Segui and Fraisse (1968).

The results of prime interest deal with the magnitude of the levels effect over categories. These data are shown in Table 9.8. Clearly we again have variability in the magnitude of the levels effect over categories, and it looks very much like the variability we obtained earlier with True RTs. Just like the previous data, the present results show that high-level terms were faster than low-level terms only for birds and tools, and for the remaining categories, the magnitude of the low-level superiority is greater for fruits and vegetables than for furniture and clothing. This is a rather striking parallel between the two sets of data, and it suggests that the variability previously obtained with True RTs is in fact due to an implicit naming stage.

There is one other point about the contrast between True RTs and naming times that is worth mentioning. The decrease in the overall levels effect as we

TABLE 9.8
Mean Naming Times (in msec) for Experiment 2 as a Function of Levels and Categories

Category of Picture	High-Level Question	Low-Level Question	High–Low
Birds	719	958	−239
Fruits	881	750	131
Vegetables	930	832	98
Tools	802	924	−122
Furniture	870	856	14
Clothing	863	799	64

moved from True RTs to naming times was mainly due to changes in responses to the bird and tool categories. For these categories, True RTs were only 24 msec faster to high-level terms, whereas naming times were 180 msec faster to high-level terms. This is considerably greater than the corresponding difference for the other four categories and is highly significant even given a relatively insensitive between-subjects comparison. The differential levels effect for birds and tools can be seen by comparing Tables 9.4 and 9.8 and should be accounted for by any theoretical statement that makes much of the similarity of the levels effect between True RTs and naming.

Discussion

Although our main concern was with the variability of the levels effect, some of our auxiliary results are of substantial interest in their own right. We have documented that pictures can be named faster at a basic than at a nonbasic level. If we are to take our results at face value, they further suggest that *tools* may function as a basic-level name. Evidence for this showed up in both our naming times and True RTs. However, treating *tools* as a basic-level term is in opposition to the results of Rosch et al. (1976), so for now we will leave this issue open.

Another auxiliary finding of Experiment 2 concerns typicality. There is no effect of typicality on the time needed to produce a low-level or specific name to a picture, although such an effect arises when one names a picture at a high or generic level. This result could not have been gleaned from the literature on naming times. That literature seems to be mainly preoccupied with frequency effects and has generally ignored semantic factors.[7]

[7]That there is a semantic effect on naming times appears to conflict with the logic used to motivate our first experiment. We had earlier assumed that if categorization times show a typicality effect, then a semantic process must be involved, but now we see that typicality effects occur even in naming. This conflict may be more apparent than real, because it seems likely that pictures are first named at the low or basic level (Segui & Fraisse, 1968) and that high- or nonbasic-level names are derived from the initial name by some auxiliary process. Because typicality effects occur only at the high or nonbasic level, such effects may be attributed to the auxiliary process rather than to the essential naming process.

For our purposes, the most important results of Experiment 2 were those dealing with the variability of the levels effect across categories. The major finding was that naming times showed a similar variability to that we obtained with True RTs but not with False RTs, at least when the False RTs were to picture—word pairs drawn from different categories. To further establish these correspondences between the two experiments, we computed correlations between naming and categorization times across picture—word pairs. For high-level terms, the correlation between naming times and True RTs was a significant .75, whereas that between naming times and False RTs (to different-category pairs) was an insignificant .20; for low-level terms, naming times correlated .73 with True RTs but only .01 with False RTs (to different-category pairs). Thus we see a pattern where naming times correlate with True RTs but not with False RTs. However, these correlations are for False RTs to different-category pairs. If we look at False RTs to pairs from the same category, such RTs show a significant .36 correlation with naming times.

So the latter type of False decision behaves, in some sense, like a True decision. What exactly is going on here? It appears that whenever a picture—word pair was highly related semantically (like all True pairs and those False pairs drawn from the same category), categorization correlated with naming, suggesting that such categorizations were partly based on a naming process. In contrast, whenever a picture—word pair was at a low or moderate degree of semantic relatedness (all of our different-category False pairs), categorization did not correlate with naming, suggesting that such categorizations were not based on a naming process. It looks as if there are two types of processes involved in categorization, and one of them, a naming process, produces decisions only for related pairs. Let us proceed to a revised model of picture—word categorization that takes this as a starting point.

A PARALLEL MODEL FOR PICTURE—WORD CATEGORIZATION

Overview of the Model

The Parallel model is portrayed in Figure 9.2. Like our previous theoretical attempt, the present model postulates both nominal and semantic comparisons, but now the comparisons are executed in parallel.

The general ideas behind the present model go something like this. The subject first accesses nominal and semantic representations for the question, with the former being fed into a name comparator and the latter into a semantic comparator. Then the picture is analyzed. Perceptual, nominal, or semantic codes may be formed for it. The nominal codes are fed into the name comparator, and this device can then use a common-code procedure to see if the names for the question and picture match. Either perceptual or semantic codes

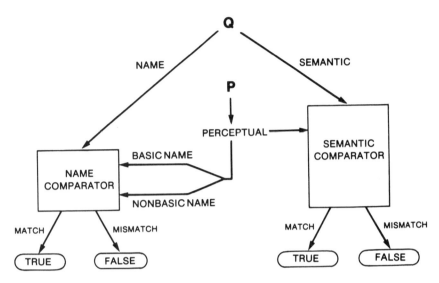

PARALLEL MODEL

(Q = QUESTION, P = PICTURE)

FIGURE 9.2 A parallel model for the picture–word categorization task (see text for explanation).

can be input to the semantic comparator, depending on whether we think this device operates via a semantic common code or by means of a translation between perceptual and semantic codes. If the former, then semantic codes for the picture must be formed and compared to the semantic representations of the question; if the latter, then the perceptual code for the picture is fed into the semantic comparator, which determines if the semantic components of the word can be instantiated by the perceptual components of the picture. These two alternatives correspond to two versions of our Parallel model. We have worked on both alternatives and found that the translation version offers a more speculative though less problematic account of our data. We present only this version in detail and then note some of the changes involved in the version that assumes a semantic common code.

The Translation Version

The subject must first access nominal and semantic codes for the question and access perceptual and nominal codes for the picture. We have made a number of assumptions about this access step. With regard to the question term, we assume that both the name and the semantic representation are fully available by the time the picture is presented, because the question is presented a second or two before the picture, and this should be long enough to access both representations. With regard to the picture, we assume that the subject first codes the picture perceptually, then uses this to access a basic-level name, and then employs that to derive a nonbasic name. Our reasoning here is as follows. Two names for the picture are needed, because the question can be at either the basic- or nonbasic-level; furthermore, the basic name must be derived earlier, because our second experiment showed that pictures can be named faster at a basic level; and finally, intuition suggests that often one comes up with a nonbasic name for a picture only by first going through the basic name (although nothing in the data forces this latter assumption upon us). The only other important point to note here is that the perceptual code presumably corresponds to an initial visual description of the input and thus contains all of the information needed to make a low-level categorization of the picture. For example, when shown a picture of a robin, one codes all of the features and not just those descriptive only of birds. The upshot of this is that pictures are coded perceptually at a low level, with their basic-level status being irrelevant.

Now consider how the system utilizes these representations. All of the representations of the question and picture are fed into name and semantic comparators as soon as these representations become available, and these comparators operate in parallel. Let us first examine the semantic comparator.[8] The device operates on the semantic representation of the question and the perceptual representation of the picture. It checks whether the abstract components of the semantic code can be instantiated by the concrete knowledge in the perceptual code. More precisely, it emits a True decision if some criterial number of abstract components can be instantiated, and a False decision if some criterial number of such components can be shown to be noninstantiable.

Let's again consider some examples to see how this works. Suppose the question was *robin* and the picture contained a robin. Then one possible component of the semantic representation would be "animateness," and to instantiate this in the perceptual code, one could look for protrusions or appendages of the object that could be used for the purpose of self-locomotion. This particular instantiation might be a rather problematic one in view of the abstractness of the semantic component involved. But as the semantic components become more concrete, the instantiation should proceed more easily. Thus, to take an extreme case with our robin example, the semantic component for red-breasted can easily be instantiated by that part of the perceptual code that gives the color of the breast. Hence one should find a criterial number of instantiations sooner as the components in the semantic representation become more concrete. Because the components in low-level questions must be more concrete than those in high-level questions, the former will be processed faster

---

[8]Many of the ideas behind the following discussion were suggested to us by D. Osherson.

by the semantic comparator. This gives us one source for the levels effects we have obtained.

Not surprisingly, the semantic comparator can also account for some of our semantic effects. For one thing, this device clearly produces relatedness effects for both low- and high-level questions. This follows from the assumption of component-by-component instantiations (i.e., comparisons); for any limited-capacity comparator, mismatches should be found earlier the more components that mismatch, and unrelated items surely contain more mismatching components than do related items. (It is not clear, however, why the low-level relatedness effect was confined to same-category pairs.) It is also possible that the semantic comparator is a source of typicality effects. We may simply assume that the perceptual representations of typical pictures are better instantiations of the question's abstract meaning components than are the perceptual representations of atypical pictures. To return to our earlier example of comparing the term *clothing* to pictured objects, one would have to instantiate the semantic component of wearableness by a perceptually given aperture; such an aperture should be far more salient in a picture of a typical object, like a pair of pants, than in a picture of an atypical one, like a scarf. Although we know of no empirical justification for this assumption about typicality and instantiation, it has some precedent (Fodor, 1975, chap. 2). In any event, this assumption clearly leads us to expect the semantic comparator to terminate sooner for typical rather than atypical items regardless of their level.

There is only one other aspect of our semantic device that needs to be noted. This comparator begins processing before the name comparator. This happens because the name comparator cannot operate until the perceptual code (the first code available from the picture) successfully accesses a name, whereas the semantic comparator operates directly with the perceptual code, with no intervening step. Consequently, items that are handled quickly by the semantic comparator rarely need to be completely processed by the name comparator. Such items should certainly include unrelated False pairs, for which a criterial number of mismatches will be found earlier. The importance of this becomes apparent when we turn to a detailed look at the name comparator.

The name comparator matches the name of the question with the two names derived from the picture and produces a True decision if the question name matches either picture name and a False decision otherwise. Because the name comparator rarely gets to finish the processing of unrelated Falses, its influence will primarily be seen on True decisions and False decisions to items drawn from the same category. This explains the correlation of naming times with True RTs and same-category False RTs and the absence of this correlation for False RTs to different-category pairs.

The other important aspects of the name comparator all concern the input times to this device. Basic-level names are input before nonbasic names, because the former are derived first, and consequently name matches are found faster when the question is at the basic level. This gives us a basic-levels effect at the naming stage. Moreover, we know from our naming study that the difference in input times between basic and nonbasic names varies across categories, and thus these differences must show up in True decisions based on names. This at last gives us a source for the variability in the levels effect for True decisions. We also know from our naming study that the nonbasic names of typical pictures are available sooner than the nonbasic names of atypical ones. This gives us another source for a typicality effect on high-level questions, because such questions tend to involve nonbasic terms. Finally, just as was the case in our discussion of the Serial model, we can follow Rosch (1975) and assume that the basic names of typical items are compared faster than the basic names of atypical items. This gives us another source for a typicality effect for low-level questions, because such questions tend to involve basic names.

Summary of the Translation Version

The foregoing gives some idea of how the Parallel model explains our findings, but these explanations are piecemeal because we treated the semantic and nominal stages in isolation. Let us try to put these piecemeal explanations together.

We begin with the levels effects. According to the model, the levels effects are due to (a) variations in the ease with which the semantic comparator can find clear-cut instantiations or the lack of them, and (b) variations in the times needed to get the different nominal codes into the name comparators. For True decisions, both kinds of variations are relevant. In the semantic stage, one can find a criterial number of matches faster for low-level questions, because the semantic components of such questions are easier to translate into the perceptual components of the picture. In the naming stage, basic-level names are input to the comparator before nonbasic names. Because basic-level names tend to be low-level names, we now have two sources for a facilitation of low-level over high-level questions. For different-category False trials, most decisions are based on the semantic comparator. Hence the levels effect for these False RTs is totally due to the ease with which one can determine failures of instantiation.

The preceding implies that the levels effect for Trues should be a mixture of two types — low vs. high effect (due to semantic stage) and basic vs. nonbasic (due to naming stage) — whereas the levels effect for Falses should reflect only the low vs. high distinction (only the semantic stage). This implication was borne out by the data. For Trues, low-level questions were answered faster than high-level questions for four of the six categories, and the reverse occurred for birds and tools, whose names are supposedly at the basic level. For Falses, low-level questions were faster than high-level questions for all categories.

Perhaps the most striking asymmetry predicted for Trues and different-category Falses pertains to the magnitude of the levels effect. The model predicts extensive variation for Trues because of the variation in naming times but predicts no comparable variation for different-category Falses because such decisions rarely involve names. This asymmetry, as we have repeatedly noted, was clearly present in the data. But there is more to be accounted for here than the correlation between the levels effect for True RTs and that for naming times. In our discussion of Experiment 2, we noted that the major change in the levels effect across our two experiments concerned birds and tools. For these two categories, True RTs were slightly faster to high-level than low-level terms, whereas the corresponding naming times were much faster to high-level terms. This effect is also interpretable in terms of the Parallel model. The reasoning is as follows. For birds and tools, the basic-level names seem to be the high-level terms. Consequently, such terms will be associated with fast responses to the extent that the task involves a naming process. Since the naming task involves only this process, whereas the categorization task includes a semantic process as well, it follows that there should be a greater facilitation of high-level terms in the naming task.

Let's move on to the semantic effects in the categorization task. The semantic stage eventuates in typicality effects at both levels, given our assumption that typical pictures can be more easily instantiated than atypical ones. The naming stage also gives rise to typicality effects: one for high-level questions due to the faster access of nonbasic names for typical items (as shown by Experiment 2), and one for low-level questions due to the ease of comparing typical names (Rosch, 1975). Lastly, the model accounts for the relatedness effects at both levels via the semantic stage. Unrelated items contain more mismatching components, and hence lead to faster terminations of the semantic comparator.

So the parallel model accounts for virtually all of our results, but it does so in a rather speculative manner. One should probably have only limited faith in it until we can demonstrate that it is consistent with the data quantitatively as well as qualitatively. But such a demonstration is beyond the scope of the present paper.

The Semantic Common-Code Version

We now want to consider briefly what happens to the model when the semantic comparator is assumed to operate via a semantic common code rather than by means of a translation procedure. All of our assumptions about accessing and comparing names remain intact. What has to be altered are our notions about the input and operation of the semantic comparator.

The changes are as follows. With regard to accessing representations, the subject uses the perceptual code of the picture to derive low-level and high-level semantic representations of the picture, with the former being derived first and fed into the semantic comparator first. This device compares the semantic representation of the question to those of the picture. It emits a True decision if either of the two representations being compared are identical or if one of these representations is a subset of the other; the latter kind of match occurs only when the question is high-level, because the first representation of the picture available is always low-level. The semantic comparator emits a False decision if it detects sufficient mismatches.

Given these assumptions, we would expect typicality effects whenever a subset relation holds between the two representations being compared, because we know from studies of semantic memory that determining a subset relation between two semantic representations produces such effects. As such subset relations are more likely to occur when the question is at a high level (remember the low-level semantic code of the picture is available first), this line of reasoning gives us a source for a typicality effect at the high level. With regard to relatedness effects, there is no doubt that our semantic comparator should produce such effects at both levels. This follows from the widespread assumption that semantic representations contain several components. The more unrelated the items, the more mismatching components and the earlier the comparator can terminate. Last, the semantic comparator produces a levels effect, because the low-level representation for the picture is always available first.

There is no need to detail here why we think this version of the Parallel model is more problematic than the translation approach we discussed earlier. Suffice it to say that the common-code version requires us to postulate two semantic representations for the picture and offers little justification for why the low-level semantic representation is available first or why the semantic comparator starts processing before the nominal one. In contrast, the translation version did not need to postulate any semantic representations for the picture, and it offered a rationale for why the semantic comparator starts first (the perceptual code must be the first one available). In the following discussion of our Parallel model, we consider only the translation version.

OPEN QUESTIONS AND FUTURE DIRECTIONS

The Parallel model does a reasonable job of accounting for our results, but it leaves a lot of questions unanswered. Some concern critical assumptions made by the model, while others are simply begged questions. We deal with the latter first.

Begged Questions

One of the best things about the Parallel model is that it accounts for the variation in the magnitude of the levels effect for True RTs. The model accomplishes this by attributing the variation at issue to the naming stage. This, however, raises the question of what determines the variability of the levels effect for naming times? That is, we have begged the question about the ultimate source of the variability.

Let us consider three types of answers to this question. The first assumes that the times needed to give basic and nonbasic names to a picture are partly determined by the length of the names. Thus the obtained variability across categories in the levels effect should be tied to a variation across categories in the comparative lengths of the basic and nonbasic names. To check this we determined the correlation between: (1) the difference in the word length of high- and low-level names of the same picture, and (b) the levels effect for that picture. This correlation was a significant .41, thus providing some evidence for the word-length explanation of the variation in the levels effect. However, we remain somewhat skeptical of word-length explanations of our results for a reason noted earlier (footnote 5, p. 154); to reiterate, although the names of atypical pictures were longer than those of typical pictures, our naming study showed no effect of typicality and hence no influence on name length.

The second answer assumes that the difference between a basic and nonbasic name for a picture might be a matter of degree, and the greater the degree, the larger the levels effect in naming (E. Markman, 1976). We can evaluate this possibility as follows. Let us assume that a name is basic-level to the extent that its referent has numerous agreed-upon attributes. For example, if *table* has X agreed-upon attributes and if *furniture* has Y such attributes, then $X - Y$ provides a measure of the "basic levelness" of X contrasted to Y. For five of our six categories, this can be determined from the norms of Rosch et al. (1976). We could thus correlate these differences with the magnitude of the levels effect across categories to see if variations in basic-levelness can account for the variability of the levels effect. When this was done, the correlation obtained was .63. Although substantial, it was not significant, due to the small number of degrees of freedom (3). All we can say at this point is that this kind of explanation still remains a possibility.

The third answer is that the variability of the levels effect is due to properties of the pictures themselves. That is, a picture can be named rapidly at a particular conceptual level to the extent that the critical features required of that concept are given by properties in the picture that are themselves salient. This seems very close to saying that a picture can be named rapidly to the extent that its perceptual code can be brought into close correspondence with its semantic code, and this of course is the principle that supposedly governs the speed of our semantic comparator. Under this view, then, there would not be that many differences between the nominal and semantic stages. However, two differences would still remain. First, only the nominal comparator would compare names qua names. Second, and perhaps more important, the semantic stage would involve a component-by-component comparison, whereas the nominal stage would operate on categories rather than their components. In any event, this possible account of the variability of the levels effect, like the preceding one, suggests that the effect is not due to names per se but rather to the categorical processes that produce these names.

Critical Assumptions

The following is a list of the basic assumptions of the Parallel model.

1. Nominal, as well as perceptual, codes are derived from the picture, and all are derived independently of the codes of the question.

2. The nonbasic name for the picture is derived from the basic name.

3. Nonbasic names are derived faster for pictures of typical items than for pictures of atypical items.

4. A name comparator is involved, and it tends to generate decisions for related items, like True items and False items drawn from the same category.

5. A semantic comparator is also involved, and it generates decisions about all items.

6. The semantic representation of a word is unlike the perceptual representation of a picture in that the former is more abstract, and typicality determines the speed with which picture and word representations can be translated into one another.

Of this list, we believe we have some experimental support for assumptions (2), (3), (4), and (5). The naming time data indirectly support (2), in that pictures were named faster at the basic level, and directly support (3). Finally, there is support for assumptions (4) and (5) in: (a) the correlation between naming times and True RTs, (b) the correlation between naming times and False RTs to same-category pairs, and (c) the relatedness effects and other detailed aspects of the data.

What about the remaining assumptions? We have already noted that assumption (6), which essentially defines the translation approach, lacks experimental support. This is a difficult assumption to test, and we do not claim to have turned up any kind of definitive evidence favoring translation over a common-code procedure. Suffice it to say that useful experiments on this issue might systematically vary the salient aspects of pictures in tasks like those we have used. For example, if one wants to assess the translation approach, then one could vary the perceptual salience of those concrete pictorial features that supposedly instantiate the abstract semantic components.

Finally, the part of assumption (1) stating that picture codes are derived independently of question codes is also open to question. In Experiment I, we disconfirmed a coding-dependence hypothesis by assuming that a picture is coded to a level dictated by the question preceding it. But clearly, other versions of coding dependence are possible. In particular, although we have argued against the feasibility of generating imaginal representations from high-level terms, there is no particular reason to insist that this does not occur for the more concrete low-level questions. If this were the case, then the kind of coding prepared in advance of picture presentation would clearly depend on the level of the question, and it would therefore constitute a form of coding dependence as outlined earlier. This notion helps us to account for at least two findings not handled comfortably by the Parallel model. First, the appearance of a typicality effect for low-level True questions in Experiment 1 and its subsequent disappearance when subjects are asked to provide low-level names in Experiment 2 are easily handled. Because a low-level image could be generated in advance of the picture in the first experiment but not in the second and because such generation is known to show effects of typicality (Rosch, 1975), we are indeed led to expect the observed dependence of the low-level typicality effect on experiment. Second, our complete failure to find semantic relatedness effects on low-level Falses would no longer be an embarrassment, because a great number of these decisions could not be based on an imaginal—perceptual comparison, and there is no reason to expect semantic effects for this sort of comparison.

Although this idea seems to have much to recommend it, we did not include it in the model, partially because it mainly helps us explain only tenuous and null results and partially out of a concern for excessive complexity. To some extent, the intricacies of the Parallel model are simply a consequence of the staggering number of significant effects in our data. But it should be kept in mind that the complexity of the model also bespeaks considerable flexibility, and this sort of flexibility is something one should reasonably expect of the processes underlying the continual task of perceiving and describing the world around us.

ACKNOWLEDGMENTS

This research was supported by U.S. Public Health Service Grant MH-19705. We thank Nancy Adams for her assistance in all aspects of the research and Ellen Markman for her helpful comments on the manuscript.

REFERENCES

Clark, H. H., & Chase, W. G. On the process of comparing sentences against pictures. *Cognitive Psychology*, 1972, *3*, 472–517.

Collins, A. M., & Loftus, E. F. A spreading activation theory of semantic processing. *Psychological Review*, 1975, *82*, 407–428.

Fodor, J. A. *The language of thought.* New York: Thomas Y. Crowell Co., 1975.

Gellatly, A. R. H., & Gregg, V. H. The effects of negative relatedness upon word—picture and word—word comparisons and subsequent recall. *British Journal of Psychology*, 1975, *66*, 311–323.

Gibson, J. J. *The senses considered as perceptual systems.* Boston: Houghton, 1966.

Kosslyn, S. M. Personal communication, June, 1976.

Kosslyn, S. M., & Pomerantz, J. R. Imagery, propositions, and the form of internal representations. *Cognitive Psychology*, 1977, *9*, 52–76.

Kucera, H., & Francis, W. N. *Computational analysis of present-day American English*. Providence: Brown University Press, 1967.

Markman, E. Personal communication, April, 1976.

Oldfield, R. C. Things, words and the brain. *Quarterly Journal of Experimental Psychology*, 1966, *18*, 340–353.

Pylyshyn, Z. W. What the mind's eye tells the mind's brain: A critique of mental imagery. *Psychological Bulletin*, 1973, *80*, 1–24.

Rosch, E. Cognitive representations of semantic categories. *Journal of Experimental Psychology: General*, 1975, *104*, 192–233.

Rosch, E., Mervis, C. B., Gray, W., Johnson, D., & Boyes–Braem, P. Basic objects in natural categories. *Cognitive Psychology*, 1976, *8*, 382–439.

Segui, J., & Fraisse, R. Le temps de reaction verbale. III. Responses specifiques et responses categorielles a des stimulus objets. *L'Annee Psychologique*, 1968, *68*, 69–82.

Seymour, P. H. K. Semantic representation of shape names. *Quarterly Journal of Experimental Psychology*, 1973, *25*, 265–277.

Smith, E. E., Shoben, E. J., & Rips, L. J. Structure and process in semantic memory: A featural model for semantic decisions. *Psychological Review*, 1974, *81*, 214–241.

Trabasso, T., Rollins, H., & Shaughnessy, E. Storage and verification stages in processing concepts. *Cognitive Psychology*, 1971, *2*, 239–289.

10
How To Do Some Things with IF

Samuel Fillenbaum

University of North Carolina, Chapel Hill

The most important general lesson to be learnt . . . is that simple deductive relationships are not the only kind we have to consider if we wish to understand the logical workings of language. We have to think in many more dimensions than that of entailment and contradiction, and use many tools of analysis besides those which belong to formal logic. . . . Instead of restricting our attention to the statement-making use of language we must consider also some of the many other uses it may have . . . and try to discover the answers to questions of such form as "What are the conditions under which we use such-and-such an expression or class of expressions?" [Strawson, 1952, pp. 231–232]

This paper considers some uses of sentence operators or function terms such as AND, OR, and IF, which "play a crucial role in language in that they permit the construction of complex propositions out of simpler propositions, specify the nature of the conceptual relation obtaining between these constituent propositions, and control or affect the sorts of inferences that may be drawn from the resulting complex propositions" (Fillenbaum, 1974c, p. 913). Attention will be focused principally on the conditional IF because of its particularly obvious and central role in the making of inferences and because of the interest of psychologists in seeking to provide some account for this term (see e.g., Wason & Johnson–Laird, 1972), but the general points to be made with regard to IF should also hold for the other connectives.

We are concerned with *uses* of IF in two rather different senses. First, we are interested in saying something about various sorts of employments of IF. Second, we are interested in exhibiting some uses to which this operator may be put in studying some general problems of psycholinguistics. As to the first matter, it is argued that IF has a family of rather different uses, and some of these will be exhibited. Then, after this descriptive work, one of these uses is considered more closely and an attempt is made to provide a conceptual analysis or account that sketches out the circumstances or conditions that control this use – the worked example deals with the use of IF in inducements (conditional threats or promises). As to the second matter, we present three cases to illustrate some uses to which an operator may be put in studying general problems of understanding and communication. First, we consider how assumptions or pre-existing knowledge about the "ways of the world" may guide or rather systematically distort the understanding of messages (Fillenbaum, 1974b). Second, in the context of a study of memory for counterfactual conditionals, we examine some ways in which information may be amplified so that different sorts of facts never explicitly provided may be remembered (Fillenbaum, 1974a). Third, we try to illustrate the potential value, not to say need, for a pragmatic analysis of linguistic messages that considers the social context in which a speech act occurs and the role it serves in that context, indicating how the illocutionary point of a statement may affect or control its logical form. The analysis of inducements serves as a test case here (Fillenbaum, 1976), thus this example seeks to exhibit the beginnings of a conceptual analysis for one very important use of IF and, in so doing, to demonstrate the value of a speech act account phrased in terms of the purposes of the speaker and the understanding by the addressee of those purposes in the relevant context.

Although linguists may take it for granted that the conditional IF can be variously employed, psychologists have often written as though the formula *If p,q* always has some single analysis regardless of the properties of the *p* and *q* connected in that formula. And, granting that the operator as used in everyday speech may be different in sense from the specification of its namesake in logic, much of the controversy about the interpretation of IF has been whether it could be better represented by material equivalence or a biconditional rather than by material implication, whether one needed to assume some sort of "defective" truth table such that the negation of the antecedent made the whole assertion irrelevant, etc. The burden of the present argument is that such an endeavor is in part misguided, and in at least two ways. First, it seems very unlikely that there is one and just one correct analysis that captures the various things that can be and are done by use of the conditional. Essentially we accept and seek to provide further support for one of the major theses to be found in Wason and Johnson—Laird (1972), who argue that the conditional "is not a creature of constant hue, but chameleon like, takes on the color of its surroundings: *its meaning is determined to some extent by the very propositions it connects* [p. 92]." Second, the endeavor seems primarily concerned with providing a truth-functional account of the connectives, i.e., an account in which the meaning of a connective is defined in terms of the truth value of the complex proposition in which it serves as a function of the truth values of the constituent propositions, but as Johnson—Laird points out (1975), there is a divergence in role "between logical calculi and the inferential machinery of everyday life [p. 16]." Although the former are devised "for deriving logical truths [p. 16]," practical inference seeks "to pass from one contingent statement to another [p. 16]." One must be concerned with the uses of connectives in the service of communication, which, given some principles of conversation, may license or even require inferences not legitimate if one considers only the truth-functional relations of logic and may block others that would be acceptable solely on truth-functional grounds. Consider an example to the latter point: Given the truth of *p* ("John drove to Washington"), the formula *p or q* ("John drove to Washington or flew to Philadelphia") is necessarily true, but someone who knows *p* to be true but asserts *p or q* rather than *p* would ordinarily be accused of misleading, because the assertion of a disjunction suggests that the speaker does not know which of the disjuncts holds (if the speaker were to embody the logical formula *p or q* with something like "John drove to Washington or the cheesecake is very tasty," he would be open to the charge of perversity, because even though the logical use of the connectives permits any *p* and *q* to be conjoined, the everyday use of connectives requires some common topic for the connected propositions). The point is not that a truth-functional account is simply wrong or irrelevant but rather that, in principle, it is at least insufficient and that there will be great problems, as yet hardly capable of being phrased, in articulating such an account with the required pragmatically oriented analyses.

It should be noted that we have been claiming that a connective such as IF has different uses. This is not the same as claiming that it must necessarily have different senses or different logical representations. In principle it might be possible for an operator to have a unitary representation, but different uses as a function of the application of relevant conversational principles. Thus, following Grice (1967), it might be argued that there are no differences in the logical representations of apparently different sentences involving AND and that the various relations between the conjoined propositions in such sentences might be suggested by the speaker and inferred by the addressee on the basis of general principles of conversation or communicative interaction. Or, the different uses or at least some of the different uses of an operator may indeed depend upon differences in underlying representation, as argued by Schmerling (1975), who on the basis of considerable linguistic evidence disputes Grice's views and questions whether conjunction in English is really a unitary phenomenon. We have essentially nothing to say on this important issue, because our main concern is with the prior matter of further documenting some important differences in the use of IF and in developing the outline of an analysis for just one of these uses. As analyses for a variety of different uses of an operator become available, one should be able to provide grounds for adjudicating between the hypotheses of "unitary" and "diverse" underlying logical representation(s).

SOME USES OF THE OPERATOR *IF*

Perhaps the most characteristic usage of the conditional by experimental psychologists is one in which the propositions involved are general and abstract and the connection between them a completely arbitrary one. This strategy is illustrated in extreme form in Taplin and Staudenmayer (1973), whose problems were actually phrased using letters of the alphabet to represent the p and q propositions, e.g., a problem might read "If there is a Z then there is an H." But this sort of procedure may be found even in Wason on hypothesis testing, in which a problem might be posed as "If a card has a D on one side, it has a 5 on the other side" (see Wason and Johnson–Laird, 1972). Obviously, in such a use of the conditional as a sort of contingent universal, the connection between the two propositions is completely arbitrary and ad hoc to the experimental situation. Merely making the task concrete and posing the rule as "If a letter is sealed then it has a 5^d stamp on it" led to enormous differences in performance. If switching from an abstract to a concrete or realistic embodiment of a rule in a contingent universal use of IF makes for large differences in performance, there is warrant for caution in generalizing any results to conditionals of quite different sorts involving temporal, temporal–causal, and (implicitly) purposive relations between their constituent propositions. Indeed, considering performance on a variety of reasoning tasks, Wason and Johnson–Laird (1972) assembled a substantial body of evidence indicating that "the meaning of component propositions may decisively influence the interpretation of everyday conditionals [p. 93]" and that content is crucial, suggesting "that any general theory of human reasoning must include an important semantic component [p. 245]." We add only that such a theory must also include an important pragmatic component that is sensitive to the sorts of things the speaker seeks to accomplish by saying what he does in the particular circumstances in which he says it (c.f. Staudenmayer, 1975). This paper is directed in part to the same issues as the work of Wason and Johnson–Laird. It constitutes an extension of their work (a) methodologically in the use of rather different procedures for obtaining data (see e.g., the use of a paraphrase task seeking to discover differences in the understanding of various sorts of conditional sentences), (b) substantively in the consideration of some uses of the conditional not treated by them (see in particular the purposive–causal use of inducements, in which a speaker seeks to control the behavior of an addressee by signaling his intentions with regard to actions of the latter – this constituting a case where explicitly there is a causal relation between the antecedent and consequent propositions but where implicitly the principal role of the conditional is purposive, i.e., its use is to get the addressee to do something or refrain from doing something), and (c) conceptually insofar as a pragmatic analysis is offered for conditional promises and conditional threats.

Before proceeding further, it might be well to mention an important and ill-understood precondition on the normal uses of IF and all sentence operators in everyday language, namely the constraint of common topic (see Lakoff, 1971, or Wason and Johnson–Laird, 1972, who speak about principles governing the "cohesion of discourse"). In this regard, of course, the operators of the vernacular differ from their truth-functional namesakes in propositional logic, which may connect any p with any q whatsoever in a complex formula. Can subjects be shown to be sensitive to the constraints of common topic in the use of IF sentences? Are topically disjoint or unrelated conditional sentences differentiated from those respecting the topic constraint? The answer is overwhelmingly, "Yes." In some work fully reported in Fillenbaum (1975a), conditional sentences whose constituent propositions were unrelated were judged extraordinary or strange on the average over 90% of the time, whereas conditional sentences respecting the topic constraint were judged extraordinary or strange on the average less than 5% of the time.[1] Such sensitivity to appropriateness conditions on the relation between the constituent propositions of a conditional (see also similar results for the OR operator in Fillenbaum, 1974c) is worth noting just because psychologists in their experimental work in this area have often proceeded as though any p and any q might be connected into a complex proposition by use of the appropriate operator of interest, as though the principal concern was to mimic aspects of truth-functional logic (for a review of much of the relevant research with particular emphasis on developmental issues, see Beilin, 1975). Insofar as there is some point to the foregoing observation, there are considerable problems in generalizing from the findings of such research to properties of the logical operators in their everyday employment.

In the present study, paraphrase and inference techniques are employed to study the understanding of various sorts of conditional sentences. It should be clear that the sentence types considered represent only some of the more important and common uses of the IF operator and that if differences are obtained for the limited set examined here, it seems *a fortiori* likely that further differences would emerge if a more extensive set were to be investigated. It is shown that conditional sentences of different sorts elicit rather different kinds of paraphrases. To the extent that the paraphrase of a sentence may be taken as indicative of the way in which it is understood, such results argue that different sorts of conditional sentences may be understood rather differently and might support or require rather different inferences. A word may be in order regarding the use of a paraphrase task to get at subjects' understanding of various sorts of conditionals, or rather at *differences* in their understanding of these. Presumably when someone paraphrases a sentence, he is attempting to (re-)encode his understanding of that sentence, i.e., to provide some alternative surface realization of its underlying semantic structure or meaning. Such a paraphrase, of itself, cannot tell us directly what his understanding of the original sentence is, although it may provide clues. However, if there are systematic *differences* in the paraphrases of sentences sharing some surface property, such as the conditional IF, then there are good grounds for supposing that there must be some systematic *differences* in the ways in which these sentences are understood, even if such findings do not go very far in revealing directly what these differences in

---

[1] Further results, including data for conditionals that respect the topic constraint but in which the connection between the constituent propositions is in some ways perverse or counter-to expectation, may also be found in Fillenbaum (1975a).

understanding may involve. Establishing the fact of difference is a necessary first step in inquiry, and this is precisely the job to which we have put the paraphrase task in seeking to show that conditionals may be differently understood as a function of some conceptual properties of the related or connected propositions.

To know what a proposition means requires, among other things, a knowledge of what is presupposed and implied by that proposition, what inferences may be drawn from it. To know what a connective means "is tantamount to knowing how to draw certain inferences on the basis of the formal patterns [p. 15]" in which it occurs, as Johnson–Laird (1975) puts it. If IF may be differently understood when occurring with different sorts of contents, it would seem reasonable to suppose that different kinds of inferences might be made in different cases. The matter of inferences is particularly of central concern in the case of propositions that are conditionals or conditional assertions, because such propositions are directly, overtly concerned with relations or contingencies among events or states and, in fact, provide an explicit machinery by which inferences may be drawn. Therefore, one needs to determine what inferences are actually, characteristically drawn from conditional assertions, whether or not they are legitimate by some criterion such as the stipulations of the propositional calculus, and whether, for a given conditional form, some inferences are more or less likely as a function of the conceptual properties of the propositions involved. We take as our principal problem the relation that is believed to obtain between a premise and its obverse, i.e., the relation between a statement of the general form *If p,q* and one of the form *If not p, not q* (where *p* or *q* might each itself be a negative statement thus permitting us, e.g., to examine the relation between *If not p,q* and *If p, not q*). To agree that a statement implies its obverse is to commit the fallacy of the denial of the antecedent. It has been argued by Geis and Zwicky (1971) that in a wide variety of circumstances, a sentence of the form *If p,q* invites the inference that its obverse, *If not p, not q,* will hold. The fallacy of the denied antecedent constitutes a particularly interesting case, because conditionals often serve as contingency statements or projections as to what holds or will happen if some condition is met, and a very natural question to ask is what holds or will happen if that condition is *not met.* We are basically concerned to determine (a) whether people are prone to succumb to the fallacy of the denied antecedent, i.e., to provide some data with regard to the contention of Geis and Zwicky, which has been disputed by Lilje (1972), who points out that Geis and Zwicky "don't have any figures [p. 541]," and (b) whether the likelihood of accepting the obverse of a given proposition as following from that proposition is affected by properties of the conceptual content of that proposition. To guard against the possibility that subjects may accept just anything as following from a proposition, we also include control items asking e.g., whether they are willing to accept *If p,q* as following from *If not p,q.* Matters of method detailing procedures and describing the sorts of items employed are given in the following.

Experiment 1: Paraphrasing

Subjects were presented with a booklet each page of which contained a single IF statement. They were asked to paraphrase or rephrase each sentence "as accurately as you can conserving its meaning as completely as possible." They were told to work on the assumption that they were trying to communicate each sentence to someone else so that the other person might get the sense of it as fully and exactly as possible and that their job was "not to improve the sentences or make them more sensible, but to paraphrase them, rewording each in a way that captures its meaning as accurately as possible." While these instructions were given to one group of subjects ($N = 27$), additional instructions were provided to another group ($N = 61$) forbidding them from using IF in their paraphrases and requiring that they "provide a sentence that maintains the meaning of the original sentence without using IF." This was done because a previous paraphrase study using IF sentences had yielded a very substantial frequency of paraphrases that often just permuted the order of clauses, changing a sentence of the form *If p,q* to one of the form *q, if p*. Although this may say something about the syntactic competence of the subjects, it is totally unrevealing as to the semantics of conditionals, and we sought to eliminate such responses in order to maximize those that might be more revealing of the semantic representation of IF in various sorts of sentences.

Let us now identify the principal kinds of IF sentences employed. There were:

1. Causal IF sentences involving (a) conditional promises, and (b) conditional threats, with half of each of these involving an affirmative proposition in the first clause and with half a negative proposition;

2. Temporal or temporal–causal conditionals (e.g., "If he goes to Washington he will get drunk"), again half phrased with an affirmative proposition in the first clause and half with a negative proposition in the first clause; and

3. Noncausal, nontemporal conditionals functioning as contingent universals (e.g., "If the truck is red it belongs to the Exxon Company"), with half the sentences again involving an affirmative first clause, half a negative first clause.

For the foregoing, there were always four sentences of each kind, i.e., four promises with an affirmative first clause, four with a negative first clause, etc. In addition, there were a number of other sorts of items. There were four law-like statements taken from Wason and Johnson–Laird (1972) each involving some temporal–causal relation between its constituent propositions (e.g., "If it is raining the girl will get wet"); these probably come closest to item 2 above. There were two items involving subsumption or class-membership ("If it is a trout it is a fish"), two items constituting definitions of a sort ("If she has a husband she is married"), and two items involving contrasted contradictories ("If it is not true it must be false"). There were also some items that were counterfactual conditionals and some items involving indirect discourse ("He asked if he could use the telephone"), plus a scattering of other items and fillers; the results for these sentences are not considered here.

The paraphrases were coded with regard to the kind of operator occurring in the paraphrase and the structural arrangement of the clauses around that operator. We identified (a) paraphrases in IF both explicit and tacit (e.g., "In case ..."); (b) paraphrases in AND; (c) paraphrases in OR; (d) paraphrases using causals (e.g., "Because ..."); (e) paraphrases involving instrumentals, usually participials (e.g., "By doing this ..."); (f) paraphrases involving temporals ("When ..."); and (g) paraphrases in which the sentence was collapsed into a single clause around the q proposition with the p proposition used as a sort of modifier (as when "If the shoes are leather they will wear well" becomes "Leather shoes wear well"); as well as using a few subsidiary codes largely relevant only to particular cases.

Experiment 2: Inferences

Subjects were presented with pairs of sentences and asked in each case "to decide whether or not you would accept the second sentence as a reasonable, natural sort of inference given the first sentence." It was stressed that they were not to regard this as a task in logic "but rather as a set of problems directed to your understanding of speech and discourse when you are figuring out what is implicit or implied in sentences that you might encounter. In each case, imagine that someone said the first sentence in the pair to you, and then consider whether or not you would accept the second sentence as implied by the first." It was stressed that they should consider the study as one concerned with their knowledge of English and their feel for the language, with an "understanding of the relation between what is said explicitly and what is left implicit in normal speech." To the extent that these instructions "took" successfully, we are tapping what subjects consider "characteristic" implications of statements, i.e., the inferences of everyday social intercourse that are involved in the understanding of speech in normal, everyday circumstances. And this is precisely what we are interested in. Whether some of the inferences accepted are regarded as absolutely mandatory or "forced" and others regarded as only invited and highly likely under normal circumstances cannot be discriminated by the present technique.

We code the principal proposition types employed as follows:

1. *If p,q;*
2. *If not p, not q;*
3. *If not p,q;* and
4. *If p, not q.*

In terms of this notation, we examined the relation between 1 and 2, and 3 and 4, in each case going in both directions, e.g., asking whether 4 followed from 3 as well as 3 from 4. For control items, we looked, among others, at sentence pairs going from 2 to 4 and from 3 to 1.[2]

There were (a) purposive—causal statements involving (i) promises and (ii) threats; (b) temporal—causal statements (e.g., "If John sees Mary he will give her the message"); (c) conditionals that involved contingent universals (e.g., "If the mushroom is red it is edible"); and also some statements involving a class-inclusion relation (e.g., "If it is a trout it is a fish"). Temporal—causal statements (b) were subdivided into two kinds as a function of whether or not the obverse of a statement was necessarily empirically true, regardless of its source sentence — this distinction can be illustrated and clarified by an example. Consider the following sentence pairs:

1a. "If he goes to Paris he will visit the Louvre."
1b. "If he does not go to Paris he won't visit the Louvre."
2a. "If he goes to Paris he will get drunk."
2b. "If he doesn't go to Paris he won't get drunk."

The sentence labeled (lb), whether or not it follows from (1a), is empirically true in its own right, given our knowledge of the world in regard to the geographical location of the Louvre. On the other hand, the truth or falsity of (2b) in its own right, is completely an open matter. We included items contrasting in this regard, call them necessary and possible second sentences, to see whether the intrinsic truth properties of a proposition might prove to be seductive in a task that actually called for a judgment of the implication relation between propositions. We not only obtained judgments as to whether or not the second sentence in a pair was regarded as following from the first, but we also determined the latencies of these judgments in order to see if there were any systematic differences in time taken to reach a decision as a function of conceptual properties of the propositions related in the conditional. Subjects were run individually in a reaction-time apparatus, items appeared in a window, and the subjects were asked to press promptly one or the other of two response keys, as appropriate, as soon as they had reached a decision. In this study, there were two groups of subjects ($N = 29$ in each group), with order in each item pair reversed for the two groups, i.e., for the two sentences X, Y of a pair, subjects in one group were asked if X followed from Y, and subjects in the other group were asked if Y followed from X; two item pairs represented each cell of the design.

Now consider the results from the paraphrase and inference tasks. With regard to the paraphrase data, we concentrate on the results obtained when IF paraphrases were forbidden, because these results are the most revealing, and we make comparisons with results in the other condition as appropriate. The principal results are shown in Table 10.1, which indicates for each sentence type each

[2] For a fuller description of the sentence types employed, see Fillenbaum (1975a).

TABLE 10.1

Percentages of Various Sorts of Paraphrases — Constrained Instructions (Entries for All Responses Occurring 5% or More of the Time)

Kind of Paraphrase	Class of Source Sentence											
	Promises		Threats		Temporal–Causals		Contingent Universals		Lawlike Statements	Class Membership	Definitions	Contrasted Contradict
	P+	P−	T+	T−	TC+	TC−	CU+	CU−				
Tacit IFs	06	05	05	06	18	14	06	07	09	06	08	08
Tacit IF = provided	09	08	–	–	14	10	–	–	05	–	08	–
Unless	–	09	06	19	–	18 (09)	06	–	–	–	–	05
Causals	–	–	–	–	–	08	13	10	10	10	28	28
Temporals	15	13	13	–	43 (15)	11	–	–	30	07	05	–
Instrumentals	15	07	–	05	10	17	–	–	–	–	07	–
ANDs	40 (23)[a]	52 (31)	35	54 (44)	–	–	–	–	–	–	–	–
ORs	–	–	24 (24)	–	–	11	07	–	–	–	–	32 (20)
Simple Sentences	–	–	–	–	07	–	58 (74)	62 (75)	34 (22)	62 (80)	32 (39)	08
In exchange FOR	06	06	–	–	–	–	–	–	–	–	–	–
Explicit IF (free instructions)	42	51	42	37	63	60	21	21	55	15	42	47

[a] ( ) indicate percentage of most popular response under free instructions.

class or kind of paraphrase found 5% of the time or more. Inspection of this table shows that there are considerable differences in the kinds of paraphrases elicited by the various sorts of IF sentences. The main results are reviewed in the following.

First, consider promises. It can be seen that paraphrases in AND are by far the most common, with 40% of the paraphrases for affirmatively phrased promises (P+) and 52% of the paraphrases for negatively phrased promises (P−) phrased in this fashion. Thus, e.g., "If you don't cry I'll get you an ice cream" is very likely to become "Don't cry and I'll get you an ice cream." P+ sentences elicit a fair number of temporals (15%), whereas P− sentences elicit less than 5% of such paraphrases. This tendency for positively phrased conditionals to elicit far more temporals than negatively phrased conditionals also holds for threats and temporal−causal conditionals; such paraphrases are also quite common (30%) for conditionals embodying law-like statements. P+ sentences also elicit more instrumentals (15%) than P− sentences (7%). Finally, not surprisingly, there is some use of paraphrases phrased in UNLESS for P− statements (9%) and hardly any such paraphrases for P+ statements.

Next, look at threats. Both T+ and T− statements elicit a considerable number of paraphrases in OR, with T− statements (54%) eliciting far more such paraphrases than T+ statements (24%); thus, e.g., "If you don't pay me immediately, I'll sue you" is particularly likely to be rephrased as "Pay me immediately or I'll sue you." Whereas T+ statements yield a lot of AND paraphrases (35%), T− statements yield rather few such paraphrases (5%). Again, temporals are used more for positively than for negatively phrased statements. Finally, UNLESS is used in 19% of the paraphrases of T− statements but in only 6% of the paraphrases of T+ statements. If one compares and contrasts the responses to promises and threats, a number of differences emerge. Perhaps the most striking of these is the use of OR paraphrases for threats, particularly in T− statements, and their virtual absence from the paraphrases of promises (in fact there was a grand total of three OR paraphrases for all promises combined, i.e., three out of a possible 488 responses). Further, although both P+ and T+ statements yield many AND paraphrases, such paraphrases that occur with great frequency (52%) for P− statements occur only rarely (5%) for T− statements. Also, although instrumentals are found with some frequency as the paraphrases for promises, they hardly ever occur as the paraphrases of threats. Finally, paraphrases in UNLESS are distinctly more frequent for T− (19%) than for P− sentences (9%). It seems fair to conclude that although both conditional promises and threats involve a causal or purposive−causal use of IF, they elicit different distributions of paraphrases.

If one considers temporal−causal statements, one finds that at least when positively phrased (TC+), these elicit a very large number of paraphrases phrased as temporals (43%); negatively phrased statements (TC−) elicit only a moderate frequency of temporals (11%) but quite a few UNLESS paraphrases (18%), with

TC+ statements hardly eliciting any such paraphrases. It is of some interest that temporal—causal conditionals also yield a noticeable number of paraphrases involving some tacit use of an IF-like operator, particularly PROVIDED (14% and 10%), something which also occurs in the paraphrases of promises but not in that of threats.[3] Law-like statements stating some causal connection between their constituent propositions are predominantly paraphrased either as temporals (30%) or as simple sentences (34%); thus, "If the bed is soft the man will sleep well" is likely to become "The man will sleep well on the soft bed." Conditionals that are really contingent universals are overwhelmingly paraphrased as simple propositions whether phrased positively (58%) or negatively (62%); thus, "If a castle has a moat it is haunted" is likely to become "A castle with a moat is haunted," which is a more direct expression of the universal involved in the conditional. A similar finding is obtained for conditionals that express a class membership relation, with 62% of the paraphrases yielding simple statements; thus, "If it is a trout it is a fish" is likely to become "A trout is a fish" or "All trout are fish." Definitions phrased as conditionals elicit a substantial number of causal paraphrases (28%) and simple-sentence paraphrases (32%); thus, "If she has a husband she is married" is likely to be paraphrased as "She has a husband because she is married" or "A married woman has a husband." Finally, contrasted contradictories yield mainly causal (28%) or OR (32%) paraphrases; thus, "If it is not true, it must be false" is likely to become "It is not true because it is false" or "It is either true or false."

Whether a conditional is phrased with the first proposition affirmative or negative does make some difference with regard to the paraphrase offered. This is true not only with regard to something rather obvious, like the greater use of UNLESS paraphrases for negatively phrased conditionals, but also in some other regards. Thus for promises, threats, and temporal—causal conditionals, a temporal paraphrase is more likely if the source sentence is positively phrased. The difference is particularly impressive: 43% vs. 11% for temporal—causal conditionals. And, as has already been noted, threats that are positively phrased elicit far more AND paraphrases than do threats that are negatively phrased, whereas, conversely, negatively phrased threats elicit far more OR paraphrases than positively phrased threats (the characteristic result in each case being a paraphrase whose first clause is positive).

We have already noted that threats and promises are differently paraphrased, with the most striking difference between them being the great use of OR paraphrases in the former case (particularly if negatively phrased) and its studious avoidance in the latter case, as though it is really impossible to phrase a

---

[3]This result is consistent with linguistic intuition, because, as a conditional, PROVIDED seems to include some pragmatic component such that the consequent proposition must be either neutral or favorable. There is something strange not to say perverse, e.g., in "Provided he buys that stock he will lose his shirt," whereas "Provided he buys that stock he will make a fortune" seems quite acceptable.

conditional promise as a disjunction (this matter is considered further later on when the logic of such promises and threats is considered). It seems clear, too, that conditionals involving promises and threats are differently paraphrased than other sorts of conditionals. Thus, for all intents and purposes, the other conditionals are never paraphrased with AND sentences, and except for contrasted contradictories (32%), OR paraphrases are also quite rare. Positively phrased temporal–causal conditionals and conditionals involving law-like statements (also positively phrased) elicit a substantial number of temporal paraphrases, much more so than do other instances. Law-like statements, definitional conditionals, conditionals that express contingent universals, and conditionals involving class membership relations, all elicit many paraphrases that are simple statements, particularly the latter two classes where such paraphrases include from 58% to 62% of the responses. Definitions and contrasted contradictories often yield paraphrases involving some causal phrasing (28% of the time for each case). In terms of all of the foregoing, it seems quite clear that IF sentences may be differently paraphrased as a function of conceptual properties of the conditional that they embody. Insofar as the meaning of a sentence is revealed by the sentences that are produced as its equivalents or paraphrases, there is some evidence that IF may have different meanings or uses in different contexts of the sort examined here.

All of the results presented above are based on responses under instructions that forbade use of IF in the paraphrases. Perhaps this has biased the results, forcing subjects to rephrase sentences abnormally. In one sense, the trivial sense that IF paraphrases hardly ever occur under these instructions, this is obviously true. The question is whether there are any more general across-the-board effects. An examination of the results under circumstances where nothing was said to forbid paraphrases in IF suggests that the use of the special instructions in the main group did not introduce any substantial artifacts. As the last line of Table 10.1 indicates, when nothing is said in the instructions regarding use or nonuse of IF, a very substantial percentage of the paraphrases do employ IF, often involving very little more than a permutation of clauses, changing *If p,q* to *q, if p* plus perhaps some synonym substitution for content words. Special instructions vetoing use of IF were employed to eliminate just such unrevealing paraphrases, which were found to be very frequent in an earlier study whose results, insofar as they overlap and are comparable, are in fact very similar to those obtained in the present study for the condition without any special instructions about use of IF paraphrases. Now, consider the bracketed numbers, one for each column of Table 10.1; these represent the most frequent paraphrases for each item class, other than explicit IF paraphrases, under the more open instructions, which permitted IF paraphrases. It can be seen that in 11 of the 12 cases this was the kind of paraphrase that was also the most popular one when IF was explicitly forbidden, in the one case (T+items) of a divergence the most popular paraphrase corresponded to the second most popular kind under the more open instructions. Thus, at least with regard to the patterning of the most common responses to the IF sentences of the various kinds, the results under open instructions and those under the constrained instructions are highly similar, providing some warrant for considering the latter results as indicative of the senses in which IF was understood in the various sorts of conditionals, and arguing against the possibility that these results are simply an artifact of the special instructions employed.

The overall results for the inference study giving the average percentage of inferences accepted for the conceptually different sentence types, in which the sentences in each pair stand in the relation of proposition to its obverse, are shown in Table 10.2 The first fact to be noted is the great frequency with which, overall, the obverse of a proposition is accepted as following from that proposition. The average value of such judgments ranges up to 90%, with a lowest value of 54%. These results do not just represent a response bias toward accepting any proposition related to a source proposition, because the largest value of accepted inferences for control items is only 18%.

We look next at similarities and differences in frequency of accepted inferences as a function of the conceptual nature of the sentences presented. There seems to be very little difference between promises and threats with regard to the frequency of accepted inferences from an item to its obverse. Perhaps the main thing to notice is how frequently such inferences are accepted, with values ranging from 81% to 90%. It can be seen that inferences tend to be accepted less frequently for contingent universals than for other sorts of items; in three of the four rows the value for contingent universals is the lowest of the five row values (in the remaining case, it is the second lowest). The difference between contingent universals and other items is particularly marked for the two rows involving the relation between 3 and 4, i.e., between *If not p,q* and *If p, not q,* going in either direction. Given two items per cell of the design, any cell for any individual subject could take a value of 2, 1, or 0 (i.e., both inferences accepted, one accepted, neither accepted). These values were subjected to analysis of

TABLE 10.2
Percentages of Accepted Inferences

Relation between Propositions	Promises	Threats	Temporal–Causals[a]		Contingent Universals
			i	ii	
$1 \rightarrow 2$[b]	85	83	70	79	67
$2 \rightarrow 1$	83	81	61	80	76
$3 \rightarrow 4$	83	86	80	85	54
$4 \rightarrow 3$	84	90	82	79	60

[a] i = second sentence possibly true; ii = second sentence factually true.
[b] Identification of proposition kind: (1) *If p,q;* (2) *If not p, not q;* (3) *If not p,q;* (4) *If p, not q.*

variance. The principal contrasts examined in the analysis were contingent universals versus the rest, promises versus threats, and temporal–causal conditionals involving necessarily true second items versus those involving possibly true second items. The analysis reveals that the obverse of a proposition is significantly less frequently accepted as an inference in the case of contingent universals than in the other cases (with $p < .01$ in both samples of the study); none of the other differences reach significance, although there are some marginal effects ($p < .05$) in one of the samples for which, in the case of temporal–causals, necessary and possible second sentences are contrasted. Analysis of the response latencies reveals that judgments for contingent universals take significantly longer ($p < .01$ in each sample); none of the other differences reach significance.

It might be noted further (to mention some results from class-inclusion sentences not reported in Table 10.2) that when one goes from 1 to 2, i.e., from *If p,q* to *If not p, not q,* the inference is accepted considerably more often even for contingent universals (67%) than for items involving a class-inclusion relation (30%); thus "If it is not a red truck it does not belong to the Exxon Company" is much more likely to be accepted as an inference from "If it is a red truck it belongs to the Exxon Company" than the inference "If it is not a cardinal it is not a bird" from the statement "If it is a cardinal it is a bird." It is also the case that a true statement involving a class-inclusion relation, e.g., "If it is a rose it is a flower" is much more likely to be accepted as an inference from its false obverse, "If it is not a rose it is not a flower" (67%), than a false statement involving a class-inclusion relation, "If it is not a trout it is not a fish" from its true obverse "If it is a trout it is a fish" (30%). Clearly, conceptual type and knowledge of the world does make a difference in the likelihood of accepting an inference.

We asked whether conditionals might be understood in different ways as a function of conceptual properties of their content and whether certain formally fallacious inferences might be drawn from conditionals, with the likelihood of doing so dependent on some conceptual properties of their content. In general, an affirmative answer can be given to these questions, the implication being that if one is interested in the everyday understanding and use of conditionals and everyday reasoning with them, then it is essential to pay close heed to the content of the elementary propositions that are related in the conditional assertions. This lesson, based on data gathered in the present study, which was principally concerned with the understanding of IF sentences, is very much the same as that argued by Wason and Johnson–Laird (1972) on the basis of a variety of reasoning experiments proper.

It seems quite clear, in terms of the paraphrase results, that in important ways the conditional is understood rather differently as a function of conceptual properties of its constituent propositions. Quite different patterns of paraphrase are obtained if the sentence is a promise rather than a threat, if it embodies a contingent universal rather than a temporal or temporal–causal connection, etc. To consider just one example, threats elicit quite a substantial proportion of paraphrases in OR. This is particularly true for threats in which the first clause is negative – over half the paraphrases of such threats are phrased as OR sentences. Except for threats and contrasted contradictories, paraphrases of conditionals in OR are otherwise quite uncommon, as may be seen by reference to Table 10.1. It is interesting in this context to recall (Fillenbaum, 1974c) that threats phrased as disjunctives ("Do that or I'll hit you") are overwhelmingly (77% of the time) paraphrased as negative conditionals. Thus there is a very intimate relation, going in both directions, between some conditionals and some disjunctives, but this relation seems not to hold generally. Here it is interesting and instructive to note some comments by Wason and Johnson–Laird (1972, pp. 61–62), who cite Galen as quoted in Mates (1961) as their authority, to the effect that conditionals with negated antecedents are really disjunctives and that "there is something special about negating the antecedent of a conditional: it yields a statement different from the rest of the species [p. 62]." Their principal example is similar to what we have been calling a *contrasted contradictory*. We stress that conditionals with negated antecedents may indeed function as disguised disjunctions but only if they are threats or contrasted contradictories, not if they are promises or involve contingent universals, etc. Simply stated, this relation to disjunctives holds only for conditionals embodying certain sorts of conceptual properties.

Examination of the data on invited inferences reveals that the obverse of a conditional is often accepted as following from it, and such examination also reveals some differences in the likelihood that these inferences will be accepted as a function of conceptual properties of the conditional involved. For example, the obverse is characteristically less likely to be accepted as an inference from a proposition involving a contingent universal than for any other kind of item. In general, for temporal–causal conditionals and particularly for purposive–causal conditionals embodied in promises and threats, what is actually phrased as a sufficient condition is very often taken as a necessary condition.

The principal lesson to be drawn from the brute facts presented so far is clear: If one is interested in the use of conditionals and the everyday reasoning that employs them, it is essential to pay heed to conceptual properties of the constituent propositions connected in these conditionals. But, to this point, we have only, at most, exhibited the fact that different sorts of conditionals are differently understood, without presenting any analysis of the conceptual properties involved that might provide the beginnings of a theoretical account. To begin this necessary work, we consider more closely one use of the conditional – its purposive–causal use in inducements (conditional promises and threats). We present data showing that subjects are sensitive to the relations among conditional threats and promises phrased with IF, AND, and OR, and we seek to exhibit something of the logic of inducements by an examination of the ways in which they may or may not be phrased. The analysis that is offered attempts to account for the phenomena in terms of pragmatic factors involving consideration of the conversational context in which inducements are employed and of their communicative role as attempts to control the behavior of the addressee, a role that depends on certain assumptions held in common between the speaker and addressee of the inducing communication. Because such an account may be considered an example of the way in which the study of the conditional may be used to develop a speech–act-oriented account of persuasive communication, this presentation is postponed to the next section.

USES TO WHICH OPERATORS MAY BE PUT

Obviously the study of the operators of English is of significance in its own right because of the ubiquity of their employment and their indispensability in permitting the construction of complex propositions whose understanding and use is in critical ways controlled by the particular operator involved. But there is yet another rather different reason to motivate interest, namely that examination of the operators may provide us with a tool or instrument for the study of some major substantive semantic and pragmatic problems of interest to cognitive psychology. We list three such problems and then turn to a consideration of work on each, which hinged critically on an investigation of the understanding of logical operators in everyday use.

The first problem is that of the ways in which knowledge of the world and knowledge of language articulate, how pre-existing knowledge of the ways of the world may systematically affect the interpretation of linguistic messages [if the significance of the relation between world knowledge and linguistic knowledge needs any justification, consult Norman, Rumelhart, & LNR (1975) or many of the papers in Bobrow and Collins (1975)]. The second problem is that of how people attain information never explicitly provided, of their understanding of and memory for information never directly encountered in a linguistic message but rather presupposed or inferable from what is said explicitly [for quite diverse examples of consideration of these matters, see e.g., Bransford, Barclay, & Franks (1972) on a constructive approach to sentence memory and Gordon and Lakoff (1971) on conversational postulates for indirect speech acts in the making of requests]. The third problem is that of "How to do things with words" (Austin, 1962), in the sense of a consideration of the relation between the illocutionary point or force of a statement and its logical form, and involves an examination of the role played by a speech act in the context in which it occurs. In an important way, all three cases involve going beyond what is *directly, literally given* in a sentence or linguistic message, and surely the inferential abilities that permit passage beyond literal understanding are particularly characteristic and significant aspects of human cognitive functioning.

Experiment 3: Pragmatic Normalization

The tendency to normalize connected discourse or stories in memory has been well known since at least the time of Bartlett (1932). It is possible that such normalization involves not so much or not only memorial processes but may largely be a consequence of the way in which strange material is initially interpreted and stored, such that extraordinary descriptions are transmuted into more mundane and commonplace descriptions in a manner responsive to our knowledge of the ways things usually transpire, given a presumption of the sensibleness of the material actually encountered. Thus, in some work "On coping with ordered and unordered conjunctive sentences" (Fillenbaum, 1971) it was found that on a paraphrase task, verb order was often permuted for disordered conjunctive sentences, such as "John was caught and followed," changing meaning, normalizing them, and assimilating the order of events to conventional order. We now consider further work on this matter (see Fillenbaum, 1974b). The work to be described extends the earlier study in two respects: (a) in that (i) a new kind of ordered conjunctive sentence is examined in addition to the kind considered before, and (ii) a class of strange disjunctive sentences ("perverse" threats) is also studied; and more important (b) in that we also sought to determine whether the subject could detect meaning changes in his paraphrases by making him review each of his paraphrases at the end and having him say whether or not there was any difference in meaning between the original sentence and his paraphrase of it and, if he felt there was, to indicate what was involved. Thus this research capitalizes on some properties of the operators AND and OR (with the latter really serving the role of a conditional) in order to study the interpretation of pragmatically extraordinary messages, i.e., sentences that are not syntactically or semantically malformed but rather are strange or perverse given the subjects' knowledge of the ways in which things characteristically happen.

There were 40 sentences to be paraphrased. There were 5 filler items at the start and then in randomized order: (a) 10 ordered conjunctive sentences in normal order (e.g., "John got off the bus and went into the store"); (b) 10 ordered conjunctive sentences with normal order reversed, these sentences being extraordinary but semantically coherent (e.g., "John dressed and had a bath"); (c) 4 ordered conjunctive sentences with normal order reversed, these sentences violating temporal entailment relations between their main verbs (e.g., "John finished and wrote the article on the weekend"); (d) 5 disjunctive sentences involving commonplace threats (e.g., "Stop that noise or I'll call the police"); (e) 5 disjunctive sentences involving conditional threats that were "perverse" in that the consequent clause indicated that the speaker would *not* bring about some undesirable event commonly to be expected in the circumstances (e.g., "Don't print that or I won't sue you"); plus a single "perverse" warning, the sentence "Get a move on or you will catch the bus."

Each of the 51 subjects, who were college students meeting a class requirement for an introductory psychology course, was run individually being given a deck of 3 X 5 inch cards each containing one of the sentences to be paraphrased and a blank deck for writing down the paraphrases. The instructions, which were the same as the version two (strong) instructions of the earlier study (Fillenbaum, 1971), stressed that the task was to paraphrase or rephrase "the sentences as accurately as you can conserving meaning as completely as possible" and that the subject was not "to improve the sentences or make them more sensible, but to *paraphrase* them, rewording each in a way that captures its meaning as accurately as possible." After the subject had finished the paraphrase task at his own pace he was told that he would have to go through his paraphrases, that he would be asked "about the remaining differences IF ANY" between each sentence and its paraphrase, and that if he did "see some shred of difference" to say what seemed to be involved. For each item, the subject was then shown the original sentence and his paraphrase and asked "Is there any difference in meaning between the sentence and your rewording?" and if this question was answered "yes," the subject was asked "What sort of difference?" After running through all the items in this fashion, if the subject had actually changed the meaning of the sentences in his paraphrases and noticed this at all during the review of the items (which was the case for most subjects), he was confronted with this fact, reminded of the instructions to preserve meaning, and asked "How come?"

The analysis of paraphrases was relatively straightforward. For each conjunctive sentence, one could determine whether or not the order of verb phrases had been maintained. Change in the order of verb phrases for the disordered conjunctive sentences almost always resulted in normalizing the sentences. In addition there were occasional paraphrases that did not change the unusual order of verbs but that elaborated or emended the sentences in such fashion as to turn them into sensible, normal sentences. The disjunctive sentences, threats, were paraphrased in various ways perhaps most commonly as conditionals. One could generally unambiguously determine whether or not these paraphrases normalized meaning. Thus, for example, given "Clean up the mess or I won't report you," both (a) "If you don't clean up the mess I'll report you" and (b) "If you clean up the mess I won't report you" may be regarded as changing and normalizing the original sentence, whereas both (c) "If you clean up the mess I'll report you" and (d) "If you don't clean up the mess I won't report you" may be regarded as conserving some of the strange properties of the original sentence.

The judgments subjects made on reviewing their paraphrases, as to whether or not these differed in meaning from the original sentences, could be coded simply as "different" or "same." The observations subjects made when they did judge a paraphrase to be different from its source sentence, and the various things said by way of explanation or self-justification at the end, were found to be codeable in a limited number of categories.

For normally ordered conjunctive sentences, meaning was preserved in 99% of the paraphrases (with 90% judged same in meaning and 9% different in meaning) and was perverted in 1% of the paraphrases (with all of these judged different in meaning). For disordered conjunctive sentences violating a contingent relation, meaning was preserved in 36% of the paraphrases (with 31% judged same in meaning and 5% different in meaning) and normalized in 64% of the paraphrases (with 22% judged same in meaning and 42% different in meaning). For disordered conjunctive sentences violating an entailment relation, meaning was preserved in 30% of the paraphrases (wirh 28% judged same in meaning and 2% different in meaning) and normalized in 70% of the paraphrases (with 43% judged same in meaning and 27% different in meaning). For normal conditional threats, meaning was preserved in 99% of the paraphrases (with 95% judged same in meaning and 4% different in meaning) and perverted in 1% of the paraphrases (with all of these judged different in meaning). For "perverse" conditional threats, meaning was preserved in 46% of the paraphrases (with 40% judged same in meaning and 6% judged different in meaning) and normalized in 54% of the paraphrases (with 34% judged same in meaning and 20% different in meaning).[4]

It is clear that ordered conjunctive sentences in normal order and normal conditional threats are hardly ever perversely paraphrased and that in each case paraphrases that preserve meaning are overwhelmingly regarded as doing just that. When subjects claim that paraphrases change meaning for these sorts of sentences, the most common ground given is that change in a particular single word led to a change in sentence meaning. Results for the two sorts of disordered conjunctive sentences and for the "perverse" conditional threats are quite different. For the disordered conjunctive sentences, 64% (contingent relation violated) and 70% (entailment relation violated) of the paraphrases involve normalization, whereas for the "perverse" conditional threats, 54% of the paraphrases involve normalization (the results for the single "perverse" warning are roughly similar to those for "perverse" threats and are not mentioned further). The differences in normalization for the three kinds of strange sentences do not reach significance if proportions of normalization of each sentence kind are contrasted for each subject by means of sign tests.

Turning next to judgments of whether or not paraphrases changed the meaning of the various kinds of strange sentences, we find that for disordered conjunctive sentences in which a contingent relation between verbs has been violated, normalizing paraphrases are detected almost twice as often as not (the figures are 42% and 22%), whereas for disordered conjunctive sentences in which an entailment relation between verbs has been violated, normalizing paraphrases are

[4] These results, insofar as comparable, are very similar to those obtained earlier (Fillenbaum, 1971), in which meaning was preserved in 96% of the paraphrases of normally ordered conjunctive sentences but for only 39% of the paraphrases of disordered conjunctive sentences violating a contingent relation.

detected less often than they are overlooked (the figures are 27% and 43%). The difference in detection rates is significant ($p < .01$) if proportions of detection of normalizing changes for the two kinds of sentences are contrasted for each subject by means of a sign test, indicating that subjects are responsive to differences in the semantic properties of these two kinds of disordered sentences even though the actual percentages of normalizing paraphrases are quite similar (64% and 70%). For "perverse" threats, we find that paraphrases that normalize the source sentences are detected less often than they are overlooked (the figures are 20% and 34%), that the detection rate for these normalizing changes is significantly less than that for normalizing changes for disordered conjunctive sentences violating a contingent relation ($p < .05$), and no different from that for normalizing changes for disordered conjunctive sentences violating an entailment relation.

Consider next what subjects say is involved when they do detect differences between strange source sentences and their paraphrases of them. For disordered conjunctive sentences of the two kinds studied, we find that the great majority of comments refer to order change, change in temporal sequence, and change in causal sequence, with 85% of the comments for sentences in which a contingent relation is violated and 65% of the comments for sentences in which an entailment relation is violated falling into these three categories. These comments are quite realistic, because just these sorts of changes have occurred in the meaning-normalizing paraphrases. If we consider the comments made when paraphrases of "perverse" threats are judged to be different from the source sentences, we again find some use of the above three categories, but now the most common observation is that the paraphrase is a sentence opposite in meaning to its source. Again, such comments are quite realistic, because normalization of "perverse" threats characteristically involves just that (see, e.g., the difference between the source sentence "Clean up the mess or I won't report you" and a paraphrase such as "If you clean up the mess I won't report you").

The results just presented raise two questions:

1. If subjects can detect differences between their paraphrases and the source sentences with regard to such significant matters as changes in temporal and causal order and changes that result in opposite meaning, then why did they provide such misleading paraphrases, given strong instructions to preserve and conserve meaning and warnings against attempting to improve upon or make the sentences more sensible?

2. If subjects cannot detect such substantial differences between the source sentences and their paraphrases, then what might be responsible for such obtuseness or blindness? What is empirically true, and presupposed in both of the above questions, is the fact that extraordinary sentences are often pragmatically normalized in the paraphrases, and one needs to ask

3. Why should this be so?

It seems plausible that the same general answer holds for all three questions. Even in the peculiar circumstances of the psychological laboratory, subjects seem to be acting on the basic assumption that *what is described in discourse will be sensible,* that what is described will conform to the customary order of events and will satisfy normal qualitative and causal relations between events or actions. If a sentence is encountered that appears to violate this assumption, one may consider it a clumsy, inadequate phrasing or description and turn it into a more appropriate version in one's paraphrase. Thus what is taken as awry or extraordinary is not the world but the linguistic account of it. As to why subjects should have provided normalizing paraphrases when they *could* detect significant differences between these and the source sentences, it may be that as far as subjects are concerned, a difference detected is not so much one between descriptions of two different sorts of events as one between two different descriptions of the same event, with the paraphrase expressing properly what is *intended and badly expressed* by the original sentence. Finally, why might subjects have failed to notice differences between the source sentences and their normalizing paraphrases? This may just constitute further testimony to the strength of the basic assumption, such that the original "malphrased" sentences and their own "improved" versions are really regarded as amounting to the same description of sensibly ordered and organized events.

The foregoing suggestions, although speculative, find support in the comments subjects made at the end of the testing, by way of explanation and justification for their paraphrases. Of the 51 subjects, 10 or 11 hardly ever changed meaning in their paraphrases, so we need to consider only the responses of the other 40 subjects. Comments that claimed (a) that the paraphrases made things clear and more sensible, (b) that the paraphrases put things into natural order, (c) that the original sentences violated expectancies, (d) that the original sentences were illogical, and (e) that they knew what the original sentences were trying to say so they said it, account for the responses of 25 of these subjects. All of them appear to be claiming, in one way or another, that their paraphrases somehow put more adequately what was badly phrased in the original sentences. In addition, there were 7 subjects who said that they misread or read incorrectly the original sentences, which suggests, if their comments are taken at face value, that they may not even have noticed the strange properties of the original sentences and that, in the very act of reading and coping with them, they corrected or normalized these sentences. Thus, for 32 of the 40 subjects, there is some evidence for the operation of the assumption that what is described in discourse must be sensibly organized. One further observation is worth reporting, almost every one of the 40 subjects who was trying to explain or justify his (normalizing) paraphrases seemed in part inarticulate and was considerably flustered. It seemed as though it was somehow very important for subjects to adjust things to conventional order and sequence and to exhibit the normal relations among events in order to say what the speaker of the source sentence must have intended or meant.

People may make the basic assumption that sentences are sensible just because they believe that the events, of which such sentences purport to be accounts, occur or are organized in characteristic ways and that it is much more likely that the world that is being described is the commonplace one, and that the description is burdened with the errors and malapropisms of the speaker, rather than that extraordinary events are being accurately and faithfully presented. It is as though people focus not on linguistic messages per se but on the information they embody or appear to convey, considering and assimilating this information in relation to their pre-existing knowledge of the ways of the world.

The term AND in one class of uses functions as an ordering or asymmetric operator, specifying a temporal or temporal—causal relation between the proposition conjoined. The term OR, when appearing in an inducement statement that serves as a conditional threat, must govern as alternative or second disjunct a proposition that involves something that the addressee does not want or wants to avoid (an account of the logic of inducements is offered in a later section of the present paper). One may violate such constraints on the normal relations of events, whether in regard to physical or social causality, and determine what happens. In terms of the results just presented, what often happens is that such pragmatically wild sentences are tamed and that people may not even recognize what they are doing when, in interpreting and making sense of such sentences, they assimilate them to the conventional relations among events. Thus this work illustrates how by a systematic misuse of some of the logical operators, one may study the interaction between prior knowledge and current linguistic inputs and demonstrate the enormous effects of the former on the latter.

Amplification of Information

Characteristically, people do not remember the particular surface syntactic form of the sentences they have encountered, rather they remember propositional content that includes not only information explicitly specified but also information that in various ways is inferable from that provided directly. Such inferred information may depend on the compounding of information from sets of semantically related sentences or, for a single sentence, may be based on the proper understanding of a lexical item such as a crucial preposition (see, e.g., Bransford, Barclay, & Franks, 1972). But more subtle types of inferences may be involved, even for the case of simple sentences, as regards the recall of what is either presupposed or conversationally suggested by a sentence as compared to recall of what is explicitly asserted in it. If, in processing information, one is responsive not only to what is directly and explicitly provided but also to what can be assumed if the directly provided information is to be coherent and employed in a normally communicative way, then a concern with the functions of presuppositional knowledge and conversational "implicatures" (see Grice, 1967; 1975) becomes inescapable. And here, particularly intriguing questions arise with regard to the possibility of information gain or amplification in memory as opposed to the more usual emphasis on abstraction and information loss.

The conceptual status and proper analysis of counterfactual conditionals have long vexed philosophers. Nevertheless counterfactual conditionals may provide us with valuable test material that is particularly useful for the study of memory for information implicit in sentences. A counterfactual conditional strictly presupposes the negation of its antecedent proposition, because one cannot coherently conceive of a counterfactual without assuming the falsehood of its first proposition. A counterfactual conditional in most conversational contexts also strongly suggests or "invites" as inference the negation of its consequent proposition but does not strictly require such an inference, because the inference is cancellable in a way that presuppositions and entailments are not (see Karttunen, 1971; and Ducrot, 1972). Thus, given "If he had caught the plane he would have arrived on time," it is presupposed that "He did not catch the plane," and in most contexts, it is at least strongly suggested that "He did not arrive on time." A counterfactual conditional may also be seen as related to a causal in which the negation of the antecedent is given as the reason for the negation of the consequent: in our example, "Because he did not catch the plane he did not arrive on time" or, more stylistically common, "He did not arrive on time because he did not catch the plane."

Given prior presentation of a counterfactual conditional, one may ask if the subject will later falsely recognize (a) the negation of the antecedent proposition, which is presupposed, or (b) the negation of the consequent proposition, which is strongly suggested if not entailed; and one may ask whether false recognition is more frequent for (a) or (b). Further, given a counterfactual conditional, one may ask if the subject will later falsely recognize its causal relative, which consists of the causal conjunction of (a) and (b), with negation of (a) given as the reason for negation of (b). This relation between counterfactual conditional and causal may be viewed as going in the other direction as well (i.e., from causal to counterfactual), because there would appear to be few, if any, occasions appropriate for the causal ("He did not arrive on time because he did not catch the plane") that would not also assume the counterfactual ("If he had caught the plane he would have arrived on time"). Naturally we are interested in comparing the frequency of recognition errors in the two directions. Two experiments in recognition memory are presented (see Fillenbaum, 1974b). The first of these experiments is concerned with memory for the simple offspring of counterfactual conditionals, and the second with memory for related complex sentences in which the original sentences are either counterfactuals or causals and for which the recognition sentences include their causal and counterfactual relatives.

The basic format of the two experiments was the same. The subjects were told that they would hear a series of sentences on tape and were requested to listen carefully, because they would later be "asked questions about the sentences."

After the original series was finished, they were told that they would hear another series of sentences and would then have to decide whether each sentence was *old* (one they had actually heard before) or *new* (one that had not appeared in the first series). The sentences were presented at a 5-second rate both in the initial series and in the later recognition series. The subjects were run in groups ranging in size from 4 or 5 to 20 or so. There were 110 subjects in Experiment 4 and 92 subjects in Experiment 5.

Experiment 4. Both the original and the test series consisted of a mixture of counterfactual conditionals and simple propositions. Whether in the original or in the test series, all counterfactuals were positive in both of their clauses, with the *if* clause always coming first, as in "If he had caught the plane he would have arrived on time," and all simple propositions were negatives, such as in "He did not catch the plane." Some physical or social nexus always obtained between the clauses of the counterfactuals, as in "If he had eaten the fish he would have become sick" or "If he had talked with the boss he would have got a raise." Matters were arranged so that there were (a) conditionals appearing both in the original and the test series (6 items), (b) simple propositions appearing both in the original and the test series (8 items), (c) conditionals appearing only in the test series (12 items), (d) simple propositions appearing only in the test series (8 items), (e) conditionals appearing in the original series whose negated antecedent appeared in the test series (8 items), (f) conditionals appearing in the original series whose negated consequent appeared in the test series (8 items), and (g) filler conditionals and simple propositions appearing both at the start and end of the original series in order to make the proportions of conditionals and simple propositions comparable in the original and test series. Each item appeared twice in the original series; after every item had occurred once, the items appeared again in a scrambled order.

Experiment 5. The original series consisted of a mixture of counterfactual conditionals, simple conditionals, and causals involving negation in both of their propositions. Simple conditionals were included as a control so that we could determine whether any systematic recognition effects obtained were simply topic effects, i.e., were due to the prior occurrence of the same or similar content. The same type of sentence content used in Experiment 4 appeared in this experiment. In the causals, the "because" clause always came second, as in "He didn't pass the test because he didn't study." The simple conditionals involved the same kinds of connections between their clauses as did the counterfactuals, e.g., "If he is treated immediately he will survive " or "If he watches the show he will be bored." Matters were arranged so that there were (a) counterfactual conditionals, simple conditionals, and causals appearing both in the original and test series (6 items of each kind), (b) counterfactual conditionals, simple conditionals, and causals appearing only in the test series (6 items of each kind), (c) counterfactual conditionals appearing in the original series whose related causals appeared in the test series (6 items), (d) causals appearing in the original series whose related counterfactual conditionals appeared in the test series (6 items), (e) simple conditionals appearing in the original series whose corresponding causals appeared in the test series (6 items), and (f) some filler items. Again, each item appeared twice in the original series; after every item had occurred once, the items appeared again in a scrambled order.

For each subject, one may determine the number or percentage of *old* responses for each item class and then make appropriate comparisons across item classes; in addition, one may determine the mean percentage of *old* responses taken over subjects for each item class. These figures constitute our basic data.

Consider first the results for Experiment 4. *Old* counterfactuals (88%) and simple propositions (53%) were recognized as *old* significantly more frequently than *new* counterfactuals (12%) and *new* simple propositions (14%); *old* counterfactuals (88%) were recognized as *old* significantly more often than were *old* simple propositions (53%); and there was no difference in recognition between *new* counterfactuals (12%) and *new* simple propositions (14%). Except for the finding that *old* counterfactuals are recognized more often than *old* simple propositions, these results are of no particular interest except to show that the situation is one in which subjects can distinguish between *old* and *new* items and thus one in which the results for offspring items are relevant. It is indeed the case that offspring sentences, whether negated antecedent (25%) or negated consequent (44%), were judged *old* significantly less frequently than *old* simple propositions (53%), but more interestingly, it is also the case that these offspring sentences were judged to be *old* sentences significantly more often than the control *new* simple propositions (14%). Finally, if we compare offspring sentences in which the consequent is negated with those in which the antecedent is negated, we find that the former (44%) are judged *old* significantly more often than the latter (25%).

In Experiment 5, *old* counterfactual conditionals (79%), *old* simple conditionals (84%), and *old* causals (73%) are recognized as *old* more often than *new* counterfactual conditionals (5%), *new* simple conditionals (4%), and *new* causals (8%), with each of these differences highly significant. Although the differences between *old* propositions are significant, with simple conditionals recognized significantly more often than counterfactual conditionals or causals, and counterfactual conditionals recognized more often than causals ($p < .05$, sign test), these differences are quite small compared to those between *old* and *new* propositions. The differences between various sorts of *new* propositions are slight and nonsignificant. Related sentences are judged *old* significantly less often than sentences that actually had appeared before, but more interestingly, related sentences are judged *old* significantly more often than their *new* controls. Further, we find that counterfactual conditionals that are related to previously presented causals are "recognized" significantly more often (47%) than causals related to previously presented counterfactuals (34%) and that the latter are "recognized" significantly more often than causals corresponding to previously presented simple conditionals (25%). As noted previously, *old* counterfactual conditionals are recognized more often than *old* causals (79% vs. 73%), so perhaps the difference between counterfactuals related to previously presented causals (47%) and causals related to previously presented counterfactuals (34%) represents only a bias toward recognition of counterfactuals. Thus one needs to correct recognition rates for related sentences by corresponding rates for *old* sentences in order to determine whether the difference between 47% and 34% is reliably greater than that between 79% and 73%. Comparing for each subject the difference in recognition rate between *old* counterfactuals and *old* causals with that between related counterfactuals and related causals, we find that the latter difference is greater for a significant majority of subjects ($p < .05$). Thus, even with this correction taken into account, counterfactual conditionals related to previously presented causals are recognized significantly more often than causals related to previously presented counterfactuals.

The basic trends of the results are quite clear in each experiment and are consistent over the two experiments. Although offspring or related sentences are recognized less frequently than *old* sentences, they are recognized more frequently than new control sentences. Listeners appear to operate on the information directly provided to them, amplifying and elaborating that information.

It might perhaps be argued that the positive findings of Experiment 4 merely represent some sort of a topic effect, with negated antecedent and consequent propositions falsely recognized, because the subject remembers having encountered some similar content in the original series (in which these contents were actually embedded in various counterfactual conditionals). This argument is not very convincing given the findings of Experiment 5, in which there was significantly more false recognition of causals related to prior counterfactual conditionals than of causals corresponding to prior simple conditionals. If all that we have is a topic effect, then there should have been no difference in false recognition of causals, whether the antecedent conditionals were simple or counterfactual. Nor would the topic hypothesis account in any obvious way for the fact that in Experiment 4, false recognition of negative consequents was significantly more frequent than that of negative antecedents. Why should this be the case if all that is involved is the recognition of propositions that had occurred earlier in some form? Finally, note that recognition involved the negation of the explicit prior contents, and we know that gist memory is generally good, so that on recall subjects can discriminate rather well between an expression and its negation. Nevertheless, a control against the topic hypothesis may be desirable, and one suggests itself readily. In the recognition series, in addition to sentences that negate the antecedent and consequent propositions of earlier counterfactual conditionals, which we might call "legitimate" offspring, one might also include sentences that assert the antecedent and consequent propositions. These might be called "illegitimate" offspring. On the basis of a topic hypothesis, no difference should be expected in false recognition of the legitimate and illegitimate offspring, or perhaps we might expect even greater recognition of the latter than the former because the illegitimate offspring do not involve negation of previously encountered materials). In terms of the position argued here, however, one would expect more false recognition of legitimate- than of illegitimate-offspring sentences.

With regard to Experiment 4, we can offer no plausible reason as to why old counterfactual conditionals were recognized substantially more often than old simple propositions (88% vs. 53%) except for noting that there were substantially fewer of the former (18) than of the latter (32) in the recognition series, and this may have resulted in less confusion for the former. A problem more directly related to the concern of the present research is posed by the finding that sentences that negate the consequent of a counterfactual conditional are significantly more frequently recognized than those that negate the antecedent of the counterfactual conditional (44% vs. 25%).[5] Recall that the negation of the antecedent is strictly presupposed by the counterfactual and that one cannot coherently conceive of a counterfactual without assuming that its antecedent proposition is negated, while it has been argued that the negation of the consequent is strongly suggested in most circumstances but does not appear to be required. Thus a sentence such as "If he had caught the plane, which he did, he would have arrived on time" seems inconsistent, although there is in principle nothing contradictory in saying "If he had caught the plane he would have arrived on time, which he did anyway because he took a fast train." Hence it would appear that, if anything, the negated antecedent is more strongly implied by the counterfactual conditional than is the negated consequent, and yet our results indicate substantially more false recognition of the latter than of the former. In order to make sense of this finding, consider the circumstances under which one might be most likely to employ a counterfactual conditional. For example, one might most commonly say "If he had caught the plane he would have arrived on time" as an explanation for the fact that he was late, a fact that may be simply expressed by negating the consequent proposition, i.e., saying "He did not arrive on time." If the fact that is being explained is somehow central or focal to the discourse, then it may be reasonable that a proposition that embodies this fact, i.e., the denied consequent, is more likely to

---

[5] Actually, recognition memory for offspring sentences was examined both for the case in which just one offspring of a particular counterfactual conditional was presented in the recognition series (with a negated antecedent provided on half of the occasions and a negated consequent on the other half) and for the case in which both the negated antecedent and the negated consequent offspring of a counterfactual were presented. Because it made essentially no difference whether one or both offspring were tested, only the pooled results are presented here.

be inferred and falsely remembered than one that only purports to give a reason for the fact, viz., the subordinate denied antecedent.

With regard to Experiment 5, it is again hard to know why there should be differences in recognition of the various kinds of *old* sentences, but here the differences are certainly not of any great magnitude, with figures of 79%, 84%, and 73% for counterfactual conditionals, simple conditionals, and causals, respectively. The finding that causals corresponding to simple conditionals are recognized more often than *new* causals suggests that in some measure, there may indeed obtain a sort of topic effect, such that a sentence involving propositional material encountered earlier may be falsely recognized. However, the finding that causals related to previously encountered counterfactual conditionals are significantly more frequently falsely recognized than causals corresponding to previously encountered simple conditionals indicates that such a topic effect cannot totally explain present results. Perhaps the most interesting result is the finding that both causals related to counterfactual conditionals and counterfactual conditionals related to causals are recognized significantly more often than their controls, with the latter effect the stronger. But why should the counterfactual relative of a causal be more frequently recognized than the causal relative of a counterfactual? Consider what is assumed or what can be assumed given, respectively, a causal and its related counterfactual conditional, e.g., the sentences (a) "He did not arrive on time because he did not catch the plane" and (b) "If he had caught the plane he would have arrived on time." One cannot very easily assert (a) without assuming or taking for granted the correctness or truth of (b), but it is not clear that the converse necessarily holds. As was pointed out earlier, (b) could be true, and yet there is no absolute requirement that the person in question must have been late, because (c) "If he had caught the plane he would have arrived on time, which he did anyway because he caught a fast train" is certainly a possible elaboration. The point is simply that a counterfactual conditional does not appear to entail the denial of the consequent proposition and thus, insofar as this is the case, does not require its related causal. It would be supportive of these suggestions if, given causals and their counterfactual relatives, subjects were more willing to accept the latter as inferences on the basis of the former than conversely.

Even though the interpretation of some of the details of the results must be quite tentative with regard to within-conditions differences, viz., (a) the difference between offspring sentences that negate the antecedent and those that negate the consequent, and (b) the difference between causals related to counterfactual conditionals and counterfactual conditionals related to causals, it seems clear that there are substantial and consistent between-conditions differences such that offspring sentences and related sentences are consistently recognized more often than their *new* controls. This occurs with regard to both simple offspring propositions (Experiment 4) and complex related propositions involving the causal conjunction of the simple offspring (Experiment 5).

Wittingly or unwittingly, subjects seem to go beyond the givens, using information explicitly provided as the basis for determining what is implicit and what can characteristically be inferred given such information. If it is the case that very much of communication depends on the ability to go beyond what is said directly in order to understand what is implied by what is said and what is revealed of the communicative purposes of the speaker who said it that way in that particular context, then the various processes of inference or natural logic involved in such elaboration of information become of great interest. To the extent that one can capitalize on properties of the operators of English in research that is directed to such problems, there is further warrant and justification for concern with these operators.

The Logic and Phrasing of Inducements

We now consider more fully the use of the conditional in inducements. This serves both (a) as an example of the analysis of one of the important uses of IF, its use in persuasive communication, and (b) as an illustration of the value of a speech–act-oriented account and an indication of how a scrutiny of the ways in which some operators may or may not be employed in phrasing conditional promises, threats, and warnings, figures in such an account. Some purposive uses of the conditional in inducements are considered. Some suggestions are made as to the relations obtaining between inducements phrased as conditional sentences, conjunctive sentences, and disjunctive sentences, and with regard to some inferences that may be drawn from inducements phrased as conditionals. Data supporting these suggestions are presented, and an analysis is offered that seeks to exhibit some of the implicit rules that appear to govern the use of the purposive conditional in relation to inducements. We are concerned with the relation between the logical form and the illocutionary force of certain sorts of sentences that figure very importantly in attempts at controlling and manipulating the behavior of others, and we consider how expectation and anticipation of consequences affect the form in which inducements may be phrased and the inferences they engender.

Essentially we look at one class of clearly purposive–causal uses of the conditional. What is said explicitly involves a causal connection, thus given *If p,q, p* on your part will be the cause of *q* on my part. What is implicit or conveyed and in a sense primary is a purposive notion, because *q* on my part is being "offered" to get something done or not done with regard to *p* on your part. In important measure this purposive role is what defines an inducement as such.

We seek to show that the relations obtaining among propositions phrased in IF, AND, and OR, are systematically affected as a function of whether a promise or a threat is involved. A conditional threat may be phrased more or less equivalently by use of IF, AND, or OR. Thus "If you do that I'll shoot you" may be paraphrased as "Do that and I'll shoot you" or as "Don't do that or I'll shoot you," for which, in the case of the disjunctive phrasing, the antecedent proposition must be negated. A conditional promise must be treated rather differently. Thus "If you do that I'll give you $100" may indeed be paraphrased in AND in a way quite parallel to the paraphrase of a conditional threat ("Do that and I'll give you $100"), but it cannot very well be paraphrased as an OR sentence with negated first proposition. Thus "Don't do that or I'll give you $100" is strange and certainly not an acceptable paraphrase for "If you do that I'll give you $100." If a conditional promise is to be paraphrased at all as a disjunction, it will require the negation of the second or consequent proposition ("Do that or I won't give you $100"), and although in general this paraphrase does appear to be acceptable, in at least one important respect it would appear to be rather different from its source sentence in that the source sentence is a conditional promise whereas the disjunctive paraphrase is really a sort of conditional threat involving the conditional withholding of an incentive, as contrasted to its conditional offer in the IF phrasing. We seek to determine whether subjects are sensitive to these paraphrase relations between IF, AND, and OR sentences, and to differences in paraphrase relations as a function of whether a threat or promise is involved. Finding that to be the case, we seek to offer an analysis to account for the findings and to show why, for example, it is difficult, if not impossible, to phrase a conditional promise in OR. Given a very elementary assumption to the effect that a person wants good consequences and seeks to avoid bad ones together with reference to the contrastive force of OR (as "otherwise"), we see that the results can readily be interpreted.

A classical fallacy in reasoning is the fallacy of the negated antecedent, thus, given *"If p,q"* and *"not p,"* people may conclude *"not q,"* a conclusion that is fallacious within the context of the truth-functional calculus. Considering the relation between a proposition and its obverse, i.e., between *"If p,q"* and *"If not p, not q,"* we have seen already that people often accept the latter as following from the former, committing the fallacy of the negated antecedent. We shall argue that given some very simple assumptions about the logic of conversation, this fallacy is really no fallacy at all in the context of conditional promises and threats. If the speaker who utters such a promise or threat is believed to be sincere by the addressee, then it must be assumed that he is offering the inducement, whether positive or negative, contingent on the actions of the addressee, and there would be no point in offering the inducement in the first place if he were going to give it regardless of the actions of the addressee, because in that case, there is no reason why it should affect the action one way or the other. Essentially this may be regarded as a case falling within the scope of Grice's principle of "quantity" in conversation, which states that a contribution to a conversational interchange should be as informative as required but no more informative than required (see Grice, 1967; 1975). Thus, given the assumption of contingency, which seems to be basic to the very sense of a conditional threat, warning, or promise, it seems very reasonable that the addressee should infer that if he does not carry out the wishes of the speaker, the inducement offered or threatened in the consequent proposition of conditional will not come about (or is less likely to come about). In this context, the fallacy of the negated antecedent is no fallacy at all but rather the most sensible inference to be made; indeed, in this context, not committing the fallacy would appear to be perverse.

We now present some data with regard to ways in which inducements may be phrased and the relations among different phrasings. After doing this, we refer back to data already presented regarding the inferences that inducements give rise to. A consideration of the inferences engendered by conditionals appears to be central to their understanding, particularly in the case of inducements that are meant to serve as guides and goads to action by bringing to the addressee's attention the consequences of his actions in an attempt to control those actions.

The following experiments are designed to reveal subjects' understanding of the relations that hold among inducements variously phrased and their characterization of various sorts of inducement statements. In the first of these experiments, subjects are presented with pairs of statements and asked whether or not the different phrasings maintain meaning; the second experiment (part of Experiment 1, previously described) involves a task in which they themselves are to rephrase inducements in ways that conserve meaning. In the third experiment, they are presented with various sorts of inducement statements and asked to characterize these as promises, threats, warnings, etc., in an attempt to discover what governs such characterizations or classifications.

Procedures: Equivalence judgments (Experiment 6). Subjects were presented with a series of pairs of sentences and for each pair were asked to decide "whether or not the two statements have the same meaning. If you believe that they have the same meaning circle E (for Equivalent). If you think the statements differ in meaning in some way then circle D (for Different)." The first sentence in each pair was always an IF sentence and involved either (a) a promise, (b) a threat, (c) a warning, or (d) a prediction of future good consequences (e.g., "If you buy that stock you will make a fortune").[6] For each of these four classes of sentences, the antecedent clause in the conditional was phrased as an affirmative or as a negative. If the first sentence in the pair is symbolized by *If p,q* (where *p* might involve a verb phrased affirmatively or negatively), then the second sentence occurring in a pair may be represented as

[6] If a warning represents a statement of future negative consequences for the addressee ("If you buy that stock you will lose a lot of money"), there appears to be no single cover term to represent a prediction of future beneficial results, of a future positive contingency ("If you buy that stock you will make a lot of money"). It is as though in the analogy form, THREAT: PROMISE as WARNING:?, there exists no single term to make the completion, although following Nozick (1969), TIP might be a candidate to fill this gap. Perhaps in the spirit of our stock market illustration, if we call a warning a "bear," we may appropriate the term "bull" for a prediction of future good consequences.

either (a) *p and q,* or (b) *not p or q,* or (c) *p or not q,* i.e., as a conjunctive or a disjunctive with negation on either the first or second proposition. The above makes for 24 possible combinations, there were 2 items for each, plus some fillers at the beginning and end for a total list of 54 items. There were 37 subjects in this study.

Procedures: Paraphrases (from Experiment 1). The procedures for this task were presented earlier in describing Experiment 1.

Procedures: Descriptions (Experiment 7). Subjects were given a series of sentences phrased in IF, AND, and OR, and told "We all know more or less that it means to THREATEN someone, to WARN someone, to PROMISE someone, etc. Now I want you to look over these sentences and for each one to decide whether it is a THREAT, a WARNING, a PROMISE, or none of these. Indicate your decision by putting either a T (THREAT), a W (WARNING), a P (PRO-MISE), or X (none of these) to the left of each sentence." The various classes employed were (a) threats, (b) promises, (c) warnings (= "bears"), and (d) tips or predictions of future good consequences (= "bulls"). The sentences were phrased as IF sentences [*If p,q* (with 12 items per class)], as AND sentences [*p and q* (with 4 items per class)], and as OR sentences [either *not p or q* (with 4 items per class) or *p or not q* (with 4 items per class)]; for examples, see Table 10.3. Including fillers, there were 100 items; there were 39 subjects in this study.

The results of these experiments are now presented.

TABLE 10.3
Examples of Items Used in Description Task

Sentence Phrasing	Example
If p, q:	
Threat	If you refuse the assignment I'll fire you.
Warning (= bear)	If you spray with DDT the birds will die.
Promise	If you wash the car I'll let you use it.
Tip (= bull)	If you marry her you will be very happy.
p and q:	
Threat	Hurt the child and I'll kill you.
Warning (= bear)	Cheat on your income tax and you will be in trouble.
Promise	Run that errand and I'll give you a quarter.
Tip (= bull)	Use plenty of fertilizer and you will have a fine crop.
Not p or q:	
Threat	Don't drive too fast or I will give you a ticket.
Warning (= bear)	Don't fail the exam or you will flunk out of school.
Promise	Don't come home early or I'll take you to the show.
Tip (= bull)	Don't close that deal or you will get a promotion.
p or not q:	
Threat	Bug me again or I won't hit you.
Warning (= bear)	Conceal the evidence or you won't be prosecuted.
Promise	Help with the problem or I won't buy you a drink.
Tip (= bull)	Solve the problem or you won't be famous.

Results: Equivalence judgments (Experiment 6). Results are generally very similar whether the first proposition in the conditional was affirmative or negative; therefore we report just the pooled data. Recall that the first sentence in a pair was always phrased in IF and that the second sentence might be either a conjunctive or a disjunctive sentence, and if the latter, either the first or second proposition might be negated. In the case of threats, the second sentence was judged to be the same in meaning as the first sentence 87% of the time if it was a conjunctive, 93% of the time if it was a disjunctive with the first proposition negated, but only 17% of the time when the second proposition in the disjunction was negated. In the case of warnings, the corresponding figures are 94%, 98%, and 16%. Results for promises and predictions of future benefits differ with regard to the disjunctive sentences. In the case of promises, the second sentence was judged equivalent in meaning to the first 100% of the time if it was a conjunctive, 22% of the time if it was a disjunctive with the first proposition negated, and 76% of the time if it was a disjunctive with the second proposition negated, and the corresponding figures for predictions of future benefits ("bulls") are 98%, 18%, and 61%. Overall, the results are quite clear: The response to threats and warnings is quite similar and so is that to promises and predictions of future benefits. The main difference between these two classes, which represent negative and positive consequences respectively for the addressee, is in regard to the response to disjunctives. If a negative consequence is involved, then characteristically a paraphrase in OR that negates the first proposition is regarded as acceptable, whereas one that negates the second is regarded as unacceptable, with the converse holding when a positive consequence is involved; the effect is perhaps slightly stronger for negative than positive consequences.

Results: Paraphrases (from Experiment 1). The results for this task were presented earlier; see Table 10.1. It need only be recalled that the most frequent paraphrases of promises and threats are in AND and OR statements, in which we found the most striking differences between these two classes of inducements. P+ and P− statements elicit a very large proportion of conjunctive paraphrases (40% and 52% respectively). T+ statements only rarely elicit such paraphrases (5%). Although there are essentially no paraphrases of promises in OR, such paraphrases (negating the first proposition of the conditional) are common for T+ statements (24%) and very frequent indeed (54%) for T− statements (note that for a T− conditional, the paraphrase in OR becomes *p or q*, e.g., "If you don't do that I'll hit you" is paraphrased by "Do that or I'll hit you"). Thus, particularly with regard to the paraphrase of conditionals as disjunctives, there are some striking differences in the response to promises and threats.

Results: Descriptions (Experiment 7). In constructing items as threats, promises, warnings, and "bulls," we employed two criteria: (a) whether a positive or a negative consequence was involved for the addressee, and (b) whether or not the speaker was making himself responsible for that consequence. If the speaker made himself responsible, it was called a promise or threat depending on whether a positive or negative consequence was involved; if he did not make himself responsible it was regarded as "bull" or warning, as a function of whether the consequence was positive or negative. Now consider the results for this task. When phrased as conditionals, threats are characteristically described as threats (66%) or warnings (33%), warnings are characteristically described as warnings (88%), promises are overwhelmingly described as promises (96%), and "bulls" are described most commonly as promises (63%) but also are sometimes put in the "none of these = N.O.T." category (21%). When phrased as conjunctives, threats are described as threats (67%) or as warnings (22%), warnings are described as warnings (83%), promises are described overwhelmingly as promises (97%), and "bulls" are again most commonly described as promises (60%) but also are described as N.O.T. (22%). It does not seem to make any noticeable difference whether a conditional or a conjunctive phrasing is employed, and these results appear sensible and obvious enough. When it comes to a disjunctive phrasing, matters become rather different, and now the sign of the consequences comes to have some interesting effects. When the first proposition of the disjunctive is negated, threats are described as threats (72%) or as warnings (23%), and warnings are called warnings (91%). However, when the second proposition is negated, over half of the descriptions for threats (54%) fall into the N.O.T. category, and a similar result holds for the warnings, with 59% of the responses falling into the N.O.T. category (although 35% of the judgments here still fall into the warning category). Clearly, there is something extraordinary about a sentence that aspires to be a threat or warning but that is phrased as a disjunction with the second proposition negated. Next, consider promises and "bulls" phrased disjunctively. If the first proposition of the disjunction is negated, then promises are often (61%) classified as N.O.T., and similar findings obtain for "bulls," with 51% of the descriptions falling in the N.O.T. category. In this regard, there is a difference between threats and warnings, which can be phrased as *Not p or q* sentences, and promises and "bulls," which cannot be so phrased if they are to maintain their conceptual status. Finally, consider promises and "bulls" phrased as *p or not q* sentences. A promise so phrased is hardly ever regarded as a promise (11%) but rather is characterized as a threat (48%) or a warning (35%); similarly "bulls" so phrased are now most commonly (65%) judged to be warnings. Thus a statement that urges the addressee to do something and indicates that otherwise a good consequence will not follow is no longer regarded as a promise or "bull" but rather as a threat or warning. It seems difficult if not impossible to pose a promise as a disjunction; we consider some possible reasons for this later. Here we make only one further observation with regard to these results and those obtained in the equivalence judgment task. Let an event presumed to be desired by the addressee be symbolized $q+$, and let an undesired event be symbolized $q-$. Then, in the equivalence judgment task, we found that a conditional promise phrased as an IF statement (of the form *If p,q+*) was commonly (76% of the time) judged as equivalent in meaning to a disjunction with the second proposition negated (of the form *p or not q+*). In the present description task, we find that a sentence of the first kind is overwhelmingly (96%) characterized as a promise, whereas a sentence of the second kind is characteristically regarded as a threat (48%) or warning (35%). Thus we have the rather striking finding that a pair of sentences may often be judged equivalent in meaning when one member of that pair is regarded as a promise and the other as a threat or warning.

In terms of a variety of results, it appears that a conditional threat or promise may be phrased not only as an IF sentence but also as an AND sentence. Matters are different if one attempts a paraphrase using OR. A threat of the form *If p, q−* ("If you do that I'll hit you") may readily be paraphrased as *Not p or q−* ("Don't do that or I'll hit you") but is strange, to put it mildly, if paraphrased as *p or not q−* ("Do that or I won't hit you"). On the other hand, a promise of the form *If p, q+* ("If you do that I'll give you $100") is strange indeed if paraphrased as *Not p or q+* ("Don't do that or I'll give you $100") but may be rephrased as *p or not q+* ("Do that or I won't give you $100"), although the latter statement is no longer regarded as a promise but rather as a variety of threat. The observations on disjunctives made above hold also for warnings ("bears") and "bulls."

The inferences subjects draw from inducement statements may be considered as revealing of their understanding of the statements and of their appreciation of various consequences of different actions on their part. The procedure and results for the invited inferences task were presented earlier; see Table 10.2 for findings. In short, with regard to conditional threats and promises, subjects very readily accept the "fallacious" inference from a proposition to its obverse, with average value for acceptance ranging between 81% and 90%. It does not seem to make much difference whether a threat or promise is involved or in which direction (e.g., from *If p,q* to *If not p, not q* or from *If not p, not q* to *If p,q*) the relation goes — subjects are very prone to commit the fallacy of the negated antecedent for propositions involving inducements.

We now seek to account for the ways in which inducements may or may not be phrased and to indicate why the fallacy of the denied or negated antecedent is so seductive in the context of inducements.

Let us make the very simple (perhaps tautological) assumption that a person wants to get good outcomes and wants to avoid bad outcomes. A conditional promise constitutes an effective inducement insofar as the person wants the good outcomes offered (and is willing to do something in exchange), and a conditional threat constitutes an effective inducement insofar as the person wants to avoid the bad outcomes threatened (and will do something or refrain from doing something in exchange).[7] The logic of this is laid out quite starkly in our notation when we symbolize a conditional promise in IF as *If, p,q+* and a conditional threat in IF as *If, p,q−*.

What happens when one goes to a conjunctive phrasing? The forms *p and q+* and *p and q−* are presumably understood with AND as an ordered or asymmetric causal or causal–temporal operator that exhibits the consequences of doing *p*, whether these be positive or negative, just as directly as does the conditional proper. So, in the first case, wanting *q+* you do *p*; in the second case, wanting to avoid *q−* you refrain from doing *p*.

What happens, finally, when one goes to a disjunctive phrasing using OR? Used in the context of inducements, the form *p or q* involves an ordered or asymmetric use of OR with the force of OTHERWISE. In the disjunctive phrasing of an inducement, the first disjunct amounts to an imperative, and the second disjunct is a statement of consequences for the addressee, whose role it is to enforce the first disjunct, i.e., to get the addressee to obey the order by choosing the first disjunct. Consider a threat *If p, q−*, which is paraphrased as *Not p or q−*. You as addressee are being presented with two alternatives, only one of which will come about; it is up to you to choose. You will generally know that the speaker wants *Not p*, so if *Not p* occurs, everything would be well. But if *Not p* does not occur, then *q−* will occur, which is something you want to avoid. Hence you know that you must bring about *Not p* so that *q−* should not come about, i.e., because you want to avoid *q−*, there is some incentive to take the other alternative, *Not p*. So this paraphrase in OR seems reasonable enough. Now consider a paraphrase for *If p,q−* in OR that negates the second proposition, namely *p or not q−*. Because you want to avoid *q−*, *not q−* constitutes a perfectly acceptable alternative, in fact the desirable alternative, and there is no reason to take the other alternative, *p*. An inducement of the form *p or not q−* is additionally strange in that it offers or seeks to command *p* as an alternative,

---

[7]It should be obvious, of course, that for a threat or promise to be reasonable, it is not sufficient just that the *q* proposition be appropriately negatively or positively signed for the hearer, with the speaker asserting that he will bring about these negative or positive consequences. The sign or extremity of sign of the *p* proposition and the relation between the signs of the *p* and *q* propositions must also be considered. Although it may be a commonplace promise to say "If you do that I'll give you $50," with *p* as a sort of dummy proposition of unspecified or zero sign, it becomes quite another matter if *p* is extremely negatively signed. Thus "If you break your mother's arm I'll give you $50" is a ludicrous and presumably ineffective promise just because of the disproportion between the negative value of the act required of the hearer and the positive value of the inducement or incentive being offered. In fact, subjects are sensitive to "felicity" conditions for inducements, i.e., conditions that must be met if a threat or promise is to be (pragmatically) appropriate or plausible. In an ancillary study, it was found that promises of the aforementioned sort, in which there is a gross disproportion between the negative value of the act required and the positive value of the incentive offered, were judged extraordinary 75% of the time, whereas garden-variety promises with, say, an incentive offered to carry out something neutral or only mildly negative for the hearer were judged extraordinary only 13% of the time (see Fillenbaum, in press).

under circumstances in which you as addressee will generally know that the speaker really wants and is trying to elicit *not p*. Because the whole point of a conditional threat is to get the addressee to choose the first disjunct desired by the speaker by offering as an alternative in the second disjunct consequences that are unacceptable to the addressee, a threat of the form *p or not q−*, in which the speaker commands an action he does not want and offers as an alternative something that the addressee does want, must appear incoherent and useless as an inducement.

The analysis for conditional promises phrased disjunctively follows parallel lines. Consider a promise of the form *If p, q+,* which is paraphrased as *p or not q+*. Because you want *q+*, you will not wish to lose it by taking the second alternative of *not q+*, so there is an incentive to take the other alternative, *p*. Thus this paraphrase appears appropriate enough, subject only to the qualification that this paraphrase in OR is really a threat not to offer some good outcome, whereas the source conditional was a promise of that good outcome. However, insofar as both statements are compelling inducements to do *p*, they may be regarded as equivalent as to their effects (both of these facts are reflected in the subjects' judgments − the first particularly in the descriptions, the second particularly in the equivalence judgments). Now consider a paraphrase for *If p, q+* in OR that negates the first proposition, namely *not p or q+*. Because you want *q+*, this constitutes a desirable alternative, and there is no reason to take the other alternative, *not p*. An inducement of the form *not p or q+* is additionally strange in that it appears to command *not p* under circumstances in which you as addressee will generally know that the speaker really wants to elicit *p*. Again we have a case in which the speaker is commanding an action he does not want and is offering as an alternative to enforce this command something that the addressee does want.

Such a conditional promise is incoherent and useless as an inducement in a way exactly parallel to the way in which a conditional threat of the form *p or not q−* is incoherent and useless. An important aspect of the difficulty with threats and promises phrased as *p or not q−* and *not p or q+*, respectively, may derive from the fact that the addressee is being asked explicitly to do something or not to do something that he understands is exactly opposite to the desires of the speaker. If a disjunctive inducement statement is to be appropriately phrased, it must begin with a command that explicitly expresses what the speaker wants the addressee to do and then must present as an alternative the relatively bad outcome that will result from not going along with that command.

The above analysis provides an account of why it is difficult, if not impossible, to phrase a conditional promise in a disjunctive form. We have already seen that the only paraphrase of a conditional promise in OR that is coherent is *p or not q+* and that this paraphrase is regarded characteristically as a threat or warning, not as a promise. Buy why should this be? Why is there this difficulty of phrasing a conditional promise in OR? If a promise is to be phrased disjunctively, then the second proposition in the OR sentence must have a positive force, i.e., it must be either $q+$ *or not* $q-$, but if the second proposition has such positive force, then, as we have seen above, it loses any incentive value toward getting the person to take the first alternative, and thus, because the person will always take the second and positive alternative, such statements cannot serve as sensible or plausible inducements. Only if the second proposition in the disjunctive has a negative force, being either $q-$ or *not* $q+$, will it serve to make the listener take the other alternative and thus function adequately as an inducement.

We have seen that in the case of conditional promises and threats people are very prone to accept the obverse of a proposition as following from it, i.e., given a proposition of the form *If p,q,* they believe that *If not p, not q* follows, etc.[8] Such implications are accepted between 80% and 90% of the time (the values range from 81% to 90% for acceptance), and it does not seem to make any difference whether promises or threats are involved. Something rather similar also holds for acceptance of obverses when IF is used as a temporal or temporal–causal term (e.g., "If John sees Mary he will give her the message"), but the connection between a proposition and its obverse is decidedly less tight when IF is used as a contingent universal (e.g., "If the mushroom is red it is edible"). Here we only seek to provide an account for this invited inference effect in the context of the particular purposive–causal use of IF involved in inducements, although such an account may also have some bearing on the interpretation of the effect for other temporal–causal uses of IF.

Why, offered an inducement of the form *If p, q,* might the addressee of such a statement believe that *If not p, not q* follows? Consider that the inducement q is being offered to get the addressee to do or refrain from doing p. Now, precisely insofar as the obtaining of q is contingent upon some action with regard to p, the inducement would lose all point or force if that contingency were eliminated. Thus, in the case of a promise if $q+$ were to come about whether or not the addressee did p, and in the case of a threat if $q-$ were to come about whether or not the addressee refrained from doing p, the conditionality of the inducement that really defines it as an inducement rather than as a simple straightforward offer of a good or bad outcome would be lost, and the statement woud have no point. If the speaker is going to give the addressee $100 regardless of what he does, or if he is going to attack him regardless of what he does, then

---

[8] The compellingness of the inference from a proposition to its obverse is paradoxically exhibited by a case in which the inference must be *disinvited* and in which the temptation to such an inference must be strongly resisted, a case for which the matter would hardly ever become salient, as it often does, unless there were a strong tendency to make such inferences. Consider a statement of the form *If not p,q* such as "If I don't see you before you leave, have a good trip," which could hardly seem curious or lead to the bantering reply "And if you do see me before then, I'm not to have a good trip?" unless there were a strong and generally justified tendency in many circumstances to infer *If p, not q* from *If not p,q.*

there is no good reason for the addressee to modify his behavior one way or the other. To the extent that the addressee believes the speaker to be sincere in his inducement statement, he must assume that the outcomes that will be offered to him will be differential and contingent upon his own action, which the speaker is seeking to control through the inducement he is offering. The "conversational implicature," to use Grice's term (1967; 1975), follows quite directly if the addressee of the inducement statement assumes that the speaker is conforming to the maxim of "quantity" in saying no more and no less than appropriate to the circumstances. The crucial point concerns the contingency between an action and its consequences. The addressee need not to assume that in the absence of his action he will certainly not receive the incentive or punishment being offered; he needs to assume only that his action will affect in some substantial or significant degree the likelihood of obtaining those consequences.

Although this general analysis applies equally to promises and threats, there is one respect in which these differ somewhat and in which the analysis has a particularly direct bearing for threats. First consider a promise of the form *If p, q+,* in which the speaker is trying to get the addressee to do *p.* Here the addressee might employ a legitimate argument form (*modus ponens*) by affirming the antecedent: He wants *q+,* he knows that *If p, q+* holds, so does *p* and *q+* will follow. But what of a threat of the form *If p, q−,* where the speaker is trying to get the addressee not to do *p*? This can only work if the addressee realizes, at least, that he must not do *p* and infers (and presumably also hopes) that if he does *not p* then *q−* will not result, which amounts to assuming *If not p, not q−,* given *If p, q−.* The point is simply this: The very understanding of the force of a conditional threat depends in large measure upon the addressee making the invited inference from the proposition heard to its obverse, and thus the "fallacy" of the negated antecedent is particularly intimately involved in the understanding of conditional threats.

The preceding discussion may be considered an attempt to reveal some properties of a particular sort of purposive—causal use of IF, for a case in which there is an explicit causal relation between the *p* and *q* propositions but in which implicitly the principal role of the conditional is purposive, i.e., its use is to get the addressee to do something or to refrain from doing something. We have tried to say something about relations holding among propositions phrased in IF, AND, and OR, which involve such a use, and to indicate the role of at least one condition with regard to the sign of the consequences, i.e., whether a threat or promise is at stake, in governing these relations. This work may be regarded as illustrating the potential value of a pragmatic analysis in which attention is directed toward the circumstances of use of a certain utterance type involving conditionals. In these terms, one may begin to understand how the illocutionary point of a statement may affect its logical form and how principles of conversation may license or even require inferences not legitimate, given only a consideration of truth-functional relations. Thus the study of inducements provides the occasion for a closer examination of the logic of one important use of IF, and such an examination reveals the value of a pragmatically oriented speech—act account of persuasive communications.

WHERE THINGS STAND

In this paper, we have sought to show that the conditional IF may have a number of rather different uses, and we have sought to offer the sketch of an analysis for one of these uses. It must be obvious that there is still a long way to go in such an enterprise and still many things to do. There are uses that we have not even mentioned (see, e.g., Fraser, 1971; and Horn, 1972) and, of those that have been mentioned, we have only really discussed one, viz. that in induce-ments. And the analysis of inducements is clearly insufficient as it stands and needs to be further developed in a number of directions [see, e.g., the problem of "felicity" conditions involving the relation between the signing or extremity of signing of the p and q propositions touched on in footnote 7, p. 205 (and considered further in Fillenbaum, in press)]. But even the little that has been done here should be enough to raise questions about the adequacy of any research on the conditional that seeks to provide some single, unique account of its uses and that focuses attention principally on a truth-functional analysis.

We have sought to provide some examples of the uses to which the study of logical connectives, the conditional in particular, may be put in approaching some general problems of interest to the psycholinguist. Again, obviously, what has been mentioned can only be taken in the spirit of illustration. There are other cases of interest for which there is already information available and cases for which it would be very important to have work by the psychologist. As an example of the first kind, work on memory for sense or gist has come to be important in recent years. It may therefore be pertinent to mention that a recent study of sentence memory (Fillenbaum, 1975b) indicates considerable confusion among different phrasings of inducement statements. Subjects encountered warnings variously phrased as conditionals, conjunctives, and disjunctives with the first proposition negated. Later their memory was tested on an incidental recognition task. There were many false recognitions of related items (i.e., sentences that represent alternative phrasings of the warnings using one of the other two sentence operators). Although verbatim correct sentences were recog-nized as "old" sentences on the average 70% of the time, related sentences were recognized as "old" on the average 52% of the time, with control sentences judged "old" only 17% of the time. As an example of the second kind, consider the suggestion made by a number of linguists (see e.g., McCawley, 1972) that some of the logical operators are very intimately related to the quantifiers, that "the operators AND and OR are in important logical respects parallel to the quantifiers ALL and SOME respectively" (Horn, 1972, p. 93). And note that in the present paper, we have identified at least one use of the conditional as a sort of contingent universal ("If the coat is wool it will wear well"), which seems to relate IF rather closely to the universal quantifier ALL. Obviously the relation between the logical operators and quantificational phenomena requires and merits further exploration, and it may turn out that study of the logical operators can provide us with a tool for the investigation of important problems concerning the understanding and use of quantifiers. For a significant start on these issues, see the work of the linguist Horn (1972), who has already shown that there is not only a syntactic and logical relation between AND and OR and ALL and SOME respectively but that there are also pragmatic correspondences in regard to what is conversationally suggested or "implicated."

Another way in which the work presented here is limited in scope needs to be noted if only to alert us to the problems that await us. We have considered only some of the simplex connectives, indeed have mainly been concerned with just one use of IF, and have had nothing whatsoever to say about the major negation operator(s), nor anything to say about what might be called complex connectives, i.e., operators that on pragmatic or semantic grounds combine more than one function (for discussion of a term such as BUT, see, e.g., Lakoff, 1971; and Fillenbaum & Rapoport, 1971; for data and comments on UNLESS, in particular considering the role of this term in inducements, see Fillenbaum, 1976). Finally, nothing has been said about the cases in which a proposition involves more than one operator, perhaps the most important and interesting class of these being the propositions in which negation operates on a complex proposition involving one of the simplex connectives. What can a speaker mean if he denies (a) "If he eats that stew he will get sick" or (b) "If he speeds he will get a ticket"? And why is it that the former denial is more likely to be understood as (c) "If he eats the stew he won't get sick" than as (d) "If he eats the stew he may or may not get sick," whereas for the latter there is much more division of opinion between (e) "If he speeds he won't get a ticket" and (f) "If he speeds he may or may not get a ticket," with this last, (f), the more common interpretation? As the very phrasing of these examples suggests, one of the principal uses of negation is to correct or falsify a preconception (Wason, 1972), "to contradict or correct; to cancel a suggestion" (Strawson, 1952, p. 8), characteristically in a dialogic context. But for the case of the negation of propositions that are themselves complex because they involve one of the sentence operators or connectives such as AND, OR, or IF, it is by no means always obvious what is being corrected or cancelled or what the governing conditions may be (for discussion of these matters with regard to negated conditionals in particular, see Ducrot, 1972; and Grice, 1967). Some data that raise these sorts of problems might perhaps be mentioned.[9] Subjects were asked to indicate what they

[9] Fillenbaum (unpublished study).

understood by the negation of various kinds of complex sentences, the task being set in a dialogic context in which they were to indicate what an overheard speaker most likely meant when he replied "No, that's not so" to a given target sentence. Under such circumstances, the denial of a causal–temporal *If p,q* proposition was interpreted as *If p, not q* almost 60% of the time, on the average, and as something like *If p, maybe q maybe not q* roughly 40% of the time, whereas the denial of a contingent–universal *If p,q* proposition was interpreted as *If p, not q* not quite 30% of the time, on the average, and as something like *If p, maybe q maybe not q* about 60% of the time.[10] At the very least, such results, and parallel data indicating large differences in the ways in which the denial of different sorts of conjunctive and disjunctive sentences is interpreted, again suggest the inadequacy of any simple truth-functionally based account, now for the negation of sentences involving simplex sentence operators.

People are concerned with communication in context, and communication in context characteristically requires going, in various ways, beyond what is explicitly and directly given. We have shown that knowledge of the ways of the world may systematically affect the interpretation of pragmatically strange messages, that people are sensitive to the presuppositions and "implicatures" of statements, and that in the context of inducements people are very prone to make inferences that are logically "fallacious" but quite compelling given reasonable general assumptions about the logic of conversation. Our position is basically similar to that of Johnson–Laird (1975), who points out that "a listener is able to draw on general knowledge to allow a speaker to leave many things unsaid [p. 50]" and argues "that people exploit a communal base of knowledge . . . this knowledge will be automatically elicited by any utterance with a relevant topic, and it can be used by the inferential machinery in order to make good any gaps in the explicit discourse [p. 51]." The interesting and difficult problems arise, of course, when one tries to formulate the underlying contextually and conversationally sensitive rules necessary to account for the ways in which the often conveyed meanings are attained. Both in terms of such general considerations and in terms of the particular examples considered in the present

[10] This last finding is of interest in another regard if one considers the relation between contingent universals phrased in IF such as "If the coat is wool it is warm" and universally quantified statements, say of the form "All wool coats are warm," in which the former sort of statement appears to presuppose the latter. We have noted above that negation of a contingent universal use of IF yielded an interpretation of something like *If p, maybe q maybe not q* about 60% of the time. But the negation of matched universally quantified sentences yielded the interpretation *Some p are q some are not q* between 98% and 99% of the time. Thus the sort of interpretation that is given essentially unanimously to the denial of the presupposed universally quantified statement is given only about 60% of the time to the denial of the entailed conditional. Obviously there is work to be done in making sense of such data on the relation between conditionals and universally quantified statements, under negation.

paper, it seems unlikely that any account that focuses on or restricts itself to truth-functional matters will prove sufficient to the phenomena.

Consider the following possibilities with regard to the analysis of logical connectives:

1. The meaning of a particular term is equivalent to that of its namesake as stipulated in propositional logic;

2. 1 is not true, but some single meaning is specifiable;

3. 2 is not true, but a number of different meanings can be identified, where to this point meaning is characterized in truth-functional terms, i.e., the meaning of a connective is defined in terms of the function that relates the truth values of the constituent propositions to the truth value of the complex proposition that results when the connective joins them; and

4. 3 may be true but is in principle insufficient, because an account of the understanding and use of logical operators must go beyond truth-functional considerations, must direct attention to what is being done and understood by the employment of a logical operator in a sentence in context, and must consider the illocutionary force of the particular speech act in which the operator figures.

No psychologists have really argued 1, many if not most have attempted to establish 2, a few have come to adopt 3, but hardly any have seriously worried about the need for 4, and perhaps the major point of the present work is precisely that 4 needs to be worried about.

What this paper has attempted to do is to show that a closer look at the uses of the logical connectives is needed and may be revealing; that if the case of the conditional has anything to suggest, it is unlikely that a monolithic account will be possible for any of the connectives; that analyses that focus on truth-functional considerations only will prove inadequate; and that a speech—act-oriented, pragmatic account that considers what the speaker is trying to do by saying what he does in the relevant context seems necessary. Perhaps all this may be taken as going a little way in the direction indicated by Strawson (1952, p. 232) when he argues "that the logic of ordinary speech provides a field of intellectual study unsurpassed in richness, complexity, and the power to absorb."

ACKNOWLEDGMENTS

This paper was prepared while the writer was supported by an NIMH Special Fellowship at the Institute of Human Learning, University of California, Berkeley. The research was supported in part by USPHS Grant MH-10006 from NIMH, and much of the empirical work presented here can be found in Fillenbaum (1974a, 1974b; 1975a; 1976). For permission to include copyrighted materials from these earlier papers I am indebted to the American Psychological Association and to Springer Verlag.

REFERENCES

Austin, J. L. *How to do things with words.* Oxford: Oxford University Press, 1962.

Bartlett, F. C. *Remembering.* Cambridge: Cambridge University Press, 1932.

Beilin, H. *Studies in the cognitive basis of language development.* New York: Academic Press, 1975.

Bobrow, D. G., & Collins, A. *Representation and understanding.* New York: Academic Press, 1975.

Bransford, J. D., Barclay, J. R., & Franks, J. J. Sentence memory: A constructive versus interpretive approach. *Cognitive Psychology,* 1972, *3,* 193–209.

Ducrot, O. *Dire et ne pas dire.* Paris: Hermann, 1972.

Fillenbaum, S. On coping with ordered and unordered conjunctive sentences. *Journal of Experimental Psychology,* 1971, *87,* 93–98.

Fillenbaum, S. Information amplified: Memory for counterfactual conditionals. *Journal of Experimental Psychology,* 1974, *102,* 44–49. (a)

Fillenbaum, S. Pragmatic normalization: Further results for some conjunctive and disjunctive sentences. *Journal of Experimental Psychology,* 1974, *102,* 574–578. (b)

Fillenbaum, S. OR: Some uses. *Journal of Experimental Psychology,* 1974, *103,* 913–921. (c)

Fillenbaum, S. IF: Some uses. *Psychological Research,* 1975, *37,* 245–260. (a)

Fillenbaum, S. A note on memory for sense: Incidental recognition of warnings phrased as conditionals, disjunctives, and conjunctives. *Bulletin of the Psychonomic Society,* 1975, *6,* 293–294. (b)

Fillenbaum, S. Inducements: On the phrasing and logic of conditional promises, threats, and warnings. *Psychological Research,* 1976, *38,* 231–250.

Fillenbaum, S. A condition on plausible inducements. *Language and Speech,* in press.

Fillenbaum, S., & Rapoport, A. *Structures in the subjective lexicon.* New York: Academic Press, 1971.

Fraser, B. An analysis of "even" in English. In C. J. Fillmore & D. T. Langendoen (Eds.), *Studies in linguistic semantics.* New York: Holt, Rinehart & Winston, 1971.

Geis, M. L., & Zwicky, A. M. On invited inferences. *Linguistic Inquiry,* 1971, *2,* 560–566.

Gordon, D., & Lakoff, G. Conversational postulates. In *Papers from the seventh regional meeting of the Chicago Linguistic Society,* (University of Chicago Department of Linguistics), Chicago, 1971.

Grice, H. P. *Logic and conversation.* Unpublished lecture notes from William James Lectures at Harvard University, 1967.

Grice, H. P. Logic and conversation. In P. Cole & J. L. Morgan (Eds.), *Syntax and semantics. Volume 3: Speech acts.* New York: Academic Press, 1975.

Horn, L. R. *On the semantic properties of logical operators in English.* Unpublished doctoral dissertation, UCLA, 1972.

Johnson–Laird, P. N. Models of deduction. In R. J. Falmagne (Ed.), *Reasoning: Representation and process.* Hillsdale, N.J.: Lawrence Erlbaum Associates, 1975.

Karttunen, L. Counterfactual conditionals. *Linguistic Inquiry,* 1971, *2,* 566–569.

Lakoff, R. If's, and's and but's about conjunction. In C. J. Fillmore & D. T. Langendoen (Eds.), *Studies in linguistic semantics.* New York: Holt, Rinehart & Winston, 1971.

Lilje, G. M. Uninvited inferences. *Linguistic Inquiry,* 1972, *3,* 540–542.

Mates, B. *Stoic logic.* Berkeley: University of California Press, 1961.

McCawley, J. A programme for logic. In D. Davidson & G. Harman (Eds.), *Semantics of natural language.* Dordrecht, Netherlands: Reidel, 1972.

Norman, D. A., Rumelhart, D. E., & the LNR Research Group. *Explorations in cognition.* San Francisco: W. H. Freeman, 1975.

Nozick, R. Coercion. In S. Morgenbesser, P. Suppes, & M. White (Eds.), *Philosophy science and method*. New York: St. Martin's Press, 1969.

Schmerling, S. Asymmetric conjunction and rules of conversation. In P. Cole & J. L. Morgan (Eds.), *Syntax and semantics. Volume 3: Speech acts*. New York: Academic Press, 1975.

Staudenmayer, H. Understanding reasoning with meaningful propositions. In R. J. Falmagne (Ed.), *Reasoning: Representation and process*. Hillsdale, N. J.: Lawrence Erlbaum Associates, 1975.

Strawson, P. F. *Introduction to logical theory*. New York: Wiley, 1952.

Taplin, J. E., & Staudenmayer, H. Interpretation of abstract conditional sentences in deductive reasoning. *Journal of Verbal Learning and Verbal Behavior*, 1973, *12*, 530–542.

Wason, P. C. In real life negatives are false. *Logique et Analyse*. 1972, *15*, 17–38.

Wason, P. C., & Johnson–Laird, P. N. *Psychology of reasoning*. Cambridge: Harvard University Press, 1972.

11
Comments on Lexical Semantics

Allen Munro

University of California, San Diego *

The papers by Fillenbaum and by Smith, Balzano, and Walker suggest two conclusions about the study of semantic factors in cognition. The first conclusion is that the psychological study of lexical semantics is an extremely important and active area of cognitive psychology. Psychologists seem to be coming to consider semantics as more central than syntax in models of language understanding. George Miller (1974) has gone so far as to suggest that the rules of syntax may be best viewed as "abstractions from, not as components of, the user's knowledge of his language [p. 408]." In this view, syntax is only a generalization from lexical semantics. Another aspect of the vitality of research in lexical semantics is the variety of approaches for testing theories that have been developed. Psychological experiments using traditional dependent measures, such as recall and recognition tests, and measures of reaction time for semantic decisions, abound. Linguistic semantic theories of lexical decomposition (such as that developed in Lakoff, 1970; and McCawley, 1968) have been extended and applied by psychologists, as in, for example, George Miller's (1972) study of similarity judgments for motion verbs and Dedre Gentner's (1975) study of how some verbs of possession are acquired by children learning English. Psychologists are even making use of subjects' judgments of semantic anomaly, contextual infelicity, and semantic relatedness, as we have seen in Fillenbaum's paper. These last dependent measures are particularly significant additions to the psychologists' arsenal, because they were for so long the sole prerogative of the linguist.

The second conclusion suggested by these papers and by other recent work in lexical semantics is that this subfield of cognitive psychology is seriously lacking in one quality that could greatly contribute to progress. That quality is the

*Now at Behavioral Technology Laboratories, University of Southern California.

benefit of a unified theoretical framework within which the results of individual studies in lexical semantics can be understood. This concern is related to the appeal for macrotheories that has been made by a number of the participants in this conference. Such a unified theory is probably essential if this area of research is to avoid becoming a sterile collection of isolated minitheories, with each closely bound to a particular experimental paradigm. I don't mean to imply here that I think that detailed theories about particular meaning structures and experimentally oriented process theories are uninteresting or unimportant. Such theories are vitally important but would be more useful if they could be developed in such a way that they relate to each other. What is called for, in other words, is a macrotheory that defines the *form* of the minitheories and that makes clear the functional interrelationships among the processes described by the minitheories.

Psychologists need such a unifying semantic theory, whose terms could be used to describe and interpret their results. I envision a psychological theory of meaning that would have for the study of semantics the effect that the transformational model in linguistics had for syntax in the 1960s. It is important not just to have a high-level, abstract, general theory by which one understands the functioning of the complete system; psychologists need a broad theoretical *framework,* within which different theories for the results associated with specific experimental paradigms could be developed. A candidate theory to fill this role already exists — *procedural semantics* — largely the product of research in artificial intelligence (Minsky, 1975; Winograd, 1975), although it has had partially independent parallel development in philosophy (Harrison, 1972) and psychology (Norman, Rumelhart, & LNR, 1975). In procedural semantics, concepts have both structural and procedural characteristics. When viewed as structural entities, concepts can often be thought of as predicates, which take as arguments other concepts. When viewed as procedural entities, concepts can be thought of as active procedures, which can call upon other concepts as subprocedures. Some possible applications of the procedural semantics approach are discussed below.

Before proceeding to a discussion of the particulars of the two papers presented in this session, I would like to make a plea for another potential source for theoretical unity (or at least mutual comprehensibility). That source is the taking into consideration of nonexperimental data in connection with the construction of theoretical accounts of certain experimental results. In particular, we should try to observe the normal operation of whatever cognitive process is under investigation in a natural setting, where it has its normal function. I think that psychologists have something to learn here from linguists about what can constitute disconfirmation of a theory. A simple logical argument against a theory should have at least the weight of arguments based on statistically significant experimental results.

THE REPRESENTATION CODE: FORM AND ACCESS[1]

Smith, Balzano, and Walker have contributed to our understanding of the processes by which names of objects may be compared with pictures of objects. They show that at least two matching strategies seem to be pursued simultaneously:

1. Using a semantic analysis of the picture, a name for the picture is found and compared with the name presented; and

2. The semantic representations of the picture and the name presented are compared.

Smith et al. have also discovered some interesting facts about the naming process itself. *Basic*-level naming can be done more quickly than nonbasic-level naming, yet naming at different levels may be independent, because typicality seems to have an effect only for high-level names. Caution is called for in interpreting the results of these experiments, however. In Experiment 1, subjects did not name pictures but rather compared pictures with just-presented names. Even in Experiment 2, in which subjects said aloud the name appropriate to the presented picture, it might be argued that the subjects did not *name* the pictures in the normal sense but rather compared the picture with the list of names they were instructed to use for the session. It is possible that subjects did not encode the pictures in a normal manner but instead only searched for features that could verify the name or names that had been presented to them.

Many instances of naming are undoubtedly far removed in complexity from the sort of comparison process just described. Chafe (1977) has been concerned for some time with the problem of how visual objects are named and has collected observational and experimental data on the problem. He points out that naming can often be an uncertain, variable, even creative act. The process of naming can be a very *thoughtful* act, involving a lot of semantic processing to decide which representation that goes with a name is closest to the representation of the perceived object. (Of course, Chafe's task is somewhat extraordinary in that he uses as stimuli objects that are not easily nameable, such as playground equipment that looks like works of abstract sculpture.)

The paper by Smith et al. touches on the controversy concerning the nature of conceptual representations. Much of the previous debate between proponents of imaginal theories and proponents of propositional theories has unfortunately been marked by successive demolitions of straw men. There is considerable evidence now that conceptual representations must have both propositional and imaginal properties. Smith et al. present convincing arguments for less imaginal, more propositional representation at a more abstract level than the basic level,

---

[1] I thank Robert Gluschko for discussing many ideas related to this section with me.

but they acknowledge the highly imaginal characteristics of concepts at the basic level.

The imaginal–propositional debate is closely related to the analogue–propositional debate, which more and more reveals the uselessness of the distinction. Bobrow (1975) has shown that the distinction between analogue and propositional representations is not as useful as any of a number of better-defined distinctions that permit a clearer characterization of the nature of a representation. Norman (1976) points out that every useful representation must be analogical in some sense. What must be specified is with respect to what processes a representation is analogical to its visual appearance. An imaginal representation is one that has analogical properties with respect to certain processes that deal with the visual form of the object represented. For example, Cooper and Shepard (1973) have shown that the psychological process of recognizing letters of the alphabet in various orientations is analogous to the physical process of rotating letters at a constant speed. Those who have been involved in the propositional–imaginal debate would do better to agree that conceptual representations must include both abstract concepts and more detailed concepts and then to discover which concepts belong to which category and what processes that operate on the less abstract concepts have physical analogues.

The major contribution of the Smith et al. paper is not, however, to clarify the nature of conceptual representation but rather to reveal an important fact about how the picture-naming process takes place. Earlier theories of semantic comparisons based on reaction time data (such as the work of Clark & Chase, 1972) imply a strictly sequential processing model, in which subjects first process one part of a display, then another part, independently, and then compare the two representations. Recent work by Potts and Scholz (1975) suggests that this assumption of independence is probably not justified. The model that accounts for the data of Smith et al. makes use of parallel processes of naming and making semantic comparisons. Although the Potts and Scholz study does not require a parallel model, both articles call into question the assumption of strictly sequential, independent processing in semantic-comparison-time tasks. Perhaps there is a need to review this literature in search of minor results in semantic comparison tasks that cannot be accounted for with strict sequential processing models.

MEANINGS IN CONTEXT[2]

Fillenbaum's study is not only a study in lexical semantics but also a study of the contextual control of word meanings. It not only treats the basic meaning of the logical connective IF but also considers what contextual factors are responsi-

---

[2] I thank Pamela Munro for her suggestions and for discussing ideas presented in this section with me.

ble for changes in the meaning of IF as well as the mechanisms by which contexts may bring about these effects. It seems likely that contextual effects are important not only for other logical connectives but for many other (perhaps all) lexical items.

Fillenbaum first shows that the lexical item IF has a family of uses. The issue of whether difference in usage constitutes difference in meaning is not resolved, but this may in fact not be an issue beyond the terminological level. Still, a problem is posed: Is IF polysemous? Do we need a number of different semantic representations of the lexical item *if* (IF_1, IF_2, etc.) to represent these different uses? Fillenbaum seems to be inclined against this solution, and he sketches the *means* by which a context can be responsible for a particular *use* of IF.

Some other semantic theorists have chosen the polysemy alternative when faced with similar decisions. This is not an infrequent issue for semantic theorists. Both Schank (1973) and Rumelhart (1975) decided to postulate four underlying predicates of *causation*. In Rumelhart's system, described in his paper on an episode schema, these can be distinguished from each other by the nature of the arguments "X" and "Y" in "X $CAUSE_i$ Y." This situation, in which the nature of the *component* propositions determines the interpretation of the whole causal structure, is closely parallel to the situation with IF described by Fillenbaum (in which the interpretation of the *whole* condition "*If p, q*" depends on the nature of its components "*p*" and "*q*". Perhaps the approach suggested by Fillenbaum here should be applied to the meaning of causation asking not "What are the various *meanings* of cause?" but rather "What contextual effects determine what the interpretation of a particular causal structure is?"[3]

Fillenbaum shows two powerful contextual effects on IF-inducements. The first is a general world-knowledge effect. Both the syntactic and the semantic structure of an utterance can be overwhelmed by a subject's knowledge of what is sensible. The second contextual effect is the interaction between the illocutionary force (or speech act in Searle's terms) of an utterance and its logical form.

Fillenbaum studies this second effect in the interpretation of threats and promises phrased as conditionals. Earlier, I made a plea for a procedural semantics approach to lexical meaning. I'd like to sketch here now it might be applied to threats.

A procedural semantics approach to speech acts (such as ASSERTing, QUESTIONing, REQUESTing, etc.) can be partially based on the analysis of *sincerity conditions* associated with speech acts, as discussed by Gordon and Lakoff (1971). Here is a partial listing of the sincerity conditions that I believe hold for

---

[3]Charles Li has informed me that in Chinese, the recognition of IF-clauses usually depends wholly on context, because there is no overt marker of conditionality, no word that means "if." Juxtaposition of two clauses ("I go to school, I become sick") is ordinarily enough, in context, to convey the conditional meaning ("If I go to school, I'll become sick").

THREATS (in what follows, *S* stands for the speaker of the utterance, *H* for the hearer, *P* for the action S wants H to perform, and *Q*– for the negative sanction to which S may subject H:

THREAT
  speaker-based conditions

.
.
.

  INTENDS (S, IF (not P, Q–))
  INTENDS (S, IF (P, not Q–))

.
.
.

  hearer-based conditions

.
.
.

  ASSUME (S, PREFER (H, P, Q–))

.
.
.

The first of these conditions means that the speaker intends to impose the sanction if the hearer does not perform the action P; the second means that the speaker intends not to impose the sanction if the hearer does the action; the last condition means that the speaker assumes that the hearer prefers doing P to having the sanction Q– imposed. For a threat to be uttered sincerely, these conditions (and others not listed above) must hold.

Now, there are many ways in which a threat can be uttered. One could say, "I hereby threaten you with Q– unless you do P." According to the Gordon and Lakoff model, two ways to indirectly convey a speech act are to *assert* a speaker-based sincerity condition or to *question* a hearer-based sincerity condition.

1. If you don't do it, I'll break your arm.
2. If you do it, I won't break your arm.
3. Would you like to do it, or would you rather have me break your arm?

To see how a procedural semantics account explains how sentences 1–3 can be interpreted as threats, imagine that the sincerity conditions for THREATs constitute part of the meaning of a particular threat. I here adopt the version of procedural semantics described by Rumelhart and Norman at this conference and treat the understanding of a sentence as the process of activating the appropriate schemata. Consider the process of understanding sentence 1 in this model. The lexical items in the sentence are responsible for the activation of their associated schemata, such as the IF-schema, the BREAK-schema, and so on. The result of these activations of simple lexical schemata is a structure of instantiated lexical schemata something like this:

4. IF(not DO(H, X), BREAK(S, ARM(H)))

(X represents the action that the speaker wants done, which would presumably be specified in the context of the utterance.) This representation does not include the notion of future tense, conveyed by the "will" of sentence 1. When the WILL-schema is activated, the INTEND-schema is also activated (that is, WILL knows that when it is activated with a first-person subject, the INTEND-schema should also be activated). Now the representation is:

5. INTEND(S, IF(not DO(H, X), BREAK(S, ARM(H)))),

which is obviously a more explicit version of the first speaker-based sincerity condition, with P and Q− filled in. This representation (sentence 5) works to activate the THREAT schema, which busily checks that none of the other sincerity conditions for THREAT are violated. If none are, and if other essential conditions are confirmed (e.g., that the speaker is actually in a position to impose the sanction), then the utterance is understood as an instantiation of the THREAT-schema.

The Smith, Balzano, and Walker paper and the Fillenbaum paper both raise a number of important issues. They share the feature of relying on logical arguments as well as experimental results, and it is to be hoped that this is the beginning of a trend in psychological research.

REFERENCES

Bobrow, D. G. Dimensions of representation. In D. G. Bobrow & A. M. Collins (Eds.), *Representation and understanding: Studies in cognitive science.* New York: Academic Press, 1975.

Chafe, W. L. Creativity and its implications for the nature of stored knowledge. In R. Freedle (Ed.), *Discourse production and comprehension.* Norwood, N. J.: Ablex Publishers, 1977.

Clark, H. H., & Chase, W. G. On the process of comparing sentences against pictures. *Cognitive Psychology,* 1972, *3,* 472–517.

Cooper, L. A., & Shepard, R. N. Chronometric studies of the rotation of mental images. In W. G. Chase (Ed.), *Visual information processing.* New York: Academic Press, 1973.

Gentner, D. Evidence for the psychological reality of semantic components: The verbs of possession. In D. A. Norman, D. E. Rumelhart, & LNR (Eds.), *Explorations in cognition.* San Francisco: W. H. Freeman, 1975.

Gordon, D., & Lakoff, G. Conversational postulates. In *Papers from the seventh regional meeting of the Chicago Linguistic Society.* Chicago: Chicago Linguistic Society, 1971.

Harrison, B. *Meaning and structure: An essay in the philosophy of language.* New York: Harper & Row, 1972.

Lakoff, G. *Irregularity and syntax*. New York: Holt, Rinehart & Winston, 1970.

McCawley, J. D. Lexical insertion in a transformational grammar without deep structure. In *Papers from the fourth regional meeting of the Chicago Linguistic Society*. Chicago: Chicago Linguistic Society, 1968.

Miller, G. A. English verbs of motion: A case study in semantics and lexical memory. In A. W. Melton & E. Martin (Eds.), *Coding processes in human memory*. Washington, D.C.: Winston, 1972.

Miller, G. A. Toward a third metaphor for psycholinguistics. In W. B. Weimer and D. A. Palermo (Eds.), *Cognition and the symbolic processes*. Hillsdale, N. J.: Lawrence Erlbaum Associates, 1974.

Minsky, M. A framework for representing knowledge. In P. Winston (Ed.), *The psychology of computer vision*. New York: McGraw-Hill, 1975.

Norman, D. A. *Memory and attention* (2nd ed.) New York: Wiley, 1976.

Norman, D. A., Rumelhart, D. E., & LNR. *Explorations in cognition*. San Francisco: W. H. Freeman, 1975.

Potts, G. R., & Scholz, K. W. The internal representation of a three-term series problem. *Journal of Verbal Learning and Verbal Behavior*. 1975, *14*, 439–452.

Rumelhart, D. E. Notes on a schema for stories. In D. G. Bobrow & A. M. Collins (Eds.), *Representation and understanding: Studies in cognitive science*. New York: Academic Press, 1975.

Schank, R. C. *Causality and reasoning* (Tech. Rep. 1). Castagnola, Switzerland: Istituto per gli Studi Semantici e Cognitivi, 1973.

Winograd, T. Frame representations and the declarative/procedural controversy. In D. G. Bobrow & A. M. Collins (Eds.), *Representation and understanding: Studies in cognitive science*. New York: Academic Press, 1975.

12
Comments on the Papers by Smith, Balzano, and Walker and by Fillenbaum

Kenneth Wexler

University of California, Irvine

I would like to discuss the Smith, Balzano, and Walker paper, not in relation to other experimental studies, but rather in terms of its own approach and also in relation to its significance for more general questions. This is partly because I think that a discussion of this sort has intrinsic interest and partly because I don't know the relevant experimental literature very well.

First, I give a quick summary of what I think the paper is about. Smith et al. are trying to understand the process whereby somebody answers the question: Is this picture a picture of an apple? The novel idea they have is that there is a kind of analysis-by-synthesis process going on in which the subject looks at the picture, *names* it, and then compares this name to the verbal name that he has already been given. This naming process of course turns out to be only part of the story, and "semantic" processes are needed as well. Although, as I said, I'm only familiar in a scattered way with what has gone on in the field of semantic memory, I suspect that most previous accounts have used only semantic and not naming processes to account for various kinds of answers to questions.

The first model that Smith et al. pose is a serial model in which the naming process is first tried, and only if it fails to provide an answer is a semantic process called in. This model encounters the following problem. Sometimes subjects are asked whether the picture is an apple, but sometimes they are asked whether it is a fruit. Call apple "basic" (more about that in a minute). The basic category will immediately pop to mind when the picture is seen. That is, the subject looks at the picture and thinks: apple. Thus he can match this description of the picture against the original question (verbal) description. Because they match, he answers yes. But because when the question is "fruit" his description "apple" does not match, another process is needed, and thus the question "fruit" will take longer than "apple." This happens in the data. Thus far so good.

But there is a further large effect in the data. Namely, there is quite a bit of variation in this "level" effect across categories, that is, vegetables have a different effect from fruits, the effect of which is different from tools, and so on. That is O.K., because one can assume that the variability is due to variable naming times. But the problem is that the variability holds only for questions whose answers should be yes. If the answer is no (for example, if the question is "apple" and the picture is "hammer"), then there is far less variability. But if the process is serial, with the naming process always occurring first, then the variability in the naming process should cause variability in the total reaction time even for false questions.

Experiment 2 shows that the variability in the first experiment is matched in a direct naming-time experiment. Then Smith et al. propose the parallel model, which assumes that the naming and semantic processes take place in parallel. The naming process time thus will not be a component of the false questions, and the lack of variability in the level effect for the false questions will be accounted for.

There are many assumptions in the parallel model, and, although there may be something I missed, it appears to be able to account for the data effects. (But if subjects don't know what a soldering iron is, basic-level tools will be slowed.) To a certain extent, it seems to me that parallel models of this kind are weaker than serial models (in the sense that models with more parameters are weaker) in that serial models are special cases of parallel models. For example, it is assumed that the basic and nonbasic names are searched for in parallel, but the nonbasic search takes longer than the basic one. Thus one can have the serial effects of one process ending before another. On the other hand, I am told that Townsend (1972) has argued that serial models are weaker than parallel models in that serial models can use the results of previous processes to feed into later processes.

The concept of "basic" level bothers me to some extent. My understanding of the work of Rosch et al. (1976) comes strictly from the Smith et al. paper. The *basic* level is the most abstract level for which the instances share many attributes. Thus "apple" is basic, whereas "fruit" is not. But is it really true that apples share "many" characteristics, whereas various instances of "fruits" don't? Or that hammers and saws don't share many attributes? Hammers and saws are tools. They are used for building things. They are often kept in workshops. And so on. Certainly hammers and saws have much in common. As do cabbages and carrots. My guess is that the word "attribute" here means "visual" attribute or at the very least sensory or perceptual attribute. Also, I am very suspicious of the quantitative definition, that is, of the word "many." Does a Gravenstein apple share more with a Delicious apple than a lemon, lime, and orange share with each other? Why isn't *citrus* basic? I simply don't think that a count of shared attributes is what is going on.

But what *is* important about the notion "basic"? Namely, that "basic" categories are those that come to mind first when an instance is shown. Thus, see an apple, and say "apple," not fruit. Smith et al. could simply define "basic" in this way, but then, of course, they would lose the independent justification for the levels effect and for why high-level "bird" questions take less time than low-level ones ("bird" is basic). But they could still get this justification from studies that asked subjects to name objects, without restricting the names. Thus, if a robin were named "bird" lots of times, then "bird" would be "basic," in the sense that it came to mind first.

If I had to think of why different levels were used to commonly name things, I suppose that the best answer is that given years ago by Roger Brown, namely that certain levels were more useful in certain cases. Thus it would be useful to name a certain fruit an "apple," because we often ask for apples. We don't go to the store and ask for two pounds of fruit very often. Unless one adopted an incredibly strong version of the Whorfian hypothesis, the cause and effect here would be that we apply the term "apple" because of its use. On the other hand, it's not nearly as important to most people whether the bird on the tree is a robin or a finch. Thus "bird" is used most often to describe these. It would be interesting to run an ornithologist in these experiments.

Despite the data, I must admit that I'm uncomfortable with the parallel model when it assumes that search for the basic and nonbasic names goes on in parallel. I don't see how I can search for whether that red thing is a fruit independently of whether it is a tomato. The attributes that I perceive are not attributes of "fruit." Rather, they are attributes of "tomato." And, I know that a tomato is a fruit. Likewise, what attributes that I can take from a picture of a whale will allow me to decide that it is a mammal?

In fact, I would say that what would be quite useful would be a theory of naming. Such a theory would help resolve many of the issues in the paper, besides being interesting on intrinsic grounds. Such a theory might want to distinguish between visual and functional features. In fact, this distinction might be helpful in the analysis in general. Consider that most of the kinds of furniture, tools, and clothing are defined by functional rather than visual features.

I'm also curious about how the models presented in this paper agree or disagree with models presented for other semantic memory tasks. In particular, it is probably true that different processes are needed for different tasks, but don't we need a theory of those processes and tasks? Is one likely to be forthcoming? If strategies of processing are different in every case, how can we claim to have learned something about, say, comprehension, without explaining these "strategies"?

This leads me to what I least understand about these studies, namely their point. Let's suppose that many models have been created that fit many different experiments. I'm sure that to some extent this is true. Where do we go from there? What kind of discussion can be offered of what the entire enterprise is about? Can these studies tell us anything about the process of language comprehension or language learning? About linguistic structures? Such a discussion would be quite welcome.

We now turn from a study concerned with the processing of semantic information to a study which deals with the results of that processing. Fillenbaum makes the very important point that the use of "logical" connectives involves far more than a simple "truth-table" analysis. We can consider the truth-table analysis to be a "semantic" analysis. Fillenbaum's point is that we have to go beyond semantics to the study of performance or "pragmatics."

To support his analysis, Fillenbaum cites a variety of experimental data in which subjects have to do various tasks, for example, make paraphrases, judge inferences and equivalences, and so on. Fortunately for us, we can consider his analyses without looking in detail at many of these results, because, generally, the results are quite in keeping with our linguistic intuitions.

Fillenbaum's major claim is that the logical connectives have different meanings in different contexts. For example, the meanings of the connectives differ depending on the particular content of the sentences that replace the variables in the formulas. In particular, the meaning of the conditional "if . . . , then . . ." depends on the content of the two sentences that would have to be filled in in the formula.

Although I do not disagree with Fillenbaum's statement that the psychological study of pragmatics is important, I would like to take a different tack in the analysis. In doing so, I follow the general analysis given by Grice and in particular some of the analyses presented by Deidre Wilson in her recent book (1975), *Presuppositions and Non-Truth-Conditional Semantics.* Early in his paper, Fillenbaum states that "it should be noted that we have been claiming that a connective such as IF has different uses. This is not the same as claiming that it must necessarily have different senses or different logical representations. In principle it might be possible for an operator to have a unitary representation, but only with different uses as a function of the application of relevant conversational principles." Fillenbaum notes that Grice presents this latter view and that others have argued for different underlying forms, but he says that the issue can be ignored for the present. It seems to me that the issue can be very important for psycholinguistics. Suppose, for example, that Grice is right and that each logical connective has only one sense but that general rules of conversation indicate how the connectives can have different interpretations in different contexts. Then these general rules of conversation will be candidates for psycholinguistic hypotheses, with quite important implications for psycholinguistic processes, such as language processing and language learning. Thus, I would like to turn to an account of these principles. I take the following essentially from Wilson (1975, pp. 95–96).

Grice's principles of conversation:
Co-Operative Principle: Make your contribution to the conversation such as
to advance its accepted purpose or direction.

Maxims
1. Quantity: (a) Don't give too much information
             (b) Don't give too little information
2. Quality: Try to speak the truth
             (a) Don't lie
             (b) Don't make statements for which you have insufficient evidence
3. Relation: Be relevant
4. Manner: Be easy to understand
             (a) Avoid obscurity and ambiguity
             (b) Be brief and orderly.

In one of Fillenbaum's studies, subjects were asked to paraphrase sentences, some of which were "strange," such as "Clean up the mess or I won't report you," or "John dressed and had a bath." Subjects tended to "normalize" these sentences, that is, to make them less strange, or, as Fillenbaum puts it, to "assimilate them to the conventional relations among events." The conclusion is, in his terms, that "people . . . make the basic assumption that sentences are sensible." It seems to me that this assumption is equivalent to the assumption that the listener behaves as if he believes that the speaker is obeying Grice's maxims plus the assumption that the world that is being described is the "conventional" world. It is perfectly clear, of course, that subjects can be induced to not "normalize" sentences if they are convinced that a nonnormal world is being described. For example, one could create the following scenario: "This morning, John was thinking so much about his work on the general theory of relativity that he did everything backward. He got up, dressed, and then took a bath. This refreshed him, but it didn't do much for his clothes."

If we now asked subjects to paraphrase "he got up, dressed, and then took a bath," it seems clear that they wouldn't "normalize" the events. The point is that humans have the ability to normalize or not to normalize, and it is this ability that we want to study.

Returning now to Wilson's discussion of Grice, we can see how Grice's principles enter into an explanation of why subjects make certain preferred interpretations. Consider the sentence:

1. I've just been reading *The Times* and I'm in a very bad temper.

[Wilson's (19).] Now, a truth-table analysis of (1) would simply entail that both of the conjuncts of (1) were true. But, of course, in conversation, the sentence would suggest that there is a causal relation between the two conjunctions, namely that the first conjunct causes the second. In other words, I'm in a very bad temper as a result of reading *The Times*. Many people, including Lakoff (1971) have suggested that besides the truth-functional sense of *and*, there is another sense, in which it is equivalent to *and so*. In one use, the symmetric one, "*p* and *q*" is equivalent to "*q* and *p*." In the second use, "*p* and *q*" is *not* equivalent to "*q* and *p*." Thus the sentence,

2. I'm in a very bad temper and I've just been reading *The Times,*

is not equivalent to the earlier sentence. But, as Wilson points out, this "ambiguity of *and*" solution cannot handle all the data, because we also have the sentences:

3. I've just been reading *The Times*. I'm in a very bad temper.

Here, because *and* is not used at all, and yet the causal interpretation still exists, we cannot attribute this interpretation to the ambiguity of *and*.

However, Grice's maxims account for these phenomena in the following way. Quoting Wilson (1975):

> Grice could account for this suggestion by appealing to the maxim of relation: The two conjuncts must be interpreted as being not only relevant to the situation in which [1] is uttered, but also to each other. One natural way of construing the relation between the two conjuncts would be to see them as causally connected. Moreover, the injunction to be orderly would dictate that events should be recounted in the order in which they happened, unless explicit counter indication is given. Hence [1] is taken as conveying more than the mere information that both its conjuncts are true, even though its semantic analysis will yield only this information about the truth of its conjuncts [p. 96].

Notice that this analysis accounts for sentence (3) in which there is no *and*. The principle to be orderly is interpreted as meaning that, unless indication is given, the order of conjuncts will match the order of events. It is interesting to note that young children bring just this common-sensical principle to bear in their interpretations of sentences, as has been amply demonstrated by Eve Clark. One can easily imagine that this principle, which states that, short of explicit marking, linguistic order follows event order, is related to cognitive abilities in general.

Another piece of evidence offered by Wilson — that general conversational principles and not various senses of *and* account for various interpretations — involves the assumption that sentence (5) is derived from sentence (4).

4. John is my friend, and John is famous.
5. John, and he is famous, is my friend.

Now consider sentence (7), which would be derived from sentence (6).

6. The Lone Ranger mounted his horse and rode off into the sunset.
7. The Lone Ranger, and he rode off into the sunset, mounted his horse.

Sentence (7), of course, is grammatical but distinctly odd. Under the usual assumption that transformations do not change meaning, if one assumed that *and* is temporal in (6), then it would be temporal in (7), and (7) should not be odd but rather should mean the same as (6). But a Gricean analysis does just the right job here. Because the *and* conjunct in (7) precedes the horse-mounting, the listener would have to assume that the Lone Ranger rode off *before* he mounted his horse — and thus the oddness of the sentence.

Some of Fillenbaum's data and arguments also implicitly support the notion that a difference exists between conversational principles and logical analyses and that they are not one and the same. For example, in the recognition memory study, there was a finding that causals related to counterfactual conditionals are not recognized as often as counterfactual conditionals related to causals. For example, if the original stimulus sentence is the causal, (a) "he did not arrive on time because he did not catch the plane" — and the "new" test item is the counterfactual conditional (b) "if he had caught the plane he would have arrived on time" — then there is greater recognition of the test item than if the stimulus and test items were inverted. In order to explain this result, Fillenbaum notes that

> One cannot very easily assert (a) without assuming or taking for granted the correctness or truth of (b), but it is not clear that the converse necessarily holds. As was pointed out earlier, (b) could be true, and yet there is no absolute requirement that the person in question must have been late, because (c) "if he had caught the plane he would have arrived on time, which he did anyway because he caught a fast train" is certainly a possible elaboration. The point is simply that a counterfactual conditional does not appear to entail the denial of the consequent proposition and thus, insofar as this is the case, does not require its related causal.

But this first implication might be a logical, "truth-table" implication of *because*. That is, "x because y" implies "not y implies not x." On the other hand, the converse "implication" is *not* an implication at all but is rather a Gricean implicature. That is, if one says, "If he had caught the plane he would have arrived on time," and nothing else is said, then the maxim to be relevant suggests that he had not caught the plane, that he had not arrived on time, and that there was a relation between the two, presumably causal. Thus *a* may be inferred from *b*. But this inference may be broken by further information, as in *c*. It would be interesting to look at all of Fillenbaum's data from this point of view.

In particular, it seems that the data about "disjunctive" threats can be analyzed in this way. For example,

8. Buy a book or I'll give you $100,

is odd. Suppose we take "or" as exclusive "or" so that "A or B" is false if both A and B are true. This is the more common interpretation of "or" in English. There are then two ways for "A or B" to be true. Either A is true and B is false, or A is false and B is true. Following Grice's maxim, we can take the first element of the conjunct in either case as occurring first temporally and perhaps even causing the second element of the conjunct. Thus, in

9. Scream or I'll kick you,

we would usually infer both that if screaming doesn't take place then there will be kicking and if screaming *does* take place then there will be no kicking.

But why is (8) odd? Because the first disjunct of (8) has the imperative form, and we can interpret (8) as a "threat." But, if one is threatening, the maxim of relevance would imply that a result of not following the order will be interpreted as bad for the threatened party. Because we usually assume that receiving money is good and not bad, (8) is odd. Of course, (8) can easily be made to sound good by producing the appropriate scenario: Consider a man who is in principle a pauper.

It is also worth noting that threats are perhaps a special case of "warnings."

10. Buy his book or John will hate you.

Sentence (10) is a warning, but not a threat. The difference, at first glance, anyway, seems to be that, in threats, the resulting bad consequences are the responsibility of, or will be caused by, the speaker. We do not even have to assume that the speaker wants the first disjunct done. Sentence (10) certainly has a reading in which the speaker is not to be interpreted as ordering the listener to buy a book or even to necessarily care about buying a book. Even more clear is (11).

11. Be a scoundrel or the world will treat you badly.

There is no inference from (11) that the speaker wants the listener to be a scoundrel. [For a discussion of some related kinds of sentences, see Culicover (1972).]

We can even have cases like

12. Be a scoundrel or I'll treat you badly.

Here the speaker, let's assume, doesn't want the listener to be a scoundrel, but he knows that, nevertheless, if the listener doesn't behave like a scoundrel, then he, the speaker, will treat him badly. (Also, the listener is not a masochist, that is, he doesn't desire to be hurt.) This is a kind of "nonrational" behavior, i.e., a type of behavior in which actions are not undertaken in a way calculated to produce (consciously) desired outcomes.

The above kinds of analyses should also apply to what we might call (on analogy with "disjunctive threats") *conjunctive inducements.*

13. Buy my book and I'll kiss you.

Of course, there are many phenomena to be discussed, and a far more explicit analysis will be necessary. Nevertheless, it seems to me to be a more promising approach to look for the explanations of Fillenbaum's interesting data not in the proliferation of meanings for logical connectives but rather in a general theory of conversational rules and of contextual interpretation. In fact, an analysis in which ambiguity is explicated by different underlying logical forms is a semantic analysis, not a pragmatic analysis. Thus, although Fillenbaum calls for the psychological study of pragmatics, he actually gives a semantic analysis. (I don't mean at all to suggest that Fillenbaum has ignored contextual interpretation. Rather, I mean that in the technical sense of semantics and pragmatics, the analysis is semantic.)

It seems to me that not only do these data seem to support an inferential rather than a "different-logical-form" explanation but that the inferential explanation is more attractive as a psychological theory. It certainly fits with the modern view in cognitive psychology of the human as an active processor, consistently making hypotheses based upon the information available to him. One would expect this kind of complex, active, perhaps nonalgoritmic (in the sense of no solution being guaranteed) processing to be particularly prominent in just this area of use, the making and interpreting of inducements, threats, etc.

To take an analogy, we know that the science of biology has discovered much and will discover more of the formal nature of biological processes and materials. Much less is known about the use of such processes and materials in, say, medicine. But most of us believe that a scientific theory of medicine will have to be founded on a scientific biology. I would argue that the analogy holds in linguistics and psycholinguistics. We know something about syntax, less about semantics, and perhaps almost nothing of a systematic scientific nature about pragmatics, which involves the use of the elements and relations studied in syntax and semantics. A scientific pragmatics, however, will have to be founded on a scientific syntax and semantics.

REFERENCES

Culicover, P. OM-sentences. *Foundations of Language,* 1972, *8,* 199–236.

Lakoff, R. Ifs, ands and buts about conjunctions. In C. Fillmore & D. T. Langendoen (Eds.), *Studies in linguistic semantics.* New York: Holt, Rinehart & Wilson, 1971.

Rosch, E., Mervis, C. B., Gray, W., Johnson, D., & Boyes–Braem, P. Basic objects in natural categories. *Cognitive Psychology,* 1976, *8,* 382–439.

Townsend, J. T. Some results concerning the identifiability of parallel and serial processes. *British Journal of Mathematical and Statistical Psychology,* 1972, *25,* 168–199.

Wilson, D. *Presuppositions and non-truth-conditional semantics.* London: Academic Press, 1975.

Author Index

Numbers in *italics* refer to pages on which the complete references are listed.

Subject Index

086647